Impact

IMPACT

How to Inspire, Align, and Amplify Innovative Teams

KEITH V. LUCAS, PhD

NEW YORK

LONDON • NASHVILLE • MELBOURNE • VANCOUVER

IMPACT

How to Inspire, Align, and Amplify Innovative Teams

Published in New York, New York, by Morgan James Publishing. Morgan James is a trademark of Morgan James, LLC. www.MorganJamesPublishing.com

Proudly distributed by Publishers Group West®

Morgan James BOGO™

A **FREE** ebook edition is available for you or a friend with the purchase of this print book.

_____

CLEARLY SIGN YOUR NAME ABOVE

Instructions to claim your free ebook edition:
1. Visit MorganJamesBOGO.com
2. Sign your name CLEARLY in the space above
3. Complete the form and submit a photo of this entire page
4. You or your friend can download the ebook to your preferred device

ISBN 9781636986555 paperback
ISBN 9781636986562 ebook
Library of Congress Control Number:
2025933846

Cover Design by:
Lawna Oldfield

Interior Design by:
Chris Treccani
www.3dogcreative.net

Scan QR Code to visit author website

Morgan James PUBLISHING Builds with... **Habitat for Humanity® Peninsula and Greater Williamsburg**

Morgan James is a proud partner of Habitat for Humanity Peninsula and Greater Williamsburg. Partners in building since 2006.

Get involved today! Visit: www.morgan-james-publishing.com/giving-back

For Mia and her generation.
There is always time to build the future you want to see.
Just don't ask permission.

With special thanks to David Baszucki and Erik Cassel
who created the environment that unlocked my potential—twice!

In memory of Joseph P. Lucas, my first leadership role model.
He coached his team to greater mastery, helped them
build careers, had their backs, put in the work, led with
urgency and integrity, and acted with decency.

CONTENTS

Foreword . . . . *ix*

Preface . . . . *xi*

Introduction *1*

PART I: Aligned Autonomy **13**

Chapter 1   Fuel by Purpose   15

Chapter 2   Live by Values   32

Chapter 3   Institutionalize Mastery   57

Chapter 4   Unlock Autonomy   87

Chapter 5   The Cascade   123

PART II: Mission Athletes **143**

Chapter 6   Define Success   145

Chapter 7   Recruit Mission Athletes   162

Chapter 8   Develop Mission Athletes.   179

Chapter 9   Coach Out.   217

Conclusion *251*

Acknowledgments *259*

About the Author *263*

Notes *265*

FOREWORD

When Keith asked me to write this introduction, I was flattered. We worked closely together from the earliest days of Roblox. Our time together included the creation of many key aspects of our core technology, and the creation of our Roblox values. We always talked about combining great people with a huge vision, and along the way, we learned a lot about how to power product and market innovation.

Keith's book is about finding, inspiring, and aligning people in order to achieve big goals. And as I thought about framing this with an introduction, I realized this topic is a lifelong learning. I'm still learning today. And I believe it's a noble pursuit. There are areas I'm working on at this very moment to help us better align and inspire the teams at Roblox. In this book, Keith shares some of our early learnings that helped eventually build what we call the Roblox Operating System—a move to systematize some of these learnings into ways to help teams innovate out-of-the-box solutions and bring them to market quickly.

There is literally a "feeling" one gets when in a meeting, whether it's with four or fourteen people—when the confluence of great people and cultural alignment snap together. It's an amazing feeling. Everyone wants the same thing, and each person brings their unique creativity to the challenge. The conversation can be intense and, at the same time, resilient. It's one of the most exciting parts of running a company. And this is a feeling that doesn't happen when people in the room are misaligned with the culture and not excited to drive forward.

A constant learning for me has been to increasingly trust my intuition. When we go off to high school or college, we are not typically in company-building mode. And because of this, we end up with relationships that come through intuition, rather than through planning or logic. In retrospect, what we typically don't know at the time is that we are trusting our intuition to pick the people we want to build stuff with—friendships, clubs, teams, and projects.

This same intuition comes to bear in the professional world, and it's often ignored. Your intuition will often "know" when someone isn't culturally aligned. Having even one person on a team of eight who is not culturally aligned can slow down the whole team, even if they are individually a high achiever. The stronger and clearer your culture, the more you can trust your intuition. And the more you can trust your intuition, the more quickly you can move in making decisions.

When great teams are properly supported and aligned, great things happen. There is shared interest in the mission and vision of the organization, and a mutual understanding around how the goals of the team can contribute. And when a team is both aligned and free to act autonomously, you will literally feel the difference.

In addition to trusting your intuition, it also takes courage to stand behind your culture. It's better to have a clearly defined culture that works for only a subset of applicants, than a broad culture that tries to work for everyone. By having a strong culture, you will turn off those unwilling or unable to operate with the team, but you will also attract those who will amplify the people and culture already in place.

So with that—onward—with courage!

—**David Baszucki**, Founder and CEO of Roblox

PREFACE

Roblox is a social platform for user-created games and virtual experiences, and in early 2012, it faced a crisis. Its revenue growth had suddenly slowed compared to its player growth, and the trend lines were diverging to a worrisome degree. I was senior vice president of engineering & operations at the time. This was not the first challenge Roblox had faced, nor was it the first time I had worked alongside its CEO and his cofounder. But the crisis of 2012 was sobering. More Roblox players—a good thing—meant more infrastructure, application monitoring, and human moderation. Scaling these costs without an accompanying growth in revenue would drain our cash reserves. And because Roblox was relatively small in 2012, the risk was company survival.

There were many potential explanations for these trends that were both in and out of our control. Maybe something in our game engine or web application was broken. Or perhaps existing players were losing interest, newer players were less willing to pay, or players were spending their money elsewhere. Or maybe players had less money to spend overall. Adding to the challenge, a few employees—including a recently hired executive—lost faith and left the company over the next year while we were working through ideas.

The revenue crisis was a challenging time, but it was also a transformative time. Why? Because the Roblox team rallied. While a few employees moved on, the vast majority leaned in, put in the work, and figured it out. And by the time the crisis passed, Roblox had not only realigned revenue and player growth but had also established a new critical piece of its growth engine, leaving the company better poised for the future than ever before. Roblox rallied.

How did Roblox turn a crisis into an opportunity? There were a few key components. First, *we believed.* Roblox had a very meaningful role in players' lives, unlocking their creativity, expanding their friend circles, and delivering adventures made for the community by the community. For all these reasons, players loved Roblox. Second, *we focused.* From the top down, revenue was the one thing everyone worked on that year, aside from the necessary activities of scaling, content moderation, and bug fixes. Third, *we iterated.* We didn't wait to act until we had the "best idea," and we didn't let uncertainty about the success of each idea reduce our speed. Fourth, *we worked from first principles,* questioning every aspect of our product. And that ultimately led to the solution—a move away from early mainstays such as avatar clothing and club memberships to big new ideas that improved the quality and sophistication of virtual experiences. And finally, *we had fun.* The team's creativity and energy were infectious, and so was our shared belief in each other. We knew we would figure this out and that Roblox and its community would be better for it.

The revenue crisis was not a one-off. Roblox repeatedly turned crisis into opportunity, so much so that Roblox's first employee coined the term *crisitunity.* There were certainly outsized thinkers during this time, but valuable ideas came from passionate thinkers across the team, and the design and engineering that transformed creativity into product was a team sport. In short, Roblox didn't repeatedly convert crisis into opportunity—Roblox's people and culture did. And that combination was not an accident.

Roblox succeeded through multiple crises because its founding CEO was an expert team builder who invested in people and culture from the start. And that's what this book is about—the people and culture needed to create, innovate, and solve problems repeatedly and better over time. Team building is not rocket science, but it is not always obvious. This book is for all those leaders who have earned their roles through subject matter expertise and innate leadership skills, and who now face the challenge of building and growing innovative teams.

During my tenure of almost ten years at Roblox, I contributed across the business with a focus on product and engineering, but my chief contribution was team building. I formed the first engineering pods (cross-functional teams) and insisted that each pod have a clear set of company-aligned vision, mission, strategy, and goals. I institutionalized the product team with a vision that product is a shared resource owned by founders, community, and employees. I held the line on hiring and retention to those most able to work as a team. And I operated by a set of values, along with my teammates, that contributed directly to our success.

My time at Roblox and more broadly my time over the years in startups, good and bad, helped me develop what I now understand to be my life's passion—empowering people to get things done together, to focus on what matters, to create and innovate, and to have impact.

What we can do alone pales in comparison to what we can achieve together, but a raw ability to get things done is not enough. *How* teams get things done is critical to enduring success. That how is a team's people and culture. It is a vision and mission that inspire and focus, shared values that drive urgency and ownership, a commitment to mastery that elevates skill, a leveraging of autonomy that maximizes brainpower and horsepower, and a team of compelling peers who fuel personal growth. The behaviors a team cultivates and the people it hires, develops, and retains are what transform a group of talented individuals into a self-actualizing, high-impact team.

The learnings in this book span my career, from PhD student to my tenures at Knowledge Revolution, Roblox, and Instrumental. They also span the other companies I've worked with as an engineer in the tumultuous aftermath of the 2000 dot-com bust and more recently as a startup advisor. And they include what I learned as a public policy student.

A high-impact creative culture takes thoughtfulness, commitment, and design. I have been part of successes and failures, and I've learned tremendously from both. As a leader, I've made mistakes, and I've had moments of fulfilling competence. The common thread through it all has been my commitment to the missions and people I've served and my passion for building high-impact, creative teams that unlock potential. I'm excited to share with you what I've learned and developed along the way.

INTRODUCTION

At one point in my career, I had reached an unexpected inflection point. I had amassed expertise in my field and developed skills in my craft. And along the way, I had accumulated a series of achievements based on this experience and my innate ability to lead. As a result, I had developed a reputation for getting stuff done and improving anything I touched. It was thus not surprising that I was regularly asked to lead bigger teams and assume higher-impact roles—roles with broad consequences for people and mission. But I was hitting a leadership wall.

Like most leaders, I had started my journey as a player/coach, working directly in the trenches alongside those I led. That worked well for small teams, but it was not the right model for building larger ones, particularly in entrepreneurial settings. Indeed, it was counterproductive. Doubling down on intensity, hands-on management, and personal heroics does not foster the broad-based creativity, innovation, and problem-solving that's critical to disrupting the status quo. I was trying to improve team performance as if I were throwing everyone on a bus and hitting the accelerator harder and harder. But the bus didn't move faster, and people wanted off.

To foster teamwide innovation, I instead had to level up my mindset and skill set. I not only had to let the team hold the steering wheel with me, but I also had to figure out how to do that while maintaining focus, momentum, and urgency. This meant transitioning my leadership from tactics to a systematic approach to people and teams. I ultimately succeeded, but only after initially failing—it is not always easy or intuitive to make room for new success strategies when others have worked so well in the past, and it took some failure to see that my approach had to change.

It turns out that this inflection point is common. Many leaders today have earned their roles through subject matter expertise, a capacity for impact, and innate leadership skills—the high-impact engineer now leading a team, the innovative scientist building a research group, the volunteer turned executive director, and the founding startup executive. Subject matter proficiency and leadership intuition can initially take leaders far, but team performance ultimately hits a wall when leaders lack team-building expertise.

Entrepreneurial teamwork—collaborative disruptive creativity toward mission—is among the most impactful, rewarding, and fun things we can do together, but it is too often derailed by uninformed, misinformed, or just plain bad leadership. In my experience, there is a leadership chasm between player/coach and team builder, much like the market chasm that exists between early adopters and the mainstream.[1] The strategies that drive early success are not quite the same as those that work as teams and products grow, and not everyone crosses the chasm.

I wrote this book for leaders across this leadership chasm—from emerging leaders who want to embrace the road ahead with confidence and competence, to those in the trenches transforming from player/coaches into team builders, to those seasoned leaders on the chasm's other side questioning why their current team-building strategies aren't leading to higher performance.

This book helps leaders build engines of innovation in the behaviors they cultivate and the people they hire, develop, and retain—self-reinforcing systems that amplify and align creative effort to convert novel ideas into impact. This book also helps leaders avoid the common pitfalls of growing teams beyond a handful of people—diminished impact, lower productivity, culture dilution, disempowerment, focus loss, and hiring bursts followed by team-resetting layoffs. Leveraging my personal experience, I address all of this team building through a specific lens—the entrepreneurial team disrupting the status quo through sustained innovation.

Why This Book?

I wrote this book for entrepreneurial leaders—the founders, executives, and individuals building teams to disrupt the status quo. And while the setting of this book is the tech startup of my lived experiences, the lessons are applicable beyond that to a general group of entrepreneurial disruptors in business, science, politics, the arts, and community service.

This book is for all those leaders charged with building and growing high-performing innovative teams. The team may need to be built from scratch, in which case this book serves as a design framework for the road ahead. Or the team may already exist but is underperforming, in which case this book serves as a blueprint for transformation. If you want to build a team that follows convention, this book is overkill. But if you want to build a team that innovates repeatedly, this book will accelerate your ability to do so.

So why this book? First and foremost, I haven't seen entrepreneurial team culture well executed very often. Cultural issues too often dominate the day-to-day of teams, restricting growth—often without anyone realizing that culture is the cause. Here are some of the specific leadership misses I have seen firsthand, all addressed in this book.

- Regularly asking why people are unfocused, misaligned, or moving slowly instead of explicitly building, measuring, and refining a culture that advances mission.
- Playing house with vision, mission, and values—creating phrasing that works in abstract but does not provide a clear North Star or filter counterproductive people and ideas.
- Getting alignment (focus) wrong—not aligning (punching in all directions), misaligning (doing what seems important but not what matters), aggressively aligning (top-down mandates), not understanding what trust means, and viewing alignment as a bad word.

- Not pursuing mastery—not creating a culture of excellence, not practicing iterative improvement, not holding the line on quality, failing to understand the audience.
- Failing to unlock individuals—not coaching through growth or turnaround, not creating opportunities for growth, not leveraging personal purpose, misunderstanding mindsets.
- Hiring, promoting, and retaining the wrong people—not having clear values or success criteria, and not assessing or improperly assessing an individual's probability of success.
- Getting exiting wrong—moving too slowly, moving too quickly, acting too harshly, operating without a transparent and clear process, not experimenting with other roles when there is opportunity, and treating a performance assessment as an indictment.

The second reason for this book is that I believe it is missing in the content landscape, as large as that is. I love to learn. To develop my own leadership skills, I've subscribed to business journals, studied organizational design in policy school, read newsletters, listened to podcasts, and learned directly from people who inspire me. I've also read some great books about being an entrepreneur. They tell us how to motivate intrinsically (*Drive* by Daniel H. Pink), set goals (*Measure What Matters* by John Doerr), develop customers (*The Four Steps to the Epiphany* by Steve Blank), iterate (*The Lean Startup* by Eric Ries), do hard things (*The Hard Things About Hard Things* by Ben Horowitz), innovate (*Insight Out* by Tina Seelig), lead large teams (*Team of Teams* by General Stanley McChrystal), lead with purpose (*The Infinite Game* by Simon Sinek), and start from scratch (*Zero to One* by Peter Thiel).

Despite all of this learning, I did not find what I was looking for. I wanted an end-to-end systematic approach for building entrepreneurial teams. So in this book, I wrapped my arms broadly around entrepreneurial culture, from the team to the individual and from the CEO to the frontline contributor. I knew from experience that all the pieces reinforce each other, and I wanted to articulate how.

There was one other motivator for me when I thought about some of the conventional wisdom on entrepreneurship. There is a school of thought that entrepreneurial success comes down to the hard-charging founder or CEO with a brilliant product mind, and everyone else needs to just fall in line. There is, indeed, some truth to that, particularly because innovation often starts with the belief and impact of just one person. But society tends to overindex and extrapolate.

The best entrepreneurial leaders I have worked with are not solo innovators, although they might have started that way. Rather, they are masterful team builders, calling individuals to go beyond instructions to cocreate and co-innovate. These leaders consistently demonstrate significant personal strength as they lead teams through risks, crises, and change. The kind of strength needed to lead creative, autonomous, and masterful teams is not fear-based power but rather adherence to a code of conduct, a dedication to team and mission, a commitment to values, and persistence in the face of headwinds. It is the strength of personal code and character. The best entrepreneurial leaders I have known have led this way—as I have at my best. I hope this book helps entrepreneurs lead confidently with the kind of strength that builds enduring teams.

Entrepreneurial Teams

The setting for this book is the entrepreneurial team. So before discussing team building in depth, let's first clarify what entrepreneurial teams are and what they do.

The people on an entrepreneurial team commit to a shared mission toward a vision of the world they want to see. By definition, that mission is disruptive in some way—launching a brand, transforming a market, starting a movement, pursuing scientific discovery, or otherwise bucking the status quo. The work of disruption is inherently nonlinear. The path is unclear, the solution emerges over time through trial and error, and the journey is marked by risk. The work of disruption is therefore creative, requiring a mindset that weaves through established rules and norms to pursue change. To make a difference, disruptive teams must continuously solve problems in order to transform creative ideas into measurable external impact. They must innovate.

Today, the term *entrepreneurial team* is often associated with tech startups, and for good reason. Consider the impact of just a few recent tech companies with entrepreneurial roots—Microsoft, Apple, Google, Meta, and Amazon in consumer and business internet infrastructure; Genentech, Illumina, and Moderna in biotech; Change.org, Benentech, GoFundMe, and Kiva in community services; Tesla and Beyond Meat in sustainability; and most recently, OpenAI and Anthropic in artificial intelligence. But entrepreneurial teams are doing much more than building technology. They are advancing science, assembling multidisciplinary teams around the globe to better understand our bodies, our world, and our stars. They are advancing policy as they build coalitions across the aisle and across oceans. They are advancing the well-being of communities through foundations and nongovernmental organizations, and building distributed teams of neighbors, employees, volunteers, and donors. And finally, entrepreneurial teams are leading the charge in business creation, from local shops to the global brands of tomorrow.

While the detailed work of entrepreneurial teams is specific to each team and its mission, there is a basic pattern. Creators get inspired by a world they want to see (their overarching vision). They develop their first hypothesis on how to realize that world (their product vision). They then search for an initial fit between a version of their product and an early market, a fit defined by strong connection and need (product market fit). These creators find this fit through a series of experiments, engaging directly with their audience and regularly iterating product and sometimes even vision.[2] And finally, for the growth-seeking, creators cross the chasm from early market fit to mass market through further experimentation and product iteration.[3]

This pattern is common among entrepreneurial teams. Facebook, Airbnb, and Uber all started with narrow offerings in features and geography, and then incorporated feedback from early customers iteratively and expanded their markets over time. Krispy Kreme started with a single store, cut a hole in the wall so eager customers could buy hot donuts, and expanded locally, regionally, and beyond, all following demand.[4] Political careers also follow this pattern. Politicians find an early fit with a core constituency who connect on message, values, and vision. They then expand this fit to broader geographies and constituencies by iteratively refining their narratives, and the best do so in a way that builds on their base. And science follows this pattern. Each new research professor must build a team of creative thinkers, rally and align those thinkers around a shared mission of independent projects, and iterate their work through successive papers. These labs ultimately find fit within their field in the relevance, impact, and validity of their work.

The patterns of entrepreneurial success suggest a few key ingredients—ingredients that must be part of any approach to entrepreneurial team building. First, *the time between product iterations is critical.* The first product experienced by an audience must be small, focused, and simple. If not, too much is invested before learning from the audience. It's the same for subsequent iterations. Second, *teams must unlock creativity and problem-solving to find fit* between product and early market. Third, *teams must harness distributed creativity and problem-solving to scale* through mass market growth. And fourth, *teams must ground their work in a vision of the world they want to see*, or products will become amalgams of tactical nice-to-haves rather than focused, high-impact must-haves. These ingredients are foundational to all that follow.

Before moving on, let's define a few terms used throughout this book. These are initial definitions that we'll revisit. *Creativity* is making something new from an internal vision, often unencumbered by the status quo. *Problem-solving* is overcoming challenges through the application of principles, creativity, systems thinking, and feedback loops. *Innovation* is the application of creativity and problem-solving in a coherent direction to realize substantive change; it is applied creativity much like engineering is applied physics. *Product* encapsulates anything you create in service of your audience, and your *audience* can be customers, clients, fans, constituents, investors, peers, or community. *Product market fit* is a critical mass of audience engagement, loyalty, and advocacy in a market segment that allows your product to grow within that segment much more easily than initially because it has become a necessity, not just a nice to have. It is the difference between starting a campfire (a combination of log selection, placement, kindling, ignition, and oxygen) and growing it (more logs and air).

What Great Entrepreneurial Teams Do Differently

Entrepreneurial teams vary broadly in their effectiveness. Some teams aren't very creative, either because they don't have a critical mass of creative thinkers (people) or because they are too tight operationally, stifling the creativity they have (culture). Healthy constraints such as deadlines, for example, often fuel creativity, but micromanagement generally constricts it. Other teams don't solve problems well, either because they lack the capacity for analysis and systems thinking (people) or lack follow-through, optimism, and focus (culture). Teams need agility to navigate uncertainty, but their long-term impact depends on the things they complete, not attempt. And still other teams fail to innovate, lacking one or more key skills needed to transform creative ideas into concrete action (people and culture). To innovate, teams must be adept at both the intriguing (product, strategy, and risk mitigation) and the mundane (details and tasks). But some teams are marvels, firing on all cylinders to have consistent impact toward mission.

Why are the marvels different? *High-performing entrepreneurial teams don't just innovate toward mission; they also create sustainable engines of innovation in the behaviors they cultivate and the people they hire, develop, and retain.* Companies such as Netflix, Airbnb, Spotify, and Pixar have been intentional in the ways they operate since their early days. Focusing on the work just ahead is, indeed, a critical survival tactic for startups, particularly in the early stages before audience and product traction. But focusing on what's next to the exclusion of building team capacity diminishes long-term impact. It makes repeated success too reliant on individual heroics rather than on a systematic mastery of collaborative creativity, innovation, and problem-solving.

Building Entrepreneurial Teams

Building a high-performing entrepreneurial team starts with a clear goal, one that doubles as a vision for team culture. That goal is *to amplify and align creative effort to convert novel ideas into audience impact.* Ultimately, teams that achieve this goal become sustainable engines of self-actualizing and self-organizing teamwork. Teams don't reach this goal all at once, nor do they sustain it without some ongoing tuning. But those that do bring much more energy and capacity to mission than their struggling peers.

Entrepreneurial team building calls leaders to create engines of innovation in the behaviors they cultivate and the people they hire, develop, and retain. The approach described in this book is a two-tiered framework that examines culture as a system and leadership as a discipline. Building on a foundation of intrinsic motivation, the first tier is a set of team-wide practices to drive focus, cultivate alignment, and unlock collective brainpower and horsepower. The second tier is a set of individual-centered practices to ensure the team hires, promotes, and retains those most likely to contribute to mission.

A Foundation of Intrinsic Motivation

Entrepreneurial impact starts with *intrinsic motivation,* described by Daniel Pink in his book *Drive: The Surprising Truth About What Motivates Us.*[5] As Pink articulates, we each have the following:

- An innate desire for purpose, and with it, we are propelled to higher levels of effort, resilience, and performance than by carrots and sticks.
- An innate capacity for mastery, and we will put in the work to build expertise, given the time and space to do so and a cause that matters.
- An innate need for autonomy, and given the room, we can create, innovate, and problem solve better than through command and control.

Purpose is a sense of meaning driven by our actions. It is our place in the world because of how we contribute to it. Mastery is expertise in a subject area; mastery is interpreted broadly in this book as both what you do (craft) and how you do it (what it takes to be a masterful craftsperson on a team). Autonomy is defined by Pink as control over task, time, technique, and team.

For context, think about a time when you worked on something you believed in, felt ownership in, and had the space to do it well. How empowering was that! Now think about the opposite—a time when the mission was uninspiring, your work was micromanaged, and the team's output was subpar. How demoralizing was that? No matter how well intentioned we are, we cannot perform at the same level in creative endeavors when intrinsic motivation is broken.

Intrinsic motivation is a key driver of entrepreneurial engagement and initiative. Purpose provides fuel and direction, mastery drives investment, and autonomy unlocks capacity. Beyond drive, intrinsic motivation also provides a basis for team culture in the *way* that humans engage with autonomy, mastery, and purpose. Purpose is *desired*, so we must inspire with a cause that pulls. Mastery is a *capacity*, so we must institutionalize and encourage it. And autonomy is a *need*, so we must give people the space to exercise it.

The Aligned Autonomy of Mission Athletes

This book builds on a foundation of intrinsic motivation to deliver an end-to-end operational system for entrepreneurial teams. The approach described is one I've developed throughout my career as a team builder and startup advisor. It can be summarized in a simple phrase that defines high-performance entrepreneurial culture—*the aligned autonomy of mission athletes.*

Autonomy is the organizing principal because only through autonomy can teams maximize the brainpower and horsepower applied to innovation and minimize the forces of soul-crushing bureaucracy. But while people need autonomy in order to unlock ownership and initiative, teams need *aligned autonomy* to effectively pursue mission. Without alignment, too much is left for interpretation—even the most capable and well-intentioned teammates often differ on strategy and tactics, let alone problem definition. Unaligned teams punch in too many directions, and even if what they do is virtuous, their impact is diluted over time. Entrepreneurial success is the result of the continuous and focused impact that builds audience passion, not the inconsistent and diluted effort that builds forgettable utility.

The alignment entrepreneurial teams need must be enough to focus effort on mission, but not so much that it stifles creativity, innovation, and problem-solving. Alignment must therefore be a minimal set of ideas that drive productive focus while leaving space for initiative and action. This minimal set includes an inspiring purpose, values that guide behavior, a commitment to individual and team mastery, and a codeveloped set of strategies, metrics, and goals.

Aligned autonomy is necessary for high-performing entrepreneurial teams, but it is not sufficient. As any experienced leader will tell you, who you hire, promote, and retain is fundamental to team culture and performance. The people entrepreneurial teams need are mission athletes, individuals committed to a shared mission who, like athletes, seek continuous improvement in personal and team performance. The best athletes seek and incorporate feedback, measure themselves against benchmarks, embrace challenges, live by values, work by principles, and own their autonomy on the field. The same is true for the mission athletes who drive entrepreneurial success.

The rest of this book dives deeper into all these ideas, exploring what it takes to build high-performing entrepreneurial teams. Part I explores the teamwide culture of aligned autonomy, and part II is about mission athletes. Both parts matter—you must do both well. Building only for aligned autonomy blunts the team's collective force. Without well-designed recruiting, coaching, and exiting practices, teams fail to amplify the capacity of contributors and fail to protect the productive from the unproductive. Likewise, building only for mission athletes dilutes everyone's contributions. Individuals may grow to higher levels of mastery, but without strong purpose and values, their collective effort is rudderless and frictional. Entrepreneurial teams need strong culture in both the team and its individuals. Now let's get started.

PART I
Aligned Autonomy

Aligned autonomy is a collection of teamwide principles and practices to drive focus, cultivate successful behaviors, fuel innovation, and unlock aligned brainpower and horsepower across the team. In short, aligned autonomy is a team's *operating system,* much like the software operating systems that unlock supercomputers—maximum power and maximum throughput.

As defined in the introduction, the overarching goal of entrepreneurial culture is to amplify and align creative effort to convert novel ideas into audience impact. As we turn now to the team, let's complement this goal with a definition of success for collective action. I define team success as the *enduring ability to advance mission with increasing creativity, mastery, and scale.*

Aligned autonomy is about building a collective innovation engine that transforms a group of well-intentioned, diversely operating individuals into a cohesive, high-impact team. It ensures that individuals work toward a mission that matters and operate in an environment that advances that mission and the team's collective competence. To build such an engine, teams must

- fuel by purpose to inspire action, direct creativity, and power through challenges;
- live by values to reinforce standards of behavior that lead to high performance;
- institutionalize mastery to differentiate in the marketplace and reduce team bloat; and
- unlock autonomy to build an ownership culture and maximize collective force.

Each of these topics is covered in the chapters that follow.

The purpose, mastery, and autonomy described in part I are the team-wide implementation of intrinsic motivation—the practices and principles that amplify and align effort. Values also amplify and align, institutionalizing standards of behavior that follow from the team's own proven success strategies. Part I concludes with *The Cascade*, an approach I developed to connect the dots from vision through execution, from CEO to individual contributor, and across the entire team.

CHAPTER 1

Fuel by Purpose

Instrumental is a tech startup that improves and accelerates hardware manufacturing through the use of artificial intelligence. It was founded ten years ago by two Apple hardware engineers who not only believed that hardware manufacturing could be changed, but also that it had to change. Identifying and correcting defects on high-volume assembly lines the conventional way—human visual inspection, pencil and paper, emergency trips across the globe, and luck—made little sense in the era of machine learning and cloud connected software. But transforming an entire industry is not easy, particularly when operational practices are entrenched.

Over the last ten years, the shared belief of Instrumental's founders propelled them through numerous challenges and roadblocks. They had to find a few visionary customers who shared their beliefs, and they had to cultivate relationships one sale at a time. They also had to build a team to bring cutting-edge technology to hardware engineers in a simple and accessible way. The founders persisted through industry downturns, geopolitical disruption, external competition, internal personnel changes, venture naysayers, and corporate saboteurs. And through it all, they built a movement of industry professionals committed to transformation. I saw the enthusiasm of this movement firsthand recently at an annual event the founders started.

Building something new or turning something around starts with belief—belief in a vision that must be realized or in a problem that must be solved, belief in an initial direction to apply effort, and belief that progress can be made. It then involves building a team to increase the creative and problem-solving capacity available to your pursuit. And to have impact, it matters less if that team is formal or informal, large or small, centralized or distributed, and much more that everyone shares a set of beliefs about where they are going and how they will get there.

Beyond getting started, belief fuels the journey. Doing something you believe in is incredibly fulfilling, but doing something that changes the world, even a little, involves uncertainty, risk, crises, and curveballs. Along the way, there are inspiring successes and times when you just have to grind through the mundane or, worse, a total mess. There are also moments of incredible affirmation and moments of self-doubt. And there is always a myriad of ideas to consider, paths to take, and people to engage. Building something enduring takes time and resilience. Belief in what you are doing and in each other is what propels you and the team forward.

Belief *inspires action.*[6] It is about what must happen, not what could happen. Belief *powers resilience.*[7] It is a well of energy that helps you not only push through challenges and doubt but also helps you enjoy the ride. And belief *filters ideas.* It helps you discard the many important ideas for the few that truly matter.

Purpose is the foundation of shared belief on entrepreneurial teams. It is the one universal reason people are on the team and the primary reason the audience exists. The other elements of shared belief matter, too, including belief in values, operating principles, strategies, and goals. Without these beliefs, as we'll discuss throughout this book, the team does not effectively transform creativity into impact. But purpose is foundational. There are a lot of things you can do with talented peers and a lot of places to do them, and there are always multiple viable strategies and tactics to pursue. Purpose is what transforms a collection of people into a motivated, focused, and resilient team. But to do all that, purpose must first and foremost inspire. It must elevate beyond a business objective to a collective calling, a *just cause*[8] worthy of effort. In this chapter, we'll explore how to fuel entrepreneurial teams through purpose.

The Benefits of Purpose

There are three interventions entrepreneurial leaders make regularly at the team level.

- Inspire the team to *move faster,* not for an external deadline but as a matter of survival.[9]
- Help the team *push through crises*, particularly ones that promote self-doubt such as the loss of a key customer or a troubling change in a critical performance metric.
- *Focus the team* on the highest-impact effort, asking them to abandon creative and sometimes great ideas that are peripheral to the team's mission and current strategy.

In short, leaders regularly need to inspire action, power resilience, and filter ideas.

Each of these interventions is tricky in its own way. Asking a team to move faster without a deadline can appear unnecessary—moving faster "just because." That is particularly true for people who are new to entrepreneurial endeavors (and their fail rate) or who have only experienced success. Similarly, optimistically rallying through crises can appear Pollyannaish, particularly when the crisis is significant. And saying no to creative ideas can appear arbitrary like the whims of the most powerful person in the room.

To be successful, *interventions require purpose-fueled narratives that cultivate a shared belief that the mission is worthy and achievable.* Specifically, interventions require the following:

- Belief in something bigger than any individual (the team's purpose).
- Belief that effort matters (this team can turn ideas into impact).
- Belief that impact matters (the status quo can be disrupted).

Purpose and its connection to the work at hand drive these beliefs, which in turn inspire action, power resilience, and filter ideas. Let's see how this plays out in three examples.

Purpose Inspires Action

While at Roblox, I helped launch its Cash Out feature, which lets creators exchange earned virtual currency for U.S. dollars. One of the most rewarding things about Cash Out was hearing stories about what people did with the money. One person paid for college. Another bought matching Corvettes for him and his dad. A creator in Europe purchased a building to start a Roblox studio. The money earned from Cash Out helped creators kick-start their futures in one way or another.

Helping young people connect with each other online and pursue their creativity was the purpose that united the Roblox team. And the more we learned about their success, the harder and faster we worked. Community engagement started with the early Roblox team: They read community forums and played games to understand what was working, what was not, and what creators hoped to do next on the platform. Those engagements motivated that team of four, and a few years later, the Roblox Developers Conferences (in-person conferences with creators) did the same for our larger team. Engaging directly with creators was rocket fuel for our efforts, and they were so inspiring that we had those conferences as much for ourselves as for the community. Afterward, we typically disrupted our product road map, prioritizing the features our creators needed over our preexisting plans. The players and creators mattered most at Roblox, and every engagement with them drove us to work harder and faster.

These experiences met all three of the requirements I listed above. Through direct engagement with our audience, we established a deep connection with our purpose. Through our creators' success stories, we had evidence that impact mattered—that we were improving people's lives. And by seeing how new features turbocharged creations, we knew we could make a difference. We didn't move faster to outpace a competitor; we did so for our audience.

Purpose Powers Resilience

As I was studying for my public policy degree, I generally knew my peers' views on policy and politics. That was the point, and the regular debates we had about society were among the most enjoyable aspects of the entire experience. But while we often disagreed about what the most important problems were and how to solve them, we worked and learned effectively together. In retrospect, that is more remarkable than it seemed at the time. We discussed issues that are typically taboo at parties, holiday gatherings, and the workplace—hot-button, divisive, intractable issues of history and the moment. Why did it work for us when it might not have worked in other circumstances? I believe it was because we had a shared belief, that regardless of what each of us thought separately, the world could be made better if people acted. That shared belief united us in a common cause and gave us a basis for mutual respect.

Shared belief in purpose has the same effect on entrepreneurial teams, uniting people on mission to drive through personal differences and operating friction. Purpose doesn't just power resilience to external forces; it also builds resilience to internal disruption. I have seen this repeatedly on the high-functioning teams I've joined and advised, and I've seen the disarray that happens on lower-performing teams when purpose is neither clear nor compelling. When a team's mission taps into a higher calling, it inspires action in the face of internal strife and external adversity. Without that inspiration, challenges are headwinds, not "crisitunities" (see preface). When teams work toward a common cause, they are robust in the face of internal differences.

To rally people through crisis effectively—driven either externally or internally—leaders must talk about the team's *why* in a way that changes the narrative from a doubt-fueled, can-we-achieve-this mission back to a purpose-fueled "this mission must be achieved." Service to others is always a great antidote to self-doubt. It is also critical in crisis to point to the impact already achieved as proof that impact can be made and matters. Effective crisis response, of course, also requires an honest assessment of the situation, as well as optimism, a credible plan, and competent execution. But it starts with a purpose-fueled narrative that speaks to something bigger, demonstrates that impact matters, and highlights the team's ability to make a difference.

Purpose Filters Ideas

I once heard Reid Hoffman, LinkedIn's cofounder, give an inspiring talk on focus in which he described LinkedIn's "wall of not doing." Any idea that was not on mission, not on strategy, or not on plan was placed on that wall—it was heard, and it was captured, but it was not pursued. Reid used this example to underscore the extreme focus that ultimately led to LinkedIn's success, specifically that the filtering of ideas is critical in order to maximize effort on what truly matters, not just on what seems important. This example, though, also demonstrates *how* to filter ideas effectively—to hear and capture ideas and then to leverage vision, mission, strategy, and plan to filter ideas in a manner that focuses creativity rather than stifling it. While I've never implemented a "wall of not doing," I have successfully guided teams to greater focus by connecting the dots between purpose and action. Purpose constructively channels creativity to filter ideas that are not relevant to mission or current strategy.

Codify Purpose

For entrepreneurial teams, mission and vision statements are the codification of purpose. Mission is a solution statement to the broader problem statement of vision. *Vision is the world you want to see*, and *mission is the team's current role in realizing that world.* For example, consider the vision and mission statements for TED, a nonprofit platform for sharing ideas.

> **Vision:** We believe passionately in the power of ideas to change attitudes, lives and ultimately, the world.[10]
>
> **Mission:** To discover and spread ideas that spark conversation, deepen understanding, and drive meaningful change.[11]

When done well, vision and mission create a universal North Star for the team, which in turn unlocks distributed action, fuels the imagination, and helps people filter out distracting ideas. So in addition to being inspiring, vision and mission statements must be clear, concrete, and credible.

People need to believe that the world they want to see is reachable and the path just ahead is achievable. Vision statements are often more enduring than mission statements because they describe a future state of the world, while mission statements evolve over time as the team achieves them. Vision statements can sometimes be inferred from mission statements, and some teams rely on this, focusing solely on mission. Don't do that. Vision and mission matter equally in realizing the benefits of purpose. Mission requires our focus because it is the next hill to climb, but vision is the mountain that reminds us of the ultimate destination.

Roblox's early internationalization efforts, for example, lacked vision. Even though the next tactical step for any vision was enabling multiple language support in our app, there was discomfort until the team agreed on a long-term vision for translation—a handcrafted experience by Roblox focused on quality, a community-driven experience focused on scale, or some mix. As a general rule, charging ahead without vision risks wasting resources (heading in the wrong direction), and having vision without mission risks not having any impact at all (no clear next step).

Vision and mission statements can be framed positively—what you hope will come to pass ("transform our enemies into allies"). Or they can be framed negatively—what you hope to avoid ("destroy our enemies before they destroy us"). Positive framing is preferred for activities that create or seek constructive change. It opens the imagination and points to a world of possibilities. Negative framing, on the other hand, constricts our mental scope to problem-solving at best and promotes problem grievance at worst. So if you want a creative and aspirational team, your vision and mission statements must embody those very attributes.

The easiest way to wordsmith your vision and mission statements, as well as understand their differences, is to look at examples. A simple internet search returns a lot of them, but the quality of the material is mixed. Good vision and mission statements should inspire imagination, commitment, urgency, and action; and they should help people sort themselves on and off your team. Bad vision and mission statements are vague, not aspirational, mundane, overly analytical, too tactical, or lacking urgency. The biggest issue you'll likely encounter in a search, though, is the confusion between vision and mission. Vision is something you have, and mission is something you pursue. Let's now look at some good vision and mission examples.

Tesla

> **Vision:** The future is sustainable.[12]
>
> **Mission:** To accelerate the world's transition to sustainable energy.[13]

The world Tesla envisions is one of sustainable energy. And Tesla's role in bringing that world to life is *acceleration*, currently through electric cars, solar panels, storage batteries, and a vehicle charging network. Tesla's vision and mission are aspirational, clear, big, and bold—they inspire.

An earlier mission statement when Tesla was focused solely on vehicles is also inspiring, but it played an additional role. That mission was "to create the most compelling car company of the 21st century."[14] The mission was not to be *a* compelling electric car company but *the most* compelling. I agree. Why bother for second place, and that was likely the point. Such a mission statement will attract people who aim for first place and turn off those who want to make modest improvements. The earlier mission statement, therefore, explicitly filtered people by their belief in the need for sustainable energy and implicitly by their desired work environment.

Warby Parker

> **Vision:** We believe that buying glasses should be easy and fun. It should leave you happy and good-looking, with money in your pocket. We also believe that everyone has the right to see.[15]
>
> **Mission:** To inspire and impact the world with vision, purpose, and style.[16]

Warby Parker's vision unambiguously states its beliefs, and there is no better filtering mechanism than belief. Potential employees and customers who believe in the same things will want to work or shop at Warby Parker. And those who don't, won't. Like Tesla's statements, these are aspirational, clear, and globally impactful in scope. The statement that seeing is a right casts the company's purpose as a human right, a cause worth fighting for.

Roblox

> **Vision:** Reimagining how people come together through communication, connection, and expression.[17]
>
> **Mission:** Build a human co-experience platform that enables billions of users to come together to play, learn, communicate, explore and expand their friendships.[18]

Roblox's vision paints a picture of a world where people engage in new ways, all predicated on communication, connection, and personal expression. It is very much a problem statement, and it underscores the reality of the field Roblox inhabits—no one yet knows what the future of immersive experiences will be, just that these experiences can unlock greater connection, learning, and play around the globe. Roblox's mission statement defines the role Roblox plays in bringing about that reimagined world by building a co-experience platform fueled by curiosity and social engagement. Although not stated but understood by all those familiar with Roblox, its commitment is to community creatives. Empowering entrepreneurial creatives is in Roblox's DNA.

Socialize Purpose

Purpose must be socialized regularly in order for it to take root and bear fruit. Purpose is a belief, and beliefs can fade without regular practice, inspiration, and stories. Practice is the application of purpose to strategy, goals, and decisions. Inspiration is the reminder of who the team serves and why. Stories are the examples of action transformed into impact.

A team's mission and vision should be shared regularly at all-hands meetings. The cadence of this repetition varies with context, including team stage, size, and situation. For very small teams that are in constant communication, frequent repetition can feel overly formal and bureaucratic. In those cases, review purpose whenever the team rethinks the path ahead (this will happen often enough). For larger teams, review purpose at each all-hands during crises or after a vision-mission rethink, and monthly or semi-quarterly otherwise. Socializing vision and mission quarterly is generally too infrequent—too much time goes by between moments of inspiration and alignment, and the low cadence reinforces an overall slower pace. Similar to socializing a team's overarching purpose, the purpose of a project or initiative should be reviewed during update meetings in order to effectively evaluate progress, learnings, and adjustments.

Socializing purpose regularly has three benefits in addition to keeping it top of mind. First, socialization naturally encourages realignment without intervention. Just being reminded is often enough to cultivate self-organization. Second, the transparency encourages peers to evaluate the alignment of each other, reinforcing a culture of focus and co-ownership. And third, the transparency also invites everyone to evaluate purpose itself—to identify when a project's purpose needs a tweak or when the team's vision and mission statements are losing relevancy.

In addition to the drumbeat of socializing purpose at all-hands and group meetings, there are a few other events that warrant repetition—when goals are set, after a big win, during a crisis, and whenever purpose is ignored or misused. When setting goals, for example, ground the entire conversation in purpose, both the team's overall purpose and the initiative's purpose. It is not always necessary to restate purpose when reviewing goal progress, but it should be among the first items revisited if anyone asks, "Why are we doing this?" Talking about purpose after a big win reinforces a belief that effort matters. And doing so in crisis strengthens the belief that impact matters, *that putting in the work is toward a greater good.*

Connect the Dots

Company vision and mission statements are common in startups. It's entrepreneurship 101. So it was not a great leap for me at Roblox to require that each engineering group articulate its vision and mission. For example, the client team that built our gaming software was asked to express its vision for our multiplatform virtual experience, as well as its current mission in pursuing that vision. Ditto for the game engine, social, discovery, and infrastructure teams.

I wanted each and every person on the broader team to be inspired not only by what we were doing collectively but also by what they were directly contributing. I also wanted a North Star for each group to unlock greater independent action, and indeed, group-level mission and vision statements yielded greater autonomy. Everyone involved understood that long-term creativity and problem-solving would align to vision, and that near-term effort would align to mission. This North Star also helped those on the front lines know when to raise a flag that vision and mission were no longer aligning with reality, furthering our collective ability to operate.

While leveraging vision and mission in this way, I came to realize that virtually everything needs vision and mission, from the team to projects, to leadership roles, to organizational changes, to cultural changes, to crisis navigation. Everything becomes easier and everyone is more effective when you clearly articulate three things: where we are going and why (vision), what's the next step (mission), and why is that the best next step in the overall journey (strategy). My leadership effectiveness improved noticeably when I started asking about the vision, mission, and strategy of each group and how those mapped to our overall vision, mission, and strategy. This calibrated collaborators, streamlined conversations, and allowed us to respond quickly to changing conditions. Ultimately, this thinking led to my development of *The Cascade* (chapter 5), which ensures that the vision, mission, strategy, and goals of each group flow from and align to the overall team, allowing teams to unlock distributed autonomy.

Protect Mission *and* Team

Purpose is powerful fuel for entrepreneurial teams, but there are a few pitfalls in its use, mostly in focusing on team health or mission to the exclusion of the other. Mission is the team's focusing belief, and people its conduit for impact. Mission and team are thus inextricably intertwined—both matter. Without an inspiring mission, there is no anchoring belief to fuel effort and no operational rudder to filter good ideas from bad ones. And without a healthy team, there is no enduring lever to transform ideas into impact.

The pursuit of mission cannot be so myopic that it creates or sustains systemic team dysfunction. Working with purpose is exciting, and working like crazy when it authentically matters is the ultimate team-building exercise, like responding to a challenge with a burst of intensity. But working hard just to do so—or when there is no plan or leadership competence—makes it hard to pursue mission with intensity beyond the few at the top calling for hard work.

Likewise, team health cannot be an end in and of itself. Individuals need to be given the space to recharge and stay fresh, like athletes taking active recoveries. But team health is a means to an end—the pursuit of mission. When team health supersedes mission impact, the entire endeavor is at risk because too much energy shifts away from audience and purpose.

High-performing teams pursue *mission through team*, a dual commitment to purpose and the principle means of its pursuit—people. Let's now look at a few specific patterns of imbalance.

Playing House

Playing house is a term I've used for more than just defining purpose. It applies whenever a team spends too much time on the meta work—like defining culture and process—and not enough time on the actual work—like building product and serving audience. High-performing teams innovate and build engines of innovation in tandem. Playing house is investing too much in the engine and too little on the impact. It is spending too much time crafting vision and mission statements early on, for example, in the hopes of guiding the team for the long haul. The mistake is believing you know what the long-haul needs at the current moment.

Do not overthink vision and mission early on. Anything is better than nothing because even terrible statements get clarifying feedback. If your vision and mission inspire and filter, you're on the right track. And if not, rework them. As a general rule, spend an amount of time proportional to your team's size. The larger the team, the more precise the statements need to be in order to guide people far removed from those writing them. So when starting out, just get it done and iterate. What matters most is communicating clearly what you're doing and why you're doing it.

Garbage Canning

There is a term I learned in public policy school called the *garbage can model.* Whenever a piece of legislation looks likely to pass, people add items to the bill in hopes that the additions pass as well. The implied visual is someone carrying a garbage can out to the curb while others frantically throw more into it while they can. The naming codifies the cynicism the practice engenders. Unfortunately, the practice is not limited to government but seems to be a defining characteristic of bureaucracy. If people are garbage canning, you might be in a bureaucracy.

The temptation to garbage can arises on entrepreneurial teams whenever the mission is tweaked in some way. That applies to either the team's long-term mission or an initiative's singular goal for the next few months. Typically, a newly framed mission has high-level leadership buy-in, if not a mandate, and enjoys widespread enthusiasm. That creates an incentive for people to reframe their favorite projects to be aligned with that mission even if they are completely unrelated. That is not necessarily ill-intentioned—purpose filters ideas, and those who truly believe in their ideas do not want them filtered out. But here is the problem. Garbage canning dilutes the filtering capabilities of purpose and, as a result, diminishes the team's overall impact.

The impetus for reframing mission is almost always to improve clarity to in turn improve filtering and focus. But when people respond by garbage canning in all sorts of projects, they dilute the mission and increase the workload beyond the focused push that was likely intended by the reframing. The answer is to hold the line on the mission's new meaning and openly push back on garbage canning. LinkedIn's "wall of not doing" is particularly useful here. Along with holding the line, iterating quickly gives people solace that while their project is excluded from this iteration, it's not necessarily excluded from the next.

Zealotry

Zealotry is a fanatical devotion to mission that can undermine success by blinding people to risk and constructive feedback. You absolutely do not want blind obedience to your mission. That is not purpose. It is not autonomy. It does not lead to mastery. You want a team of authentic believers for all the benefits that purpose offers, but you need a team of *independent thinkers* to drive creativity, ownership, autonomy, and mastery.

Purpose is a tool for focus and inspiration, but the pursuit of mastery requires feedback, and feedback requires intellectual independence. Purpose should be questioned in good faith as a means to an end—to improve its ability to inspire action, power resilience, and filter ideas as the team and audience grow. Additionally, the strength of the team's purpose and the team's commitment to it should not blind people to risk and opportunity. That would be like missing out on a key industry inflection point such as the transition from film to digital photography.[19] Foster an environment of productive intellectual independence, and coach those whose belief passes into the realm of closed-minded zealotry.

Loyalty

If bottoms-up zealotry undermines autonomy and mastery, then top-down demands of loyalty to cause undermine the ability of purpose to inspire action and power resilience. Such loyalty asks people to put the mission and team ahead of everything else in life, not just in crises but all the time. Each person on the team operates in a unique multidimensional context, optimizing their net purpose across career, friends, family, finances, and personal calling. The team's purpose is the one belief everyone shares across the team, but it is not the only belief that each person holds. The purpose needed on entrepreneurial teams is the one that powers resilience and creativity, not the one that eclipses all other considerations. People cannot endure conflict with their personal priorities and responsibilities for very long. The better way to inspire action—a sustainable way that also fuels team member retention—is to align personal purpose with team purpose, a topic we'll cover in chapter 8, "Develop Mission Athletes."

Be an Entrepreneur of Beliefs and Ideas

A product manager[20] once said to me, "The engineers refuse to do what I ask. Can't you just make them?" This came early in my tenure as chief product officer of Roblox and at a pivotal moment for defining the product team's culture moving forward. I did not want the antagonistic relationship between product and engineering I had seen on other teams, and I accepted the role with a vision that product was a shared resource— no single team owned it. The product manager's idea was also contrary to my sense of ownership. If something's not working, it's on you to fix it.

I told the product manager he had to make the case to the engineers and *earn their effort.* He had to inspire with a product vision, connect that vision to the feature being requested, and explain why this feature mattered most next to the audience and our company. Engineering was a market for the product manager's ideas, and he had to attract collaboration, not demand it. His call to action was to become an entrepreneur of beliefs and ideas. He had to cultivate engagement through influence and collaboration. This set the tone for the product team moving forward.

Entrepreneurial teams need alignment, or their impact is diluted across too many directions. But entrepreneurial teams also need constructive and creative dissent, not just of strategy and tactics but also of the fundamentals such as vision, mission, and values. While it is not productive to question everything all the time, questioning the status quo is the heart of entrepreneurial endeavors. You cannot build a team of entrepreneurial change agents if you stifle debate. Instead, you must lead entrepreneurial teams as an entrepreneur—evangelizing beliefs and ideas, listening to others, inviting questions, channeling debate, incorporating feedback, and working with the team to develop a plan that everyone owns.

The Belief That Matters Most

Each team is different. It has a unique set of talents, opportunities, and challenges. The talents and opportunities are the spark—the successes and adrenaline hits that show direction and propel everyone forward. The challenges are everything that holds its back, not once but at each successive plateau of mastery it bursts through. A substantive part of this book is about the beliefs that propel teams through these challenges, such as purpose, values, strategies, and goals. But there is one belief that matters above all else—belief in the team itself, regardless of where everyone came from, what they collectively know and don't know, and what it seems it can and cannot do. And the basis of that belief is effort because that is the one thing the team absolutely controls. Belief in team is the result of doing, not thinking. It is the iterative improvement of skill and the impact of successive contributions. So, when in doubt, act. Pick up a shovel and make a difference. And by making a difference, you will come to believe.

CHAPTER SUMMARY

Purpose is the foundation of shared belief on entrepreneurial teams.

A clear and compelling purpose

- *inspires urgency,* intrinsically and not by artificial construct;
- *fuels resiliency* to help teams push through crises;
- *focuses* teams on their highest-impact efforts.

Entrepreneurial purpose is codified through *vision* and *mission*. Vision is the world you want to see, and mission is the team's current role in realizing that world. Mission levels up with impact.

Vision and mission create a universal North Star that unlocks distributed action, fuels the imagination, and helps people filter out distracting ideas. It is best to frame them positively.

A team's high-level vision and mission are its macro purpose, its North Star. Aligning to that is a collection of micro purposes for sub-teams and individuals. A micro purpose creates aligned, distributed action in the same way macro purpose creates aligned, collective action.

Purpose must be socialized regularly in order for it to take root and bear fruit. Purpose is a belief, and beliefs can fade without regular practice, inspiration, and stories.

Regularly socializing purpose

- naturally encourages realignment without intervention;
- encourages peers to evaluate and course correct each other;
- invites everyone to evaluate macro purpose regularly against changing conditions.

In addition to socialization, purpose must be protected from some common pitfalls:

- *playing house*—spending too much time on meta work and too little on mission work;
- *garbage canning*—diluting purpose by artificially aligning far-afield ideas;
- *zealotry*—the fanatical devotion to mission that creates blind spots;
- *loyalty*—top-down requirements of loyalty to cause above all else.

Lead entrepreneurial teams as an entrepreneur—evangelizing beliefs and ideas, listening to others, inviting questions, channeling debate, incorporating feedback, and working with the team to develop a plan that everyone owns.

CHAPTER 2

Live by Values

left a startup a number of years back after realizing our values didn't line up. I did not then understand values the way I do now, but I knew we did not align in fundamental ways beyond style. I had been very excited about the company when I joined. The people seemed smart and experienced, and the mission was altruistic and compelling. My mistake during the interview was equating the virtue of the mission to the values of the team, and as a result, I ignored red flags, such as a lack of transparency in discussing the financials.

During my interview, the company's cash runway was communicated verbally rather than as a spreadsheet. I then learned after joining that we would run out of money much faster than had been suggested. That financial pressure soon revealed other operating values that concerned me. Problems were not solved quickly, obvious personnel changes were not made, and our funding strategy relied on new prototypes instead of the (problematic) technology stack we had been working on for months. Ultimately, the team's values around transparency, commitment, and urgency were too different from mine for me to continue. I don't even remember whether the company had official values. The behaviors were all that mattered.

Values establish a *standard of behavior* for a team, both for its individuals and in aggregate. Should people act with urgency, deliver quality, put the customer first, or all of the above? If vision and mission are the team's "why," then values are its "how." They define effective collaboration across the team, creating operational cohesion and consistency. A team with effective values is like a computer leveraging all its hardware to the fullest, distributing work to all its processors, and solving multiple problems in parallel—maximum power and maximum throughput. But just as computers require engineering, so do values.

When done well, values encourage a set of behaviors that correlate most with positive impact for *this* mission on *this* team right *now*, as opposed to aspirational and unfamiliar traits that are often less actionable. The best values codify existing *shared success strategies* such as the operating behaviors of the founders or high-impact individuals—proven behaviors already in practice but not yet ingrained across the team. Like purpose, values need to be codified and socialized in order to have impact, but what ultimately matters most is living them. The codification is the standard, but the actions are the reality.

Values matter throughout a team's evolution, but they evolve with the team as it grows. What's needed for the first five people in both content and polish is generally different from what's needed to maintain standards across a team of thousands when individuals no longer know everyone else. The precise meaning of a value, for example, is less important for smaller groups when everyone can talk directly with the source of truth (e.g., the founders). On larger teams, precision matters as new team members learn from those who learned from others. In this chapter, we'll explore how to build a system of values that drive team success as it grows.

The Purpose of Values

Early in my career, I didn't really think about values. I had mine (though I couldn't always articulate them), and I intuitively associated with people who shared them. But like all things strictly intuitive, there was a lot of trial and error in what I embodied, what I looked for in others, and how I coached. It was often accidental, and accidental culture typically underperforms.

The next phase of my evolution was in the late 2000s, when I started seeing values discussed in startups, and I helped develop them at Roblox. My thinking at this point was "values as guideposts"; that is, concrete traits to model, look for in candidates, and discuss in reviews. But while the words were clear, my embrace of the values themselves was still a little squishy—not always consistently defined nor applied. As a result, while the team I influenced was more aligned, individuals were too often confused or surprised by my wielding of values. Enter phase three.

As a team expands, initial small differences in operating approach magnify. Your interpretation of our shared value of "urgency," for example, might be "act fast with high uncertainty" while mine might be "act fast to reduce uncertainty." This tension is in fact healthy—you often need to do both. But sometimes it causes operational friction, particularly if we each are leading teams that amplify our differences. These teams will ultimately develop conflicting subcultures.

This type of friction happened at Roblox as the team grew, but luckily, our CEO saw it. He then led a transformation of values from "behavioral guidepost" to "cultural cornerstone" (my phrasing). Values were carefully *designed* for clarity, illustrated with exemplars, explicitly used in hiring, promoting, and exiting, regularly discussed in meetings, and intentionally role modeled by executives. The team gelled on an entirely new level. Conversations became easier because we didn't just have a common language; we had shared belief. And the values impacted everything, from people to projects to product to community. Ultimately, we reached a level of efficiency and consistency that allowed us to expand from tens of people to thousands.

To be effective, a team's values must serve two overarching purposes: They must establish a behavioral North Star that drives mastery and unlocks autonomy, and they must define who gets hired, promoted, and exited to reinforce that North Star. For both of these, the best values are based on *shared success strategies*—proven behaviors already in practice but not yet ingrained.

Values based on established success strategies are aspirational in a specific and important way: There is proof they can be achieved and proof that their achievement leads to impact. And because no one, not even an exemplar, hits the benchmark in all values all the time, values based on success strategies inherently call for individual and team growth in the pursuit of their mastery. Values thus drive mastery when they define an achievable standard of excellence for individuals and the team.

Values based on success strategies also unlock autonomy. If everyone understands what generally leads to success, they can be trusted to operate that way even when acting independently. This is especially true if peers are encouraged to hold each other to account, and it's here that incentives align—autonomy grows for all as values become ingrained in each person.

Values based on success strategies are also good predictors of impact—positive outcomes map to value hits and failures map to value misses (not exclusively, but generally). As such, values are *the* foundation of individual accountability and thus must define who gets hired, promoted, or exited, as well as who quits. Values, of course, need to be socialized, and the pursuit of mastery on entrepreneurial teams typically requires coaching. But the people who are hired, promoted, and exited reinforce values much more than socialization and coaching—new hires reflect the latest standards, promotions signal alignment, and exits highlight incompatibilities.

Growth-oriented, mission-driven, impact-seeking people—the people you need most on entrepreneurial teams—view hiring, promoting, and exiting as the core articulation of culture. If you hire mediocre performers, that's your culture. If you promote incompetence, that's your culture. If you fail to exit disruptors, that's your culture. But if you hire people who inspire and raise the bar, promote those who amplify others' success, and exit those who disrupt the team, then that's your culture. We'll explore this topic in detail in part II, "Mission Athletes."

Create a Values System

While the best values codify shared success strategies, the most effective ones also constitute a system, complementing and balancing each other. *Complementary values* reinforce and expand on each other, while *balancing values* prevent the dysfunctions of excess in any particular value.

In the early days of Roblox, for example, the value of "work hard" was complemented by "have impact." Working hard was a commitment to each other, and having impact was guidance that not all effort has the same quality. These two values also complemented each other in another way: Working hard is a mission input, while having impact is a mission output. Together, these two values established a behavioral North Star of working hard toward impact.

While complementary values combine to form a behavioral benchmark, balancing values offer guidance on how separate benchmarks operate together. Consider an "act with urgency" value that, in isolation, can lead to low-quality output as people focus on speed. An urgency value should be balanced by a mastery value such as "deliver quality." By design, a robust value system has intellectual tensions like this to remind everyone to make constructive trade-offs—trade-offs that can only be resolved in the moment and in the trenches.

When designing your value system, also be aware of two common dysfunctions—*aspirational values* and *inauthentic values*. By their very nature, aspirational values attempt to shift culture. They are thus harder to live by than established success strategies, and they need additional support to take root. If you want a measurement culture, for example, you won't get one by simply adding a measurement value. You'll also have to consistently reinforce that value by socializing its connection to mission success, championing exemplars, celebrating wins, and investing in measurement infrastructure. And ultimately, living that value must impact hiring, promoting, and exiting for it to become ingrained. Failing to live by aspirational values creates a culture in which values don't matter—the opposite of what's needed. Given the commitment required, teams should thus have at most one aspirational value at a time and commit to living it.

If a poorly implemented aspirational value can cause damage, inauthentic values can be downright deadly. These values are the output of leaders who are either too lazy to be thoughtful or, worse, intentionally manipulative, holding others to a standard they personally have no intention of hitting. And sometimes these values are simply the product of someone who is incapable of introspection and thus unaware of the dichotomy. This is the team with a value of "serve the customer" led by someone who never engages directly with the audience and discounts their feedback. Imagine the confusion when team members, in the name of this value, aggregate feedback to steer the product road map, only to be chastised for wasting time and lacking personal conviction. These teams devolve over time into checking with key leaders for too many decisions, thus undermining mastery and autonomy—and the people you need most will self-select off the team. Inauthentic values create a culture of inauthenticity, which in turn undermines intrinsic motivation, the very thing needed on entrepreneurial teams.

Value System Examples

Let's now turn to some examples of value systems.

Team-Specific Value	Higher-Level Abstraction
Respect the community	Service
We are responsible	Ownership
Take the long view	Vision
Get stuff done	Impact

Table 1: Roblox, 2024[21]

The wording of Roblox's stated values in table 1 is specific to its mission, experience, and style. "Respect the community" reflects Roblox's commitment to its players and creators, one that has existed from the start and is core to its success. And the phrasing "get stuff done" reflects the down-to-earth yet serious culture of the team. To understand how these values operate as a system, consider how these four team-specific values map to the higher-level values of service, ownership, vision, and impact. These values complement each other (ownership and service) and balance each other (vision and impact). The short list communicates efficiency and simplicity.

Team-Specific Value	Higher-Level Abstraction
Self-organize	Ownership
Get stuff done	Impact
Inspire others	Mastery
Work hard	Effort
Respect the community	Service

Table 2: Roblox, Early 2010s[22]

There is a clear connection between Roblox's values from the early 2010s and its values in 2024. As officially worded, only two values survive over time—"get stuff done" and "respect the community." But looking at their higher-level abstractions, most of the values continue with one noticeable difference—effort and mastery are dropped in favor of vision. The other substantive change, though, is the movement of "respect the community" from the last to the first position. Order matters. Placing this value first better reflects Roblox's commitment to its players and creators. These first two examples show how values evolve with the team.

Patagonia[23]

- Quality
- Integrity
- Environmentalism
- Justice[24]
- Not bound by convention

Patagonia's "quality" value is expressed in its clothing. The other four are consistent with Patagonia's recent conversion to a charitable organization with its profits funneling back to environmental causes.[25] This transition will inspire all those who believe what Patagonia believes, which can increase sales and thus charitable giving. Henceforth, every believer will associate purchasing Patagonia clothing with contributing to the environment,[26] thus creating a positive incentive for sales—not a guarantee, but a positive force nonetheless. That takes us back to quality.

The population of consumers who value the environment *and* have money to spend on outdoor clothing is Patagonia's market. The higher the quality of Patagonia's clothing, the deeper its sales penetrate this market. Lower-quality clothing only attracts the staunchest of environmental advocates, while high-quality clothing "crosses the chasm" to the mainstream.[27] Together with Patagonia's mission and vision, the last four values define a "belief market," and its product quality dictates market penetration. Values are a system.

Netflix[28]

- Judgment
- Selflessness
- Courage
- Communication
- Inclusion
- Integrity
- Passion
- Innovation
- Curiosity

Netflix's list seems long. I prefer a shorter list that can focus behavioral effort. It's easier to remember and use in feedback, and you make faster progress when focusing effort. So if you're starting out, start smaller, and iterate. In Netflix's case, though, the proof is in the pudding. Netflix is a clearly innovative company that has achieved outsized success. It has also been intentional and public with its culture from its early days.[29] I can see its values at play both in what I experience as a consumer and in what I have learned about its early streaming technology.

Consider, for example, Netflix's early use of the then relatively new Amazon Web Services (AWS). At that time, cloud computing resources were a bit unstable, and online servers would occasionally disappear. Committed to delivering a stable, high-resolution, fast consumer viewing experience, Netflix shielded consumers from these instabilities by building an automated management layer on top of AWS, a layer now provided in part by AWS itself. Chaos Monkey is just one example of this early layer.[30] Chaos Monkey was automated code that randomly shut down cloud servers to ensure that Netflix engineers built systems resilient to individual server loss. As a result, Netflix remained available even when specific AWS computing instances failed. This effort exemplifies great judgment, product integrity, passion, innovation, and curiosity. I don't think it's a given that Netflix would have achieved the same success without its innovative tech and the values that supported it.

U.S. Army[31]

- Loyalty
- Duty
- Respect
- Selfless Service
- Honor
- Integrity
- Personal Courage

These values strike me as pure—simple, clear, timeless, fundamental—human values. They reflect the commitment and enduring service of the United States military. The U.S. Army is an incredibly large organization that engages in continuous adaptation, innovation, and rapid deployment. It may be a bureaucracy, but it actively engages in bureaucracy-busting activities to achieve high performance in the field such as the daily all-hands described in General Stanley McChrystal's book *Team of Teams*.[32] The U.S. Army is a great source of organizational research and development, from goal setting to operational autonomy. It is worth studying U.S. military organizational design, operations, and logistics when scaling any team—and there's no shortage of books on the subject.

Culture Is What You Do, Not What You Say

When something needs to get done, I move fast. I've developed a skill for speed over the years, but the drive is innate. When something that matters is unfinished or not on track, I am incredibly uncomfortable. Moving fast competently is a skill I have developed, as well as one I share with Roblox's CEO and his cofounder. In the early days of Roblox, any engineer could hear any one of us ask questions about speed. Why is that going to take so long? Could we do it in half the time? How long will it be until a first version is released so we can start iterating with players? The questions were fueled by experience—coupled with every question about speed was a willingness to change the requirements, change the project scope, or rethink the entire idea. And we didn't just communicate speed; we lived it. The speed at which we made decisions, responded to crises, and got stuff done set the tone and pace for the entire team.

Now consider a counterexample. The leaders of one startup I advised expressed frustration about how long it took everyone to complete projects, but they also consistently took a long time to make decisions. Leaders shouldn't make rash decisions, but in a startup, most decisions are made with high uncertainty. Entrepreneurial leadership is about managing that uncertainty, making decisions, and fixing mistakes. Decision-making time is one of the key timescales that sets team pace. So when the founders belabored tough decisions, they unintentionally set a slower pace for the team. Everyone's decisions extended through analysis because that approach was interpreted as a team success strategy and currency for personal success. Culture was never what the founders said (move faster); it was what they did (think carefully).

There is an important caveat to building team culture—you get to design it, but you don't technically get to set it. There is always a gap between the culture you codify and what your team realizes by its actions, and only the latter matters. The values you write down and socialize are your *codified values*, a shared benchmark of productive behavior. That benchmark is an essential building block of culture, and codifying it allows for easy socialization (e.g., posters and mugs). But culture is what you do, not what you say. That means the team also has *realized values*, ones defined by behavior, and those values actually define a team's culture.

Realized values are defined by the high-impact things you do each day—how you set goals, who you hire and retain, who has voice and influence, who you celebrate and ignore, who you promote and sideline, how you respond to success and failure, and how you manage someone out. Realized values are also defined by the mundane—meetings, assessments, documentation, team structure, middle management, messaging volume, personal reviews, disruptions, distractions, and policies. In short, *everything you do, allow to be done, or allow to slide defines your team's culture*. It doesn't matter what you say.

The gap between your realized and codified values defines your dysfunction. There is always a gap, as there is in each of us between our best and worst selves. It's the size of the gap that matters, and large gaps equate to inauthenticity. To prevent this, demand first and foremost that people hold you to account, and support those who speak truth to power in the name of mission and values. Leaders of any kind, formal or informal, cannot hold others to account effectively or enduringly unless they live by the values they preach. Second, hold others to account, and don't shy away from the difficult conversations that are needed when someone is not walking the walk. Finally, walk in the shoes of your team in order to understand the values they experience every day. And if that's not what's codified, make it right.

Performance Values

Erik Cassel, Roblox's cofounder, was an extraordinary engineer and human. He was smart, urgent, and dedicated, all while being easygoing. It took a lot to ruffle Erik's feathers, which is why he made a lasting impression on Roblox's culture when he expressed significant frustration with some newly hired engineers early in the company's history. Those engineers shipped their code one morning, as was the custom, and then promptly left for lunch to celebrate, which was 100 percent *not* a custom. Equally promptly, the site started having issues. Erik asked for a patch, only to realize that the engineers had left. He called one of them and said to return immediately. Once the site was healthy again, Erik pointedly reminded them that their job was not to ship code but to ship and support code. The job was not finished after deployment but only after issues were resolved and performance returned to normal. Everyone involved got the message.

Erik echoed what I had also heard from David Baszucki, Roblox's CEO, and what I had heard earlier at Knowledge Revolution, Dave's first company. True ownership goes beyond performing a task to fully owning the impact of what you do. This value of ownership spread throughout Roblox as the team grew, and it became a superpower. Everyone was expected to own projects broadly and deeply, from having a long-term vision to thinking through every operational detail, including logistics, metrics, and community impact.

The following values map most, in my experience, to high-performing entrepreneurial teams. These values are not just good models of constructive behavior; they are also effective guardrails to the misalignments, inefficiencies, and dysfunctions I have seen most often—the moments when people bristle at being questioned, abdicate responsibility, accept mediocrity in themselves and others, move too slowly, or fail to do what matters. They are meant to inform your values, not define them. Your codified values must be specific to your team and its success strategies.

Here's the list. Note that each value also has a paragraph explaining it. Single words are sufficient with a handful of people because they can easily discuss nuance. But as a team expands, the nuance needs be codified as well.

- *Impact*—Our purpose is to make a material difference in the world around us, specifically toward the mission and vision we seek. We measure that by the impact we have on our audience, and we believe that impact ultimately matters more than inputs. We engage directly with our audience members, act toward their aspirations, and reduce their pain. We believe that our success is only achieved through their success.

- *Integrity*—We live our values. We do what's best for our mission, our audience, and our team, even when it's hard. We commit to acting with integrity with each other, the product we're creating, the organization we're building, and the audience we serve.

- *Ownership*—We accept full responsibility for both our inputs and outputs. We embrace the scope of everything in our charge, both in what we do now and what we choose to defer. We have each other's backs but operate without that expectation, fully thinking through opportunities, risks, and issues on behalf of the entire team.

- *Transparency*—We are one team. Everyone's work impacts everyone else because we each have a stake in each other's outcomes. We share freely what we are doing, why we're doing it, and how we're doing it. We also seek mastery in personal skills and creative collaboration. Mastery requires feedback, and feedback requires transparency.

- *Mastery*—We embrace a path of continuous improvement for ourselves and our collective action. We define standards, measure inputs and outputs, seek feedback, and keep raising the bar. We know that mastery requires focus, so we channel effort to the impact that matters most. We understand that mastering hard things sometimes means failure. We use failure to learn, and we fuel the climb toward greater mastery by the inherent value of its pursuit and the merit of our shared purpose.

- *Urgency*—We choose to act, and we measure our progress in hours, days, and weeks, not just months and quarters. We recognize that time is a finite resource, and if we squander time, we waste our resources, our advantages, and our audience's patience. We assume there is always a risk that's moving faster than we are. We understand that urgency is a skill to master and seek ways to move swiftly without moving recklessly.

Integrity, ownership, and transparency are complements. Together, they define a foundation for leadership, and because everyone leads in some way (see below), they are the basis for teamwide behavior. Mastery and urgency balance each other. They each advance a core success strategy but together blunt the excesses of each other. Mastery unchecked leads to overbuilding and bureaucracy. Urgency unchecked reduces quality and undermines long-term strategy. Impact complements all values as a reminder to do what matters, not just what's important. If you do not ultimately target impact, you risk "playing house"—building a team that feels as if it's operating well, but that feeling doesn't translate to results. Results matter. Don't play house.

Purpose is not and should not be listed as a value. Purpose is codified in your team's vision and mission. Purpose and values are therefore complements. Taken together, mission, vision, and values are the team's "why" and "how" and serve as the core building blocks of its culture.

Everyone Leads

While not an explicit value, "everyone leads" is a natural by-product of the performance values laid out above. A purpose-driven individual seeking impact, pursuing mastery, and acting with integrity, transparency, ownership, and urgency is a leader—regardless of title.

If there is one false dichotomy that is more damaging to our collective impact than any other, it is this: There are leaders, and there are followers. That is simply not true. By the authority of your role or the inspiration of your individual performance, you lead. Whether you embrace it or abdicate it, you lead. Intentionally or unwittingly, you lead. Seasoned or novice, you lead. For good or bad, you lead. The leadership of your ideas, actions, and initiative is just as impactful to collective success as the decisions a few at the top make. In fact, your ability to inspire and align creative action is more important to your team's success than any authority a title lets you wield.

Everyone leads is a value of active ownership and shared coaching. Everyone, regardless of formal role or skill level, is called to lead the team in some way. We all have the capacity to lead, and what varies from person to person is the "what, how, and why." Some lead technically by rich example, others lead formally and through organizational prowess, and others lead informally and speak truth to power. Some lead because it calls to them, and others lead only as a means to an end. But because we look to each other for social cues, insights, and inspiration, everyone leads even when they are not explicitly called to do so. *Who you are, what you believe, and what you do matter.* They shape the world around you and influence outcomes, even if you aren't trying. So it's good to try. Everyone leads is therefore a call to action—own what you do, and lead.

Everyone leads is amplified by autonomy, mastery, and purpose. We are more inspired to lead if we have a compelling purpose. We have more capacity to lead if we develop mastery in the skill sets we lead and in leadership itself. And we have more ability to lead if we're given the autonomy to act. My experience bears this out. Hiring, promoting, and coaching for leadership have been critical to developing entrepreneurial team performance. Doing this effectively requires holding a tension between two beliefs—the belief in everyone's capacity to lead and the acknowledgment that some people are not willing or able to become the leaders your team needs in a time frame that helps your mission. The first belief makes it the job of organizational leaders to help people find their leadership "how, what, and why." The second belief makes it their job to exit those who cannot lead effectively on *this* team for *this* mission right *now*.

Removing people from the team who cannot or will not lead is critical to the health of an entrepreneurial team. It is not enough to hire for greatness (a common tech mantra) and then coach leadership. Absolutely invest in the team. Coach reluctant leaders, vary the "how" and the "what," and appeal to their "why." But after all that, you must exit people who cannot lead in some way. Why? If not everyone leads, then whoever doesn't lead has to be actively managed. That creates pressure to expand the formal managerial layer of your team, which expands the team size. That, coupled with the inherent inefficiencies of larger teams, produces bureaucracy, which is the kryptonite of creativity and innovation. Everyone leads is a hiring mantra, a coaching mantra, and an exiting mantra. Make sure you have a great recruiting approach and an effective coaching machine, but in the end, make sure everyone leads.

Building a culture where everyone leads requires maturity, both in the way it is socialized and in the way it is realized. Everyone leads is not a call for anarchy and uncoordinated action, nor is it a recommendation for consensus-driven decision-making. The best leaders understand that they are part of a team—that different team roles have different information and perspectives, and thus they have different responsibilities and authorities. Everyone leads is a call for shared ownership and an acknowledgment that who we are matters. It is not a mandate to run rogue.

Focus, Urgency, and Health

I once hired someone I was more than on the fence about. I had become impressed with the candidate's skills, but I had also become concerned that they might negatively impact the team's productivity, being inflexible to others' ideas and caustic to feedback. I moved forward nonetheless, hoping I could coach the concerns and confident in my ability to exit. It was a big miss, and the person's short stay on the team was disruptive and frustrating to all involved.

This is a classic error of inexperience—discounting the negative impact of disruptors on the team. And in making this error, I failed to protect *team health.* Team health is a topic discussed throughout this book, from motivating intrinsically to aligning purpose to exiting people with decency. These definitions are generally understood, even if less generally executed well. What is not generally understood, in my experience, is a critical component of team health, the one I missed above: protecting the morale of the productive from being harmed by the counterproductive.

Every new hire has risk, but hiring a question mark is the wrong kind. The right kind of risk, as my then boss coached me, is that the person turns out to be less awesome than everyone imagines, not that they turn out to be less disruptive than everyone fears. A critical job of a people leader is to protect team health. So when in doubt, exit the person making everyone miserable, don't promote those who will not make the team better, and don't hire the question marks.

Engineering an effective value system takes work, typically over time and multiple iterations. But the rewards for a growing team in distributed autonomy and mastery are significant. For new endeavors, though, when time is of the essence and the team is small and likely familiar, a formal value system might be too much effort for too low of an impact. And you might not have enough data yet to craft an effective system for this particular group and mission. So then what? Is there a North Star of North Stars? Yes.

If you can only do three things, these three will take you very far.

1. Focus on what matters.
2. Act with urgency.
3. Protect team health.

In my experience working as a contributor, leading teams as an executive, and advising startups, I've learned that success and failure hinge on focus, urgency, and team health more than anything else. What about product market fit? You bet. But the best path to finding it is extreme focus, rapid iteration (urgency), and some great critical thinking. What about cash management? Yep. Focus and urgency help here too (in addition to being appropriately cheap). What about disruptive people? Absolutely. But these people don't last long if you protect team health. The steep learning curve people climb when joining their first effective startup is typically about focusing more brutally, making decisions more quickly, iterating more frequently, and exiting someone more rapidly than anywhere else they have ever been. That's what it takes.

A value system is a means of institutionalizing success for distributed autonomy and mastery as a team grows—building a system that is greater than the sum of its parts. If you don't need to do that yet, then just make sure your team is focused, urgent, and healthy. But if you do need a system, then gut check that system with these same three things. No matter how big the team or how sophisticated its performance system, if the team cannot focus on what matters, act with urgency, and protect the productive from the counterproductive, the team won't perform effectively regardless of everything else you do. Focus, urgency, and team health are all that's needed on a small team and essential to maintain as it grows.

The Value of Fun

There is nothing more fun to me than solving problems and making a difference alongside talented and committed people, particularly when the challenge is high. It is not just fulfilling and rewarding, though it is both. It is also *fun*. The problem-solving, boundary-pushing, comradery, teamwork, and war stories inherent in entrepreneurial endeavors create professional relationships—and deep friendships—that are profound. The way I think about my most valued teammates, for example, sounds a lot like the way my uncle describes the friends he made in the army. The fun realized on an entrepreneurial team is based on mutual respect, collective creativity, shared purpose, and mission impact. It's the enjoyment of solving problems with engaged people and the meaningfulness of developing friendships with others in the trenches.

Beyond the fun inherent in entrepreneurial teamwork, the right kind of fun also fuels performance. People are inherently social, and our comparative strength as a species stems from our desire and ability to organize and collaborate in large numbers.[33] Having fun together cultivates a mental looseness that better supports creativity, innovation, and problem-solving than being under high stress. The right kind of stress, like a creative constraint, inspires creativity. But too much of the wrong kind of stress (e.g., unrealistic goals and dysfunctional relationships) squashes the key attributes needed to cultivate entrepreneurial teams. And because long-term team performance relies on retaining your highest contributing members, there is also value in the fun that causes people to miss their teammates when they're on vacation.

So what is this right kind of fun? The easy wrong answers include Ping-Pong tables in the engineering room, social pressure to attend daily team lunches, and mandated "fun" events after hours (all real-world examples). All these activities force high-integrity contributors to carve into time with their family and friends in order to have an impact. This type of fun, one not aligned with mission and imposed broadly on all, has the opposite effect on desired performance. It creates stress and undermines the merits of purpose. The right kind of fun reduces stress and advances purpose. *The right kind of fun* supports the mission, and the wrong kind replaces it.

If you want to be proactive and encourage fun, there are two good tactics. First, don't get in the way. Extremes aside, if you see two people laughing in the hallway, don't think it's a waste of time. Think of it as a mutual investment that will benefit both parties the next time they're finishing a project at midnight. The second tactic is to support the activities naturally emerging on your team such as sponsoring outings that are already happening. Roblox, for example, gave an entertainment budget to any group of employees who were socializing outside of work. The policy was widely enjoyed and aligned with our then value of "self-organiza-tion."[34] So to support the right kind of fun, create an inspiring productive environment, allow for the space needed to cultivate friendships, and then follow the team's lead as it organically has fun.

The trickiest part of fun is when you codify it as a value because it can undermine the two main functions of a value system—to provide a North Star of behavior and to define who gets hired, promoted, or exited. Unless fun is mission-related—such as being a Disneyland cast member in a Goofy suit—fun should be supported organically rather than as a codi-fied value. Even at a gaming company, you are not going to fire someone for not being fun, and if you're not going to do that, then a "have fun" value undermines the accountability that values provide. But for Goofy? Goofy had better be fun. And when fun *is* core to the mission (Goofy), balance a codified value of fun with other values (being character-authen-tic) to guardrail against extremes. But if you create a fun value when it's not mission-critical, don't be surprised if you get asked to put a Ping-Pong table in your engineering room and your best achievers leave one by one.

The value of fun when it is not mission-critical is what I call a *lifestyle value*, a third dysfunction alongside the previously discussed *aspirational values* and *inauthentic values*. Lifestyle values reflect the environment their authors seek to build and thus act as a North Star, but they are not used to define who gets hired, promoted, or exited. As a result, these values have little cultural weight and are suggestions at best. At a minimum, life-style values dilute the potency of a values system to guide the team. But these values do more harm than that. Lifestyle values codify the notion that people don't have to be accountable to a standard of behavior—that the values are optional as long as . . . what? Do you have impact? Do your peers like you? The answer is actually unclear when accountability is lost. By all means, shape the social environment you want, whether that is fun, intense, loud, quiet, competitive, or collaborative. But the cul-ture described in this book is about entrepreneurial performance. *You can define the environment you want, but leaders have an obligation to build a culture that performs.* And for that, lifestyle values should not be confused with the codified values that define who gets hired, promoted, and exited.

Values vs. Principles

Operating principles are another way to support distributed autonomy and mastery. They are fundamentally different from values, although they are sometimes confused. In this book, values are *standards of behavior*, and principles are *standards of work*. Values define you as a collaborator on the team, and principles define the ground rules for how work is performed. Values apply to the team at large ("get stuff done" or "act with ownership"), while principles are specific to a group or domain (visual design principles or coding standards). Beyond this book, these terms are often used interchangeably, and there is nothing special about my choice here beyond making a distinction between standards of behavior and standards of work.

Operating principles should not be unbreakable rules. Instead, they should be offered as guidelines that can be creatively and collaboratively stretched and challenged. Innovative experts break the rules, but they don't ignore the standards. Principles are a definition of excellence developed by the team (and sometimes its audience), and as such they promote mastery. And in codifying such standards, principles also unlock autonomy—everyone can be trusted to take initiative when a baseline for excellence is defined.

While operating principles can foster both mastery and autonomy, use them with caution. Principles add process. You have to draft them, get buy-in, periodically review them, and hold each other to account. As with many people practices, use a just-in-time approach, doing only what's needed to eliminate frustrating friction. There are usually strong signals when you need to define operating principles. One of the strongest, for example, is an unresolved intellectual tension, like a team repeatedly debating "the best" design or a stakeholder constantly rejecting output.

Guiding team members to define principles in these cases solves a problem and removes friction. People appreciate that, so it's a pull. But proactively introducing principles before they are needed is akin to building stuff no one has asked for—it's pushing a solution to a nonproblem that incurs costs to maintain. And because culture is what you do, not what you say, premature principles build a bureaucratic culture, not an efficient one. Instead, iterate. Invest an amount of time in proportion to the team size and need, preferring the least specificity needed to clarify work product. Doing more might seem important, but it doesn't matter. Be lean.

Values and Brand

In 2015, when Roblox was transitioning from niche to mainstream and scaling its team, we revisited our values. At first, there seemed to be two sets of values—values to guide our behavior and values to guide community behavior. After all, there were two separate but related groups. I asked whether these should be some sort of Venn diagram—some core values relevant to both with specific values for each. Our new chief business officer answered without hesitation—they needed to be the same.

Operationally, the simplicity of a single set of values is much preferred to the complexity of multiple sets. Imagine the employees working on product features for community interaction. Remembering and correctly applying both sets of values is hard at best and infuriating often. And think about the marketing team having to support a recruiting site and a community site. Each set of values requires different messaging. It's a mess. Multiple sets of overlapping values create a culture within the team of complexity and bureaucracy. But even worse, it creates a culture between the team and its audience of inauthenticity—the team lives by one standard, and the community lives by another. Conversely and powerfully, one set of values for all reinforces that everyone is on the same team—employees and community alike—all working together to advance the mission that serves the audience. That is what you want—one team, one mission.

That brings us to brand. At its core, a team's brand is the articulation of who they are, what they are doing, and why they are doing it.

Mission, vision, and values are that articulation. Putting in the work to express your vision, identify your mission, and define your values is the kind of brand exercise that leads to authentic belief and material impact. Having an authentic brand is one of the best ways to find the people who believe what you believe—audience, investors, partners, and employees.[35] Your team's values are your brand values. They are the values that apply to your product, how you engage with your audience, and how you ask your audience to engage with each other. If you are changing the world around you in a meaningful way, you are building a movement, and movements require shared beliefs and shared values in order to grow.

Iterate and Evolve

One of Roblox's early values was "work hard." Roblox always had a culture of intensity, not hours—your focus and pace mattered much more than your time. Early team members understood this interpretation through shared experience. As the team grew, though, newer employees tended to interpret the "work hard" value as an antiquated mandate rather than a shared commitment, like the call of a taskmaster of an ancient human-powered ship. The confusion is not surprising. "Work hard" was shorthand for the early team but confusing for the uninitiated. So to cultivate the desired culture as the team expanded, the value had to evolve, first requiring better socialization but ultimately replacement. Had the value not evolved, Roblox would not have been as able to effectively reinforce a shared commitment to impact.

Values must evolve with a team as it matures. The values appropriate to the first five or ten people who worked together previously don't always translate as originally written to larger teams of new acquaintances. The spirit usually remains the same, but the codified values evolve. And if they don't evolve, you may lose your behavioral North Star to misinterpretation and thus lose the filter needed for hiring, promoting, and exiting. Iterating values allows you to invest in culture proportionally to team size. For the first few teammates, your values can simply be "let's work with the best people we've worked with before." Codified values start to matter as hiring gets distributed, decisions happen asynchronously across a larger team, and the values are passed on by people who didn't learn them from the founders. Without well-designed and socialized values, culture gets lost in translation as the team grows.

There is one critical caveat to iterating—each iteration must serve a foundational purpose, such as addressing a common misunderstanding or codifying a repeated lesson learned. Values are core beliefs. They should feel enduring, not ephemeral. As such, changing values dramatically and often can undermine their potency. As a former colleague recently put it, people don't take values seriously when they are swapped out regularly: "Once you work at a company for five years and witness four changes of value sets, it kinda doesn't matter." Do iterate your values for effectiveness as your team grows, but also keep them focused on enduring shared success strategies.

CHAPTER SUMMARY

Values are standards of behavior for the team, both for individuals and in aggregate.

The best values are shared success strategies—proven best practices to protect and ingrain.

The purpose of values is twofold: to establish a behavioral North Star that drives mastery and unlocks autonomy, and to define who gets hired, promoted, and exited to reinforce that North Star. North Star values that lack accountability build inauthentic cultures.

Values constitute a system in which individual values complement and balance each other.

The values you write down and share are the team's codified values—the North Star. But the team's realized values are what ultimately matter. Everything you do, allow to be done, or allow to slide defines your team's culture. It doesn't matter what you say.

Six values correlate strongly to entrepreneurial team performance—impact, integrity, ownership, transparency, mastery, and urgency. Impact is fundamental. Integrity, ownership, and transparency are complements. Mastery and urgency balance the excesses of each other.

The natural by-product of these six performance values is that everyone leads—informally or formally, intentionally or unwittingly, for good or for bad, in embrace or abdication.

A simpler set of values can be used in a team's early stages before a values system is needed or as a gut check in later stages when systems get sophisticated. Those values are focus on what matters, act with urgency, and protect team health.

Beware of three common dysfunctions in a value system—aspirational values (anticipated rather than ingrained success strategies), inauthentic values (values designed for the team but not lived by its leaders), and lifestyle values (values that cannot be used for accountability).

In addition to values (standards of behavior), teams also need principles or standards of work. To foster creativity, principles should not be rules but rather guidelines for mastery.

Values and principles should start with the minimal set needed to align behavior and work, and then iterated to meet the needs of each moment. Expect values to iterate more slowly.

CHAPTER 3

Institutionalize Mastery

Humans have an innate capacity for mastery and will put in the work to build expertise if given the space to do so and a cause that matters.[36] Mastery is the pursuit of higher-quality craft, which in turn leads to more effective impact (more people served, or served better, without a proportional increase in inputs). Unlike purpose and values, which flow to individuals from a central definition, the pursuit of collective mastery is typically a grassroots effort—individuals and groups pursue mastery, and the entire team regularly improves. To institutionalize mastery, leaders must therefore codify and reinforce conditions across the team to ensure that people engage in mastery's pursuit.

As we'll discuss in the next section, mastery has many benefits for entrepreneurial teams, but mastery is hard work. This puts some requirements on the way that mastery is pursued. By definition, the pursuit of mastery requires advancing through a series of never-ending and increasingly difficult challenges. To push through this hard work, individuals must authentically connect with and enjoy what they master so they feel rewarded by mastery itself,[37] not just the benefits that expertise may bring (e.g., social status, opportunities, and compensation). Pursuing personal mastery without personal connection is simply not sustainable.

But connection is not enough to sustain mastery's pursuit on entrepreneurial teams. Individuals must also see that mastery connects directly with their success on the team, so they invest in mastery, not just the tactics that get them ahead. And teams must see that mastery is connected directly to mission success, so people are inspired to reinforce mastery in each other. Mastery must thus be celebrated, demonstrating what it looks like and that it's achievable. People and groups must also have the space to exercise mastery so they can invest the time needed for advancement. And the bar must be raised continually so everyone raises their expectations.

There is an important corollary to institutionalizing mastery—mastery is earned, not given. Mastery must therefore be owned by those who seek it. The job of entrepreneurial leaders is thus not to create mastery (mandated training) but to create the conditions for mastery's pursuit and then to hold people and groups accountable for seeking it (self-directed learning in all its forms). The condition that matters most by far is who you hire, develop, and retain. Stack the team with mastery-seeking individuals, and you are well on your way to institutionalizing mastery (we'll discuss this further in part II). But team composition is necessary, not sufficient.

Regardless of who's on the team, if you don't institutionally support mastery, then mastery will not flourish. Here are my ingredients for institutionalizing mastery.

- Show what mastery looks like so individuals and groups have clear benchmarks.
- Promote mastery as a first principle to inspire its pursuit and give license to seek it.
- Foster and support states of flow to help individuals get absorbed in their craft.
- Measure culture effectively and regularly to reduce operational friction and distractions.

These and other topics are explored throughout this chapter, starting with why mastery matters.

The Benefits of Mastery

The primary benefit of mastery is mastery itself—the ability at higher levels of mastery to have greater mission impact in both efficiency and effectiveness. People with greater mastery in their trade—athletes, craftspeople, engineers, artists—can achieve higher levels of performance than others (effectiveness) but also often at greater efficiency, having learned to channel effort with greater focus toward what matters. The difference between Olympic swimmers and everyone else, for example, is the honing of every element of a stroke to maximize the conversion of energy into motion—arm angle, torso rotation, kicking strength, the timing of each element, and the rhythm of the overall stroke.[38] In addition to the benefits of mastery itself, mastery also differentiates, keeps teams small, and retains mastery-seeking people. Let's explore each of these.

Mastery Differentiates

Steve Jobs famously said "It just works" in numerous product demonstrations to highlight a key differentiation for Apple. He was referring to the seamless integration of hardware and software systems that operate to the user's benefit automatically without user intervention. "It just works" encapsulates a significant amount of behind-the-scenes design and engineering to transform the complex, not into something simple but into something invisible.[39]

In the age of the internet where both information and optionality are abundant, products need to stand out from the crowd to win against direct competitors and indirect substitutes. And it doesn't matter whether you're an app in the App Store, a service company, a media brand, a politician, or a nonprofit—today's reality is an abundance that crowds out every message.

Standing out requires mastery. It can be the mastery of the product itself in serving an audience (always the best starting point), the mastery of a product's audience strategy to achieve critical mass early, or the mastery of a team's operational efficiency to serve an audience better, cheaper, and faster than anyone else. But make no mistake—it is mastery.

Like the writer who picks up steam once they know what they're writing about[40] or the sculptor who works more deliberately once the statue reveals itself,[41] teams should pursue mastery in the things that matter most to their differentiation—the proprietary algorithm, distinctive growth mechanic, unique customer service approach, unrivaled design principle, underserved audience, or operating advantage. Nondifferentiated activities (things that anyone can do and often everyone does) can receive less attention, but core differentiation and intellectual property cannot. In the face of abundance, mastery wins.

Mastery Keeps Teams Smaller

Whenever people came to visit Dave Baszucki's first company, Knowledge Revolution, in the late 1990s, they always seemed taken aback by the small size of the engineering team. Knowledge Revolution's professional engineering product, Working Model 3D, had a simulation team of just three people, all with PhDs in computational physics. The application team, also composed of three people, was similarly stacked with expertise, led by the unparalleled Erik Cassel and staffed by some of the smartest and most creative engineers I've ever worked with.

This small team shipped software to Boeing, Lockheed Martin, Ford, and other household names to design complex and mission-critical products. Their productivity baffled outsiders, particularly companies with hundred-person engineering teams, but it was no surprise to me as I worked alongside my teammates. It was also no surprise when the first version of Roblox, a real-time, multiplayer, 3D virtual experience (Working Model 3D on steroids) was built by just Dave and Erik.

Masterful teams require fewer people than mediocre ones. By definition, mastery in personal skill enables a handful of elite performers to achieve more than masses of low-mastery individuals. Masterful software engineers, for example, not only solve problems more quickly than when they started, but they can also handle greater complexity and solve bigger problems individually than a small team of lower-skilled engineers. I have seen repeatedly how the loss of an elite contributor—Roblox's Erik Cassel, for example—necessitates the build-out of an entire team.

Beyond skill, mastery in principles and tools reduces team communication and support activities, typically resulting in better outcomes from fewer people. Codified principles, for example, allow people to work with less instruction, resulting in more efficient onboarding. And the automation of common tasks codifies standards, resulting in fewer errors and less work.

The smaller team size that results from mastery also allows codified culture to be realized more easily. Communication loop times are faster, which means that ideas are shared more quickly, and questions get answered more fully than on larger teams. Cultural measurement is also faster and more precise on smaller teams because you can more easily engage directly with a greater percentage of the team. And cultural reinforcement is more effective because it is achieved through a smaller group of more intimately connected leaders.

Mastery, of course, is achievable on larger teams; it just takes more work and commitment, particularly in the face of the communication friction, cultural dilution, and bureaucracy that increase with team size. In general, more people and practices are needed as teams grow in order to engineer systems for mastery and autonomy, as well as to support a growing audience. As a result, teams can hit a tipping point when people-growth becomes inevitable. Mastery optimizes this growth toward critical mission need and away from the common growth dysfunctions of momentum hiring, "butts in seats" strategies, and spirals toward mediocrity.[42]

One final note: Keeping teams small is not a synonym for "everyone works more" or for unsustainable working practices. Rather it's a design principle to remain intentional about culture with team growth. The most effective teams I've experienced did work extreme hours in emergencies, but otherwise worked with intensity through a normal work schedule. Systematically pushing to extremes is typically a sign of a bad business model, a lack of focus, or an ineffective team. Reducing team size through mastery allows teams to expand along lower personnel growth curves, which in turn leads to easier culture socialization and a greater focus on mission.

Mastery Retains Mastery-Seeking People

As discussed in Daniel Pink's book *Drive*,[43] mastery fuels individual engagement, particularly when coupled with a compelling purpose. When people contribute in ways that are both satisfying and challenging, they become internally motivated to improve their craft, which in turn increases their productivity and impact. And when that impact is toward a mission that matters, contributors can connect the dots between effort and purpose, furthering the incentive to engage with their work.

These two factors—rewarding work connected to inspiring purpose—engage individuals. And in my experience, deep-seated engagement contributes significantly to longer-term retention (people also need to have impact without excessive friction). An environment that broadly supports mastery toward purpose is more likely to engage, develop, and retain the intrinsically motivated individuals best suited for entrepreneurial endeavors.

Beyond connecting inspiring purpose to rewarding work, entrepreneurial teams have one other ingredient to drive retention through mastery—masterful peers. When creative people work alongside others who are also seeking mastery in an environment that fosters its pursuit, they are more likely to remain on the team. And here's why: Purpose-driven people join teams to make a difference, and growth-oriented people join teams to develop. Institutionalized mastery attracts and retains these very people, the ones needed most when facing the unknown—those seeking to create and solve problems better and better over time through personal and collective growth.

Establishing a critical mass of mastery seekers shares mastery's ownership with the team, relying on distributed self-correction instead of top-down policing. Mastery seekers are supported and inspired by peers, and nonseekers self-select out or get organically rejected by the team. And because individual mastery is the foundation of team mastery, institutionalizing mastery leads to continuous improvement in aggregate effectiveness, raising the likelihood of long-term success. This higher probability of collective success helps retain the mastery seekers and growth seekers dedicated to mission success.

Mastery Exemplars

Mastery is easier to institutionalize if you know what it looks like. Here are a few of the many examples of mastery at Roblox. I have not experienced a team more dedicated to mastery than early Roblox. Mastery is ultimately specific to each team and mission, so find and showcase your exemplars to inspire mastery's pursuit.

The Mastery of Expertise

Roblox was fortunate to have two exceptional technical leads in its early days: Matt Dusek, technical lead of our web stack,[44] and Arseny Kapoulkine, technical lead of our gaming stack.[45] Matt and Arseny have different personal backgrounds but share critical professional traits.

Matt was Roblox's second employee, as well as an automotive race instructor, a road biking enthusiast, and a philosopher (no one was more renowned for naming variables and services at early Roblox than Matt). Matt is also one of the most precise and crisp systems thinkers I've worked with, and that thinking is chiefly responsible for the distributed system design that scaled Roblox through 10x growth multiple times.

Arseny is among the most profoundly capable and prolific engineers I have worked alongside (I often don't even understand his tweets). He routinely took on the most hardcore of hardcore projects, including real-time virtual lighting, a cross-platform high-throughput rendering engine, and Roblox's Lua runtime. Like Matt, Arseny guided the gaming stack through multiple 10x growth spurts, continuously improving graphics, performance, and security.

So how did Matt and Arseny achieve their expertise, and how did they translate that expertise into team mastery? Matt and Arseny share two key traits. First, they serially dive deep—identify something personally compelling, learn from first principles, develop knowledge and hands-on skill, and drive toward expertise. Second, they are compelling communicators in both clarity and conviction. As such, they became force multipliers, solidifying principles and patterns, and sharing them through hands-on engagement with team members.

These interactions not only demonstrated the mastery that could be achieved—setting the bar—but also accelerated the mastery of those they guided, elevating the entire team. When speed was critical or a new pattern needed to be established, Matt and Arseny kick-started projects personally, defining standards and paving the way for subsequent development. And they shared a commitment to mastery that compelled them to push through others' discomfort in reaching higher levels of performance. Without the mastery of Matt and Arseny and their commitment to it in others, Roblox technology stack would not have differentiated itself as it did.

The Mastery of Detail

Leif Malcomson joined Roblox just as we started growing out of our managed data centers (third-party-owned physical servers) and were exploring owning and managing our servers directly. Leif had a background in enterprise IT and had previously built several small data centers. Building our own data center was a necessity, but it was also intimidating. No one at Roblox had yet done what we were about to do, and the data center had to work on launch. It also had to be more stable, more cost-efficient, and easier to maintain than anything we had yet experienced.

Leif dove in with complete dedication, pursuing a mastery of detail that was a marvel to watch. His pursuit was iterative but ultimately all-encompassing, leveraging both his prior experience and newly acquired knowledge. Leif started with server specifications (the types, capabilities, amounts, and growth expectations). He then conducted a competitive bidding process, helped negotiate terms, and ultimately helped pick our launch partners. In parallel, he did the same with our physical hosting facility, ensuring our needs would be met through multiyear growth. Leif then progressed to rack configurations, network bandwidth and redundancy, environmental cooling, physical security, power redundancy, and local in-person support.

The most visible testament to Leif's attention to detail was his server wiring template. In a data center, servers are wired to networking equipment, and there are multiple connections per server and dozens per rack. Our early data center had tens of thousands of these connections. Leif's mastery was to standardize wiring through color and size. Every connection had a specified color and length. The result was something much easier to get right the first time and to debug if anything was wrong—two critical needs given the remoteness of our data centers.

But Leif did not just design the wiring; he also enforced it, ensuring that anyone who touched our servers abided by the design. Not only was our data center more reliable than any we had yet experienced, but thousands of servers were maintained by just Leif and one helper. Leif's wiring specification also enabled us to rack servers quickly, allowing us to grow rapidly week after week. Leif's mastery of details allowed Roblox to differentiate itself operationally and maintain a small operations team, which was critical to cost management in the early days.

The Mastery of Tools

Chad Flippo was recruited to Roblox by Matt Dusek with the recommendation that Chad was the best database and systems engineer he knew. I came to believe that as well and learned that Chad was also incredibly hardworking, dedicated to mission, generous to team, and capable of developing technical expertise in any area we needed.

When Chad joined Roblox, we had a handful of web servers backed by several databases, all hosted by a third party. Chad's initial work was to scale our databases and automate common tasks. But his mission soon expanded to include web releases, first creating basic deployment tools, then adding the ability to roll code back on failure, and ultimately rolling out and back by application farm (independent server groups each dedicated to specific functionality).

At each turn, Chad dove deep to understand not only what was needed by the team but also which needs were achievable through tools, either third-party or (mostly at that time) homegrown. With that learning, Chad progressively built expertise in managing every aspect of web deploys, database migrations, and server maintenance.

The ultimate challenge was the migration of the entire stack to our own data center, contributing on the software side what Leif contributed on the physical. Our goal was to comprehensively own every aspect of our data center, and our strategy was to maximize the use of tools, monitoring, and automation to improve uptime, performance, and cost. The systems that Chad built were the key to achieving this ownership.

As he had done before, Chad dove deep, learning our needs, understanding system characteristics, and iteratively building a comprehensive tool set. Ultimately, Chad's tools managed tens of thousands of servers across data centers around the world. These tools also allowed us to move our entire web stack back and forth between data centers with minimal downtime, an amazing feat given the technology of the day.

What Chad developed has since been realized in the marketplace in entire companies and open-source projects. Thanks to Chad's mastery, Roblox ultimately operated its distributed server farm with complete ownership and just a handful of people. That added to Roblox's operational differentiation and helped keep the team small.

The Mastery of Execution

One of the most complex product transitions we completed during my Roblox tenure was the phaseout of one of our two virtual currencies. At the time, Roblox had one currency tied to the U.S. dollar—*Robux*—and another that could float—*Tickets*. Tickets were acquired through site visits to incentivize daily engagement, and Robux were purchased directly by users.

Tickets had run their course. We no longer needed to incentivize daily engagement. Tickets also encouraged botting and hacking (a testament to our community's talents and enthusiasm). Additionally, the product complexity of dual currencies inhibited innovation. Removing Tickets, though, was a daunting challenge. It took away a beloved feature, was a pervasive technical and product extraction, and had the potential to negatively impact our revenue. There was no one more suited to this challenge than Christina Shedletsky, well known at Roblox for her work ethic, tenacity, and smarts. She was also among the most experienced with our virtual economy, having launched our virtual goods catalog (avatar clothing and gear) with John Shedletsky.

Christina developed a comprehensive plan that spanned the tech stack, product feature set, virtual economy, business strategy, analytics, community, and messaging. She thought through every detail and involved internal stakeholders in all key decisions. She also sought feedback, not only across the company but also across our community. Ultimately, her plan was a masterful combination of strategy and execution, culminating in a one-month community transition that converted a takeaway into a mini-game.

Instead of simply explaining the decision and moving forward, as most would, Christina hosted a celebration of Tickets, creating exclusive, limited-edition virtual goods available only to *Ticket* holders. The approach was not just fun but also intentionally economic. The increased demand for Tickets offset the devaluation effects of their phaseout (if Tickets phased out without this demand creation, they would immediately become worthless compared to Robux). By the end of the transition, active users had burned through their Tickets in exchange for virtual goods that forever established them as "early Robloxians."

The transition was a complete success, changing my hopes from a do-no-harm outcome into a realized community win. Of course, some players still missed Tickets, but there was no debate about Christina's commitment to the community and thus Roblox's commitment. Christina's mastery furthered Roblox's differentiation in community commitment and engagement, which in turn fueled community loyalty and retention.

The Mastery of Speed

The earliest version of Roblox lacked the ability to program games. Instead, players created experiences by arranging predefined gaming elements in their virtual environments. The rationale was usability—it is easier to create a game with smart objects than to script a game by hand. But there was a critical downside: reduced creativity, both in achieving creator vision and in the diversity of experiences that could be created. The best games would be throttled creatively by the best tools developed by Roblox rather than grow with the mastery of our community.

The story is that Erik Cassel, a believer in giving creators scripting power, implemented the scripting language Lua into Roblox in a single day and showed a prototype the next day. There are no words that beat working code, and Erik Cassel was known to speak through code. Erik was Roblox's cornerstone of masterful speed—fast *and* competent. He shipped code while the rest of us were still trying to figure out what we wanted to do. And when the code he shipped wasn't quite right, he quickly changed it. Erik once told me that everything we did was a prototype, and we'd make better the things that people actually used, with one caveat—the prototype had to deliver enough quality and functionality to accurately gauge people's interest.

Erik was the embodiment of Extreme Programming,[46] a software practice that holds fast time-to-market as its North Star and pursues it through rapid iteration. Erik developed this mastery over years through the advancement of his technical prowess and an enduring commitment to speed—from the rapid, third-party integrations at Knowledge Revolution to the multitude of complex projects he shipped at Roblox.

Erik lived competent speed, improved with experience, and role modeled it for the team. Erik's mastery of speed added to Roblox's differentiation in continuously delighting the community, and his raw personal capacity kept the team smaller in those early days.

The Mastery of Urgency

Moving with urgency is critical to entrepreneurial success. In the face of uncertainty and competition, the combination of focus, speed, and iteration outperforms everything else. But it is one thing to move with urgency individually and quite another to realize urgency across a creative team. The latter can feel mysterious to the inexperienced, and doing it in a way that intrinsically motivates a team takes true mastery. In my experience, there is no one better at inspiring team urgency than David Baszucki, Roblox's founding CEO.

I have worked with Dave in multiple companies, and he has consistently inspired people to exceed their own expectations, achieving more impact in less time and often with less effort than at first imagined. Leaders are often called "pacesetters," and Dave shows why. As a leader reporting to him, it was easy for me to lead with urgency because it came down from the top.

So what is the essence of Dave's mastery? There are a few key ingredients. First and foremost, Dave is personally urgent—he walks the walk. He is also an enthusiastic believer in what he drives toward, and that enthusiasm is infectious. Dave also has inspiring vision, which fuels a race to finish the current projects in order to move on to the next ones. And he is an incredibly curious problem solver, which allows him to plow through objections to find a faster path to any outcome.

Dave is also responsively dynamic, extending goalposts if ideas get traction and stopping projects that don't yield results. As part of this, Dave checks in regularly, setting the pace of results by the cadence of his check-ins. And finally, Dave is iterative, driving long-term vision through a series of short-term bursts.

Like Erik, Dave cultivated this mastery over years through the development of his leadership skills and a commitment to urgency as a competitive advantage. From the stories I've heard about his college projects, from my experience with him at Knowledge Revolution, and through his leadership at Roblox, Dave has lived urgency, gotten better over time, and role modeled it consistently. Working together with urgency and speed,

Dave and Erik created Roblox's secret operational sauce—a raw, get-stuff-done power. Thanks to Dave's mastery, the team focused on what mattered over the merely important, keeping the team small through repeated growth surges.

The Mastery of Community

John Shedletsky, Roblox's first employee, built or helped build some of the platform's most engaging features—the virtual economy, a currency trading system, user-to-user advertising, and the avatar catalog, to name just a few. But John's mastery was in establishing Roblox's community culture and identity, going beyond pure gaming to something unique, something that powerfully reflected its audience's native familiarity with memes, gaming, and the internet.

John engaged the Roblox community with unparalleled creativity. If some creatives think outside the box, John rejects the box entirely or never even saw it. John built some of the earliest gaming hits on Roblox, showing what could be done while delivering uniquely engaging experiences. Among these was *Nuke the Whales*, an irreverent game that produced a lot of community conversation because, surprisingly, it did exactly what its name suggests. And that is the point—it was not expected. Much more than anything we could say, Nuke the Whales showed players that Roblox was not just about fun, but also about surprise, irreverence, and imagination. It was the right antidote to homework, school, and rules.

John's creations didn't just entertain; they also engaged the players to be creative in response. Nothing shows that more than Roblox's first Egg Hunt. John built a meta game in which employees entered games and dropped eggs from the sky. The eggs were collected by players, each revealing an in-game tool or virtual good. One egg blew up the entire level being played with everyone in it (in a cartoony, nonpermanent way, of course).

The players *loved* Egg Hunt, and some rapidly built new places that were simply giant bowls to collect the eggs. It is an understatement to say that disrupting any game on the platform randomly at any time for a week, let alone destroying entire instances, was surprising. This is simply not something the average person who's optimizing engineering investments would think to do. But John did because he is unconstrained by convention and enjoys play—two things that also describe the Roblox community.

John's mastery of community came from his direct engagement with the community and a deep well of creativity. He was on the forums every day, entertaining as hero and villain in real time. One popular avatar T-shirt was "Blame John," which captured a recurring community sentiment with each bug found. John also created games in Roblox Studio and understood firsthand the frustration many creators had with our tools. And John used the product, causing a stir whenever he joined a game. His mastery of community helped Roblox differentiate itself, not just among other games but also among all the entertainment options available to young people.

Mastery as a First Principle

Mastery must be codified and reinforced as a first principle in order to inspire its pursuit and give individuals explicit license to seek it. Mastery takes work. It requires individuals to overcome challenges and to invest in continuous learning and improvement. Mastery also requires a mindset that can be at odds with short-term thinking—mastery plays the long game, sometime sacrificing near-term speed. Putting in the work and making speed-mastery trade-offs is much easier when every team member knows that mastery is foundational to both individual and team success.

To embrace mastery as a success strategy, individuals must witness mastery in their peers, which means the team must hire people who seek it. People must also see that mastery leads to impact and its absence to poor performance, which means both need to be called out during retrospectives. And everyone must know that leaders "walk the walk," which means that leaders hold themselves and the team to account when mastery is on the line.[47] Finally, every individual must be accountable for their own pursuit of mastery, which means it must impact promotions and exits. The best way to achieve all of this is to make mastery a codified value, explicitly or through similar terminology. And because culture is what you do, a value of mastery must be realized every day through all the ways described above and more.

The term *mastery* conjures different images for different people. For me, I think of a craftsperson or concert pianist. But mastery applies to anything that can be learned and then improved with experience. There is subject matter mastery—design, engineering, finance, marketing, and sales. There is operational mastery—logistics, infrastructure, product roll-outs, and audience engagement. And there is people mastery—inspiring action, coaching performance, and team building. There is really no role on the team that cannot be coached toward higher levels of mastery, but that only happens consistently if you name it.

In my early leadership, I did not call out mastery explicitly, and we all suffered for that miss—not in the performance of any single project or task (thanks to the dedication and talents of the people I've worked alongside) but in the friction it sometimes took to get the mastery needed. Asking a team to pursue mastery in the moment can seem arbitrary, like the whims of the person at the helm. And by not naming mastery explicitly, you don't connect the dots between the pursuit of excellence and long-term success, both for the team and the individual. So call out mastery by name. Inspire everyone to answer its call. Connect the dots to success. And then hold people to account for its pursuit.

Mastery Through Flow

Flow is my connection to mastery, and in my experience, there is no mastery without flow. Flow is an immersive state that crowds out all other input[48] to produce deep, productive focus. It's not just that the activity fills the mind but that the entire mind and body are applied to the activity. It is the programmer working with headphones on for twelve hours straight, the writer isolating in a cabin to finish a book, and the runner who feels they could run forever. Flow also leads to greater confidence[49]—the ability to focus, iterate, and persist through flow fuels the belief that the team has the capacity for impact, both as individuals and collectively.

Without flow, I remain tactical. My problem-solving is incremental, and my creativity is constrained. With flow, however, I can see more clearly and more thoroughly, which allows me to achieve greater creativity and problem-solving over longer periods of time. Flow is thus not just about remaining focused for longer; it is also about achieving states of higher creative performance that elevate impact. It is more and better, not just more.

Flow is fundamentally about leveraging skill to pursue a goal in such a way that the activity is a reward in and of itself.[50] The effort of flow is a pull toward things that strike your curiosity and leverage your talents in order to impact the world around you, and the application of flow increases your capacity to do so. To that end, flow is not about what you like to do but rather about the kind of skill developed through deep connection—a pursuit more akin to a calling than a choice. This connection starts with curiosity and grows with investment: The improvement of deeply connected skill creates a virtuous loop that increases connection with mastery.

Flow is a powerful performance tool for individuals and groups, but it can be tricky to enter and easy to disrupt. Entering flow generally involves properly tuned goals, real-time feedback, reduced distraction, and an alignment with skill. Goals need to be clear and properly balanced between challenging and achievable:[51] If a goal is too easy, people get bored; if it's too hard, they get discouraged; and if it's too vague, they lack focus. Feedback within flow is critical to engagement because it leads to continuous course corrections and incremental achievement. Feedback loops are therefore foundational to productive flow, whether it is a task-based flow that lasts hours or a project-level flow that spans weeks. Reducing distractions is also critical to flow, keeping people in the zone by lowering context-switching costs. A single notification can disrupt a flow state in seconds that might have taken minutes to enter.

Flow's benefits in focus, creativity, confidence, and satisfaction contribute directly to mastery's power to engage and retain individuals. Flow fuels mastery and is essential to teams that create, innovate, and solve problems.

Micro Flow

Micro flow is the optimization of environment in order to achieve flow throughout a day or week. This is the individual or small group working uninterrupted in short bursts of time. As already described, entering flow requires clear and targeted goals, rapid feedback, and dedicated time. And staying in flow requires the elimination of disruptions and distractions. Goals can be optimized for micro flow by iteration, breaking any larger problem into a sequence of smaller ones. For mastery to be owned, the iteration strategy must be defined (or at least codeveloped) by the person in flow. Outside of apprentice-like relationships, top-down task breakdown is a form of micromanagement, which does not lead to mastery.

Feedback in micro flow is about rapid prototyping—the ability to make small changes, see their effect, and then make additional changes, all in rapid succession. In practice, this is writing then reading, sculpting then observing, doing then testing. In software engineering, for example, the most productive coding environments are those with the ability to code, compile, test, deploy, and debug in quick loops. Waiting even five minutes for a deploy breaks flow, so high-performing teams invest in their build pipelines. But if slow feedback loops disrupt micro flow, two things destroy it—real-time messaging and meeting bloat. Let's look at each of these in turn.

Real-Time Messaging

Unless your role is to answer real-time messaging (like a customer service agent), real-time messaging is a productivity killer. Hearing a ding, seeing a notification, or feeling a phone buzz knocks people right out of flow, and the resulting context switch delays their return. Teams have a harder time being creative, solving problems, and navigating complexity if they cannot sustain flow.

The highest-impact people I know have long do-not-disturb blocks or disable messaging all together. Instead, they schedule communication blocks once or twice a day. Another strategy is flow isolation—scheduling time in a single-person workspace, working at home in the mornings, going to a coffee shop, or sitting in a storage closet (personal experience). As with iteration strategy, messaging discipline must be personally owned, but it is much easier to do so if it's encouraged and supported. A good place to start is to talk about the importance of flow to mastery and then role model it and defend it.

Meetings: A Tragedy of the Commons

While messaging disruptions can be personally managed, meetings are a modern-day tragedy of the commons.[52] You can create flow blocks on your calendar and turn off messaging, but if everyone does this randomly, it effectively means the reverse—that anytime is meeting time because there are no universally available times.

Meeting overload is a failure in the market for time and thus requires coordination to solve. One solution is to establish meeting-free times each day or each week. But given the complexity of globally distributed team dynamics, coordinating flow blocks is not always easy. Another strategy is to consider the inverse—specify blocks set aside for meetings and real-time messaging, leaving it to individuals to manage their flow outside of these blocks. Both of these approaches address the *supply side*—the amount of time available for meetings. Teams can also support micro flow by addressing the *demand side*, the amount of time demanded for meetings.

Demand side approaches are a bit easier to manage, have immediate benefits, and thus are a better place to start. Typical tactics include the following: preparing for meetings to make sure they are focused; managing meeting conversations to keep them efficient without stifling critical discussion; regularly pruning meeting attendance to those most likely to act or most impacted by action; and regularly killing meetings that lose value. My best practice for the last idea is to ask attendees on a regular basis whether the meeting has value and then explore changes in format, focus, attendance, or even existence. I also look for organic signals—people no longer showing up, arriving late, leaving early, minimally engaging, or being annoyed the entire time.

Another way to reduce demand is to create meeting subscriptions (like a Slack channel) for those who want to track updates and decisions but not attend the meetings. This keeps people in the loop while reducing in-meeting attendance. Subscriptions also give people the opportunity to have ad hoc discussions with meeting leads or attendees for issues they deem material.

Meeting subscription channels should be read-only for everyone but the one or two who are running the meeting. The goal of subscription channels, as opposed to project collaboration channels, is to broadcast information to a larger audience than those who are attending. But to maintain the flow of the individuals driving initiatives, channels should not become yet another medium to manage. Putting the activation energy on subscribers to seek out project leads organically culls input to things that truly matter.

The optimal approach for managing meetings is team-specific and changes as a team grows, so you'll have to find what works for your team. Meeting management is an active topic across blogs, newsletters, and journals, so developing a set of best practices is tractable. But regardless of how you specifically accomplish it, make sure everyone has time for micro flow, or you'll undermine mastery regardless of what else you say or do.

Macro Flow

Macro flow is the optimization of collaboration to achieve sufficient flow over the course of weeks and months. If supporting micro flow is about protecting creative blocks of time, then supporting macro flow is about protecting the rhythms of productivity that span many blocks of time. Macro flow is thus more subtly undermined. It might take weeks of context switching to realize that the team is working on too many disparate projects rather than focusing on strategic impact.

The principal disruptors of macro flow are improperly tuned roles and poorly utilized goals. Good role design maps the entirety of team scope clearly onto differentiated roles and responsibilities, reducing friction among collaborating teammates—macro flow is challenging if someone is inadvertently meddling in your goals because they have overlapping responsibilities. Good role design also distributes mastery across the team to maximize individual engagement and retention. Good goal design supports team flow with clear objectives, iterative sequencing, and concrete feedback loops. And good goal execution remains focused on those goals unless hypotheses-busting information is uncovered (more on this in chapter 5, "The Cascade").

Roles for Macro Flow

If roles are not distinct with well-understood mission, scope, and priorities, then effort among teammates can be duplicative if not downright counterproductive. Consider, for example, the natural tension between a head of operations who is mandated to maintain uptime for a growing website and the head of finance who is mandated to reduce costs. Who owns server capacity?

The head of finance will err on the side of cost management and lack the tactical insights needed to maintain uptime. As a result, server acquisition will be too low, thus creating site issues. These issues in turn will create fire drills for the operations team, disrupting its macro flow. To preserve that flow (not to mention user experience and enterprise value), the decision cannot be exclusively financial. At the same time, the head of operations does not have any natural incentive to cut costs, so cost efficiencies will be flat at best. The high-impact answer is for operations to own tactical server additions and for finance to own strategic cost targets. Operations stays ahead of user growth *and* has imposed long-term cost targets—targets it achieves through macro flow.

In this real-world example, the high-impact answer was negotiated quickly by the parties. It was a win for autonomy and mastery. But this example is also a bit of an exception. It is not always obvious that roles need to be negotiated, just that operating friction exists. This friction disrupts macro flow as one person or group inadvertently works against the goals of another. To preserve this flow, teams should define and differentiate roles as a system for collaboration, with roles balancing and complementing each other much like values do (see chapter 2, "Live by Values"). But there is a critical caveat to highly prescriptive roles.

Projects with high uncertainty require creativity and flexibility, both of which are at odds with highly prescriptive predefined roles. There is thus a healthy tension between the operational efficiency of role design and the creative flexibility of dynamically negotiated roles, a tension only resolved in context. The mastery is not to pick a single approach for the team at large but to apply each where it maximizes value—negotiated roles for early-stage projects, projects in transition, and crisis response; and designed roles for projects where the path is relatively clear.

Good role design also ensures that there are no mundane roles on a creative team—anywhere. Mastery is distributed across roles rather than funneled to a few specific ones. This is not to be nice, and it is not in service of a particular worldview. Rather it is about maximizing performance and retention. If every role has something to master, then every role can be staffed by a growth-oriented person whose engagement and retention increase with mastery's pursuit. And the more mastery-seeking people on the team, the smaller the team needs to be, leading to benefits in communication and efficiency.

Distributing mastery across the team also prevents the rise of a two-tiered system of elite creators and mundane task-doers. This dysfunction not only undermines the team's identity as a masterful one but can also create an unhealthy dynamic. And here lies another caveat: One person's mundane is another's path to mastery. Some people like to clean up, organize, fix bugs, create spreadsheets, or live in the minutia. That's what gives them energy. And some people hate the very same things because that's what saps their energy.

Distributing mastery across the team is about designing roles that seek mastery. Consider someone tasked with stacking shelves in a break room. If that's the job, mastery is limited—you can stack things conveniently and neatly, but then you tap out. However, if the person's mission is to increase employee retention (through benefits) and productivity (through communal mental breaks), and if that person is also given a budget and a mandate to measure impact, the path to mastery opens up. Now you get experiments with different snacks, snack request lists, snacks that represent the eating diversity of the team or the seasons, and changes to the physical environment. If every role has a masterful path, the team will become more than the sum of its parts.

Goals for Macro Flow

Goal design for macro flow is about iterating on a larger time frame—breaking down a complex objective into a series of manageable milestones that distribute external impact, and thus risk, over time. But to fuel mastery, each iteration must also raise the bar, calling teams to operate just beyond their current capacity. A team's ultimate performance goal is to grow to meet the needs of the mission over time, and often what's needed in the future is not where the team is today. High-performing teams thus look ahead, not just in terms of mission milestones but also in terms of mastery milestones, and they use iterative goal setting to continuously level up. There are two approaches in particular that are helpful with this effort.

First and foremost, a high-performing team's objective must meet the moment—it is not about what can be done but what must be done. The best-performing teams identify where they need to be in a month, quarter, or year and then "back out" how to get there. That backing out is the iterative design that turns the seemingly impossible into the tangible, both for a team's output and its capacity. For short time periods, iterations are about small projects that build toward something bigger. But for longer time periods, iterations also include building team capacity.

Second, high-impact teams have a mechanism to evaluate goal quality. Autonomy requires that individuals own their goals, which means they have a strong hand in shaping them. But individuals are not always the best judges of difficulty, and it sometimes takes a coach to craft right-sized challenges. The boundary between too easy and impossible is defined by discomfort. Comfortable goals are below a team's limit, and hopelessness is generally beyond it (but not always). Discomfort is the sweet spot. To ensure a mastery-seeking calibration, goals should be challenged and defended before becoming final. Operationally, goal calibration for mastery can happen in tandem with alignment calibration—in goal reviews prior to the launch of a new strategic effort. Just be intentional about both mastery and alignment when assessing goals.

In addition to good goal design, minimizing goal disruption is also critical to macro flow. It is disruptive to change goals before their completion, particularly if no disruptive learning has occurred. To be clear, entrepreneurial teams face uncertainty, which means that plans can and often must change. But there is a big difference between changing plans based on learning and changing them based on whim. In the face of incomplete information, moving too quickly (repeatedly) disrupts flow and minimizes impact over time, but moving too slowly can be deadly. The dividing line between these is a single question: Has learning disrupted the foundations of the current plan? If so, goals should be disrupted. But if not, disruption is whimsical and will disrupt the macro flow of those seeking external impact. For entrepreneurial teams, mission impact is defined by what a team completes, not by what it attempts.

We will dive deeper into goal setting in chapter 4, "Unlock Autonomy."

The Year of Getting Things Done

Toward the end of 2014, soon after I became chief product officer of Roblox, it became clear to me that 2015 should be a year of growth, similar to the year of revenue we had in 2013 (see preface). Our annual growth in 2014 was a very respectable 30 percent (approximately) in players and revenue, but I, like others on the team, felt that we could do better.

Part of it, to be honest, was personal to us—we had seen other companies grow faster and felt that we should be in that same league. But more than that, we believed in Roblox and the headroom it surely had both in North America and internationally. Dave, our CEO, loved the idea, and in typical Dave fashion, he soon started peppering me with questions, metrics, product features, and timelines. Dave is so smart, creative, and energetic that it is sometimes more stressful to have a good idea than a bad one (good ones are always better, of course). We set a target of 100 percent annual growth by the end of 2015, a doubling in players and revenue.

I then worked directly with Dave and a small group of leaders across the team, both formal team leads and informal thought leaders. This cross-disciplinary growth team met throughout the fourth quarter of 2014 to brainstorm, evaluate ideas, and build a road map—roughly twenty-six releases across the entire product that involved virtually every team. We then met every two weeks throughout 2015 to steer the overall project.

After some false starts and a few personnel changes, we executed most of our road map, culminating in over 100 percent annual growth in 2015 and approximately 400 percent growth in 2016. There were other factors that contributed to this growth, including some external forces and work done in 2013 to financially incentivize creators. But our road map targeted growth through specific feature enhancements (mobile-friendly content sorts, mobile developer tools, faster game joins), and we saw the direct positive results of those product changes on our growth.

Looking back, my biggest accomplishment that year was not the initial push to name 2015 a year of growth. And it certainly wasn't that I had all the growth ideas. I developed a few by talking directly with creators, but most came from all corners of our team. My biggest accomplishments were protecting macro flow and driving projects to completion across the entire team—staying focused, tracking progress, holding teams to account, removing friction and roadblocks, dynamically folding feedback into the plan, and reporting status to the entire company.

When I say in this book that high performance is defined by what you accomplish, not what you attempt, this is what I mean. We not only attempted a comprehensive road map but also delivered most of it. And we only moved on after achieving outsized success, believing that our resources would be better applied to our next strategic focus. The year 2015 was not just a year of growth; it was a year of macro flow—a great agile road map with the space to get stuff done.

Measuring Culture

A lot of corporate culture and employee satisfaction polls are terrible. In my experience, poll creators veer off track from what matters toward the mundane, and I suspect it's because they forget why they're creating polls in the first place. Consider two examples.

Poll #1

[Includes a link to a one-sheet summary of mission, vision, values, strategy, and goals]

- How much time each week do you get to work on what you think truly matters for our audience, our mission, and the team?
- How much time each week can you work uninterrupted for at least one to two hours to dive deep on a project?
- What blocks you most often from entering flow?
- What creates the most friction in your work? The most stress?
- What aren't we doing that we should? Why?
- What should we stop doing and why?

Poll #2

[Paraphrased from an actual poll]

Happy Friday!

- How do you feel about the company?
- Would you recommend this company to a friend?
- How likely are you to be here in one year?

If I received the second poll without the first, my answers would be "bad," "no," and "10 percent." The first poll is about the individual's experience, how the organization can help them achieve greater mastery, and how it can better serve its audience and mission. The second is about the company's appearance and how it will fare in the near future. The first poll is mission- and service-oriented, which role models mastery and accountability. The second is self-absorbed. Both polls reinforce culture, but only the first poll reinforces the one you want.

At the highest level, the purpose of measurement is to quantify the gaps between what you intend to happen and what actually happens so that you can take concrete action to reduce those gaps. For entrepreneurial teams, the two most important gaps are the one between your codified and realized culture and the one between your intended and actual impact (see figure 1). The first gap measures input effectiveness—how close the team is to its stated performance standards. That is what you directly control. The second gap measures output effectiveness—how impactful the team is in pursuing mission. That is what ultimately matters. The performance tweaks you make to your team's operating environment must be informed by both of these gaps.

Figure 1: The Two Gaps

Measuring the gap between desired and actual impact is more straightforward than measuring culture, even in cases when impact is qualitative. You can measure performance metrics, take audience surveys, hold town halls, use the product yourself (please), and best of all get out there and talk to people. But don't just ask the audience whether they are satisfied with the product or experience. Instead, ask why they use it, what they hope to do because of it, and what's getting in their way, either because of something the product does or does not yet do. And then measure what they do because what they do matters more than what they say about satisfaction. And once you have insight, help audience members pursue their purpose more effectively.

Measuring the gap between codified and realized culture is more challenging. Codified culture is defined by vision, mission, and values—concrete shareable ideas. Realized culture, conversely, is defined by harder to measure practices—alignment to codified culture, alignment to codeveloped strategy, metrics, and goals, and the ability to disrupt any or all of these when it matters. Realized culture is also defined by what individuals experience daily—efficiency or bureaucracy, problems solved or unsolved, speed or inaction, transparency or opacity, understanding or confusion, short huddles or long meetings.

Putting these characteristics together, realized culture is about these three fundamentals:

- Are individuals inspired by what they do?
- Are they able to work effectively toward mission?
- Is everyone working in the same general direction?

If you want to be serious about measuring culture (you should), and if you want to measure culture to drive performance (ditto), then you must know how these questions are answered by your team. Use them to craft surveys and gather statistics, but even better, talk with people.

Finally, there is a misconception I've seen in more than one company, one that I suspect is broader still—that asking people whether they are productive shows less commitment to people and culture than asking whether they are happy. Likely, the former feels crass and more focused on the bottom line than on the individual. I reject this framing. A leader's primary commitment to each individual is to protect their ability to pursue something that matters to them, to grow in mastery and autonomy, and to get stuff done so they can spend more time on all the other things that matter (family, friends, community, self). Framing surveys by the three fundamentals of realized culture shows a greater commitment to the individual than simply asking about their happiness. We'll explore these ideas further in part II, "Mission Athletes."

CHAPTER SUMMARY

Mastery is the never-ending attainment of higher-quality craft, which leads to more efficient and effective impact. Humans have innate capacity for mastery.

Mastery has many benefits for entrepreneurial teams. Mastery differentiates from the crowd; mastery keeps teams smaller, reducing bureaucracy; and mastery retains mastery seekers.

Institutionalizing mastery codifies and reinforces conditions across the team to ensure that people engage in its pursuit, both individually and collectively, leveling up capacity broadly.

Mastery is easier to institutionalize if you know what it looks like, so identify your exemplars.

Mastery must be codified as a first principle because seeking mastery is hard, requiring persistence in the face of the challenges inherent in next-level tasks and the distractions that abound.

Mastery's pursuit requires flow—the ability to enter an immersive state of sustained activity that crowds out all other input to produce deep productive focus.

Flow can be tricky to enter and easy to disrupt. Entering flow generally involves properly tuned goals, real-time feedback, reduced distraction, and an alignment with skill. As such, a critical job of entrepreneurial leaders is to foster and protect flow states for individuals and teams.

Fostering and protecting flow happens on two levels: micro flow and macro flow.

Micro flow is the optimization of environment to achieve flow throughout a day or week. Micro flow is helped by rapid-feedback tools and disrupted by real-time messaging and meeting bloat.

Macro flow is the optimization of collaboration in order to achieve sufficient flow over the course of weeks and months. Common macro flow disruptors are improperly tuned roles and poorly utilized goals.

Measuring culture is critical to entrepreneurial team growth, but what you measure matters. The purpose of measurement is to quantify the gaps between what you intend to happen and what actually happens so you can take concrete action to reduce those gaps. The two most important gaps are the one between codified and realized culture, and the one between desired and actual impact.

CHAPTER 4
Unlock Autonomy

Modern warfare is being dramatically transformed by the rapid innovation of autonomous vehicles, or drones. Once large, heavy, slow moving, and costly, drones are now cheaper, more nimble, more diverse, and more abundant.[53] And because military drone manufacturers are simply too slow and too expensive, drones are now being sourced commercially and assembled from a mix of off-the-shelf and custom parts.[54] Battlefield conditions are driving the demand for drones, and recent advancements in aeronautics, artificial intelligence, materials, batteries, and manufacturing are driving their adoption.[55] But what is driving the military innovation?

Certainly rapid iteration is a significant innovation driver—drone designs are evolving rapidly in the face of similarly evolving advancements in anti-drone tactics and defense systems.[56] But more critically, the most innovative drone development is happening in small incubators across the battlefield, not in an isolated central facility. Aligned on mission and strategy, and granted the space to operate, battalion commanders are crowdfunding and buying drones directly from commercial manufacturers.[57] And once acquired, drones are modified in the field based on local real-time data.[58] As a result of this battlefield autonomy and the experimentation it unlocks, drone designs have exploded in size diversity, from the handheld to the half-ton, and in mission diversity, from air to land to sea.[59] Drone innovation is not only impacting military tactics, but it is also becoming a factor in strategic balance-of-power calculations.[60]

Humans have an innate need for autonomy—control over "task, time, technique, and team."[61] And when autonomy is paired with purpose and mastery, humans can create, innovate, and solve problems better and faster than through command and control.[62] As a general rule, the people most suited to entrepreneurial endeavors need to operate with high degrees of autonomy. It is hard to be creative or solve problems if your operating space and solution set are overly constrained. Yet leaders who build entrepreneurial teams sometimes approach autonomy hesitantly and inconsistently, either in small amounts or by ping-ponging between passive management and micromanagement. There are two reasons for this at the team level.

First, it is not always clear to everyone involved just what autonomy means for a team that has collective interests and responsibilities, and that confusion creates operating friction. Autonomy is not compatible with micromanagement, which diminishes intrinsic motivation, but neither is it being an unaccountable black box—this undermines trust. Productive autonomy is aligning to the team's mission and strategy, seeking input on key decisions, answering questions, and being open to feedback. People need autonomy in order to reach their highest levels of creative performance, but teams need *aligned autonomy* to have substantive impact—to apply sufficient force in a common direction and for enough time to make a difference.

The second reason leaders are sometimes hesitant and inconsistent with autonomy is that institutionalizing it is not always easy. It is not hard, but it does take effort to create an environment that enables the trusted delegation of ownership. To make such an investment, it helps to understand why autonomy matters—that it is not just a cultural preference but actually increases team performance. It is then critical to know how to build a team that operates with creative autonomy while also aligning to what matters.

Of all the elements of team culture, autonomy is the trickiest. If minimally directed, I can craft my role's purpose, live by my own values, and set my own mastery bar—we wouldn't be much of a team, but we might at least be high-functioning collaborators. But the one thing I can't do is grant my own autonomy. My competence may earn me operating space, but autonomy must be granted—not just once, but repeatedly in the face of setbacks and epic fails. A team's ability to unlock autonomy therefore hinges on its leaders' commitment to autonomy. Most efforts to unlock autonomy fail because leaders misunderstand the trust that's needed, focusing too much on the delegate's probability of meeting expectations while doing something novel.

In this chapter, we discuss a more reliable basis of trust: trust in a system of peers and practices designed to guide distributed decision-making and self-correct errors. Leaders who embrace this kind of trust transform from task managers into systems engineers, and in return they reap the benefits that autonomy offers—the maximization of horsepower and brainpower, the ability to expand creativity and effort with team size, and the retention of those most suited to entrepreneurial endeavors. We'll first explore the benefits of autonomy, followed by the system needed to unlock it. We'll conclude this chapter with a look at some special cases.

The Benefits of Autonomy

Autonomy on entrepreneurial teams has three benefits.

- It maximizes the brainpower and horsepower available to mission.
- It increases the team's ability to grow by distributing creativity and effort.
- It attracts and retains the people most suited to entrepreneurial endeavors.

Let's look at these one by one.

Brainpower and Horsepower

Building something new requires creativity and problem-solving beyond the product you are creating. You need additional brainpower and horsepower to seize opportunities, face challenges, and maintain focus. When building something new, you are internally working on your craft *and* externally guiding your ideas through a landscape of ever-changing needs and competition. Creating "the thing" is just table stakes. Finding and growing an audience for your idea is what ultimately matters, and growth has uncertainty. Is anyone receptive? Who is receptive? How many are receptive? How passionate are they? Why? And what's needed for the wider market?

High-performing teams maximize the brainpower applied to hard problems by leveraging intellect across the team. It is far better to enter uncharted territory with a team of independent thinkers who share beliefs than to be the only one in the room who can identify opportunities and solve problems. In addition to brainpower, building and growing something new takes considerable horsepower in both absolute and relative terms. In absolute terms, there is a growing amount of work in any successful endeavor—building a product leads to supporting the audience, which leads to expanding the offering, which in turn leads to supporting the audience even more. And in relative terms, no one can continuously climb to higher heights without recovery, which is impossible if there aren't enough people to share the load and the lead. Distributing creativity and effort across the team maximizes the brainpower and horsepower available to mission.

Creativity and Effort

Autonomy is the delegation of ownership across the team. As such, it enables distributed creativity, innovation, and problem-solving—the small group designing a landmark product in relative obscurity (the first iPhone), the actions taken globally 24/7 that keep the lights on (a real-time operations team), the multitude of critical decisions made by individuals each day (a rapidly growing company). Autonomy allows teams to move faster by distributing goals to individuals and small groups to be performed in parallel.

Distributed autonomy is structurally more scalable than command and control because parallelism can be expanded with additional autonomous individuals or teams, and growth is not limited to the ideas that fit inside one person's head. Of course, as we'll discuss, this parallelism requires alignment, or diverse contributions will be ineffective or downright counterproductive. But when it works well—when everyone is aligned on vision, mission, values, strategy, and goals—distributed autonomy is a marvel of human achievement.

Distributed autonomy means that a serious problem can arrive in the dead of night and be solved in another time zone before the day begins at headquarters. And it means that small groups can respond to changing conditions with speed and agility without getting bogged down by hierarchical approvals, like the battalion commanders rapidly iterating drone designs on the battlefield. And it also means that leaders have a sophisticated performance monitor in each person on the team, increasing the team's collective ability to identify and respond to issues and opportunities. Autonomy increases a team's ability to grow by distributing creativity and effort.

Attraction and Retention

Autonomy attracts and retains those most suited to entrepreneurial endeavors—the creators, innovators, and problem solvers needed to disrupt the status quo. The rules, incentives, and top-down directives of command-and-control leadership optimize programmatic work (highly repeatable and prescriptive tasks) through narrow alignment that, *by design,* discourages deviations from the norm. This is the opposite of what you need when innovation is critical.

In the face of high uncertainty, when learning is achieved through rapid experimentation, you must normalize disruptive thinking—aligned, yes; productive, certainly; but disruptive, nonetheless. Culture is what you do, not what you say. If your behaviors reward following instructions more than being creative and taking initiative, then expect to attract people who want to do the former and repel everyone else. But if your leadership unlocks autonomous contribution and celebrates creativity, expect to attract and retain creative contributors who are intrinsically motivated for mission success. Autonomy attracts and retains the people you need the most.

The Right Kind of Leadership

My first career leadership role was relatively easy. I managed a few senior software engineers responsible for a desktop application. The vision and mission were clear, and our values aligned. It was essentially a project management role, one that benefited greatly by the engineering practice of daily stand-ups. Alignment and risk were triaged and resolved daily—no heavy lifting.

As the scope and size of my teams grew over the years, the frequency of check-ins diminished as my role morphed into coaching a collection of independently operating groups—projects that needed more space than a day to see impact. But as the time between check-ins increased, so did the risk—risk of project misalignment (wasted effort), mishandled emergencies (impact on audience and culture), and delays (real and opportunity costs). As the risk increased, I initially struggled with the tension between supporting autonomy and managing risk. That struggle led me to the classic dysfunction of leaders who lack a system for autonomy: pendulum swinging between passive management and micromanagement.

Passive management is ineffective abdication. It is poor leadership often masked in a stated belief in autonomy but driven by inexperience or a willful lack of ownership. While a hands-off approach might be momentarily enjoyed by those experiencing it, it is not healthy for the people involved or the mission. Passive management robs people of valuable coaching that can level up their mastery. There is also a high correlation between passive management and scapegoating—deflecting blame to the person doing the work, and away from others also responsible for its success. And finally, because passive leadership doesn't always come from an authentic or seasoned belief in autonomy, there is no commitment to autonomy when things go off the rails, hence the swing toward micromanagement.

Micromanagement is nonscalable disruption. It is the removal of agency from someone else. Micromanagement is the elimination of autonomy, the roadblocking of mastery, and the undermining of purpose—the very things that fuel creativity, innovation, and problem-solving. If passive leadership is a system without feedback ("fire and forget"), micromanagement lives at the opposite end of the pendulum—a system without much creativity or collective wisdom. That might work for a bit, but it doesn't scale beyond the bandwidth of a leader or two, and it is unnecessarily limiting in overall team capacity. Micromanagement is not effective leadership, and neither is passive management. And riding the pendulum from one to the other is a false choice.

This book is, in part, a formalization of the practices I learned to support autonomy robustly while also managing risk effectively. In short, I learned to work with CEOs and executives to ensure we had clear and compelling vision, mission, and values. And I worked with them further to draft an overarching set of strategies, goals, and metrics. I developed ways to funnel frontline feedback upward, for both the value of the information and the value of being heard. And I asked those on the frontlines to develop their own set of strategies, goals, and metrics that would guide their execution. I coached those ideas for alignment and impact and negotiated check-in cadences. Finally, I promoted a culture of transparency, curiosity, examination, and mastery.

The difference between micromanagement and this book is the difference between task management and systems engineering. Competent leaders of intrinsically motivated teams build systems optimized for team-based creativity, innovation, and problem-solving—systems defined by practices, principles, and feedback loops. These leaders engineer the system and coach the participants. They are more involved, more in the loop, and have greater long-term control over performance than top-down micromanagement leaders. They coach teams through objectives, continuously helping them level up and achieve better outcomes. And they engineer the entire organization for enduring mastery and aligned autonomy.

This type of leadership is not a blend of passive management and micromanagement. It does not abdicate, and it does not remove agency. It is detail-oriented, continuously setting the bar higher by identifying gaps in performance or impact. It solves problems alongside others as a partner, ensuring that all expertise is leveraged, including their own. It actively participates in the team's engagement channels, cultivating an openness to informal feedback and arriving ready to contribute to formal activities. It is willing to disrupt when hypotheses get busted by data and willing to be disrupted when others do the same. Competent entrepreneurial leadership is enthusiastic and curious. It is committed to the team's growth. And most of all, it is a true believer in mission. These leaders unlock teams through aligned autonomy and the pursuit of mastery toward purpose. This is not for everyone, and many who try fail. But success is exhilarating.

The Right Kind of Trust

Trust is the cornerstone of autonomy. Autonomy means delegating ownership to an individual or team to pursue an objective. The ownership and control may not be unlimited, but they are still delegated. This is impossible to do without trust. In my experience, though, people often think about this trust in the wrong way—"Can I trust this person to do this really critical thing?" Can you? Maybe. It depends on the person and the thing. Do you trust an expert to do anything, even things for which they lack capacity? I sure don't. And what about the most critical, existential, can't-fail things? Do you delegate them and stand aside passively until they're resolved one way or another? I don't. And if someone has a 98 percent success rate at a task, does that mean you trust them to get it right the next time? I wouldn't. I'd just trust that they have a 98 percent chance of getting it right. But all this misses the point.

You of course need to trust each person on your team, or the team can't be very functional. This kind of trust rests on a shared commitment to the team's mission, values, and success, and on a shared capacity for impact. Although this kind of trust certainly helps unlock autonomy, it is not sufficient. Predicating autonomy solely on trusting a person to achieve an outcome is fragile, and leaders who think this way fall into the passive-micromanagement trap. Ping-ponging between "so-and-so is awesome, let them run with it" and "so-and-so now sucks and can't be trusted anymore" does not build teamwide autonomous capacity.

To unlock effective autonomy across an entrepreneurial team, you must engineer a system for distributed work that relies on a specific kind of trust—*trust in a system of peers and practices designed to guide distributed decision-making and self-correct errors.* I call this *trusted autonomy*. Here are its key ingredients.

- *Transparency* so any stakeholder can assess progress, opportunities, and risk; this lets everyone involved solve actual problems, not red herrings.

- *Alignment* to vision, mission, values, and codeveloped strategy, goals, and metrics to ensure that autonomous creativity and problem-solving have common direction.

- *Iteration* through feedback, steering, and constructive disruption to adjust to changing conditions, solve multidisciplinary problems, and continuously improve over time.

Individual performance aside, the extent to which you do not trust in autonomy is the extent to which you are not comfortable with the system you have built. Are people at odds with the team? Are they not building for the long term? Are they pursuing the wrong strategy? Don't blame the people. Engineer your system. Get the system right, and the rest follows.

Transparent Autonomy

Transparency is the first ingredient of trusted autonomy. With the right kind of transparency, those vested in or accountable for an outcome can properly assess progress, opportunities, and risk. And they can solve actual problems instead of struggling to get through obfuscation. In this book, transparency is defined as the sharing of ideas and information to develop confidence in an outcome. I prefer this definition because it gets to the heart of what entrepreneurial transparency is trying to achieve—a shared understanding of how things do or should operate in order to have impact. Establishing shared confidence in outcomes builds the right kind of trust, one not simply accrued from past performance but one earned in the moment through competence and openness.

To establish shared confidence in an outcome, the information shared must be both necessary and sufficient. Sufficient transparency is providing the complete context needed by others to assess risk, steer response, and contribute to solutions. Sharing too little breeds mistrust because everyone knows there's more to the issue than what's been shared. Necessary transparency means limiting information to what matters. Sharing too much also breeds mistrust because it suggests an inability to focus on the critical. Oversharing and undersharing both undermine trust and chip away at the benefits of expanded brainpower and horsepower.

In addition to sharing information that's necessary and sufficient, the dialog of transparency must be a bidirectional conversation that is open to questions and feedback. Transparency underscores the shared stake each person has in the team's outcomes. It is a continuous commitment to each other to seek the maximum brainpower available for decisions and ideas. Open, necessary, and sufficient transparency develops the confidence needed for autonomy to take flight. Let's now look at a few concrete examples to drive this home.

Table 3 lays out the baseline transparency for three high-level scenarios, along with the timelines for proactive information sharing. These scenarios capture most of what people experience on entrepreneurial teams. Project Updates apply to product development, strategic initiatives, organizational changes, and operational projects, among others. Emerging Issues include strategic landscape changes, project derailments, operational issues, and personnel issues. Crisis Response happens anytime a substantive detrimental event occurs, whether by the team's actions, its inaction, or an external force.

The timeline for sharing information in each of these scenarios is different, but the information shared is thematically similar—necessary and sufficient for what has happened, the plan and timeline for response, and an invitation for input on that response. And of course, also common to these three scenarios is openness to feedback and ideas when sharing information.

Example	Necessary and Sufficient	Timing
Project Update	Reminder of strategy, goals, and plan. Goal progress and completion risk. Learnings and changes to approach. Decision-making review and preview. Creative collaboration on works-in-progress. [If needed] Disruption and reset.	On a regular cadence or on substantive changes in assumptions.
Emerging Issue	What is the issue? Who does it involve? Who does it impact? How long has it been going on? What's been done toward resolution? What is the path moving forward?	Depends on severity. Low-impact issues: after they are understood and a solution is in place or in progress. High-impact issues: ASAP with estimates of impact and response.
Crisis Response	What is the issue? What is the impact? What is the response plan and timing? [Retrospective] How did it happen? [Retrospective] How was it detected? [Retrospective] What will be done to mitigate risk or improve detection and response?	Immediate notification of awareness and effort, followed by regular updates.

Table 3: Necessary and Sufficient Transparency

As with all performance values, transparency must be more than a codified value—it must be lived. To do that, the environment must support and invite it. In reality, there is always some cost to being transparent. Even in the best of circumstances, transparency invites inspection precisely because asking questions develops confidence. That cost, though, is generally outweighed by the chief benefit of feedback—improved mastery. But if the costs of being transparent outweigh the benefits, people will become less transparent over time. If you discourage transparency by what you do or allow to be done, your culture becomes opaque regardless of your stated values.

Here are a few easy ways to discourage transparency.

- Get mad when people make mistakes.
- Punish people when they make mistakes.
- Don't help people think through and resolve their mistakes.
- Seize control of an issue upon hearing about a mistake.
- Drift from assessing risks to micromanaging tasks.
- Fail to be personally transparent.

Add anything else that makes people pay an unreasonable price for being transparent. Expecting transparency in the face of blame, social stigma, and loss of agency is not reasonable.

Creating a transparency-friendly environment through your actions is critical, but it's only half of the story. Culture is also defined by who gets hired, promoted, and retained. Not everyone is comfortable with transparency. Maybe they once were or will be again, but they are not transparent on your team right now. Unless you turn around or exit low-transparency people, you will not build a high-transparency culture.

Resistance to transparency is generally easy to spot. Here are a few examples:

- Unwillingness to discuss details; talking in circles.
- Failure to proactively share risks and the plans to mitigate them.
- Traffic-copping communications ("Talk to me only").
- Actively reinforcing silos ("It's my call as VP of . . .").

If anyone on your team does any of these things, coach them to a higher standard of leadership. Calling people out directly on opacity and discussing transparency as a value are often enough to turn them around.

But after coaching, exit any nontransparent people. If you don't, expect to be regularly surprised by undermitigated risk—systems that fail, personnel issues that demoralize, audience pain that turns into churn. Also expect to burn excessive energy solving problems because critical facts only get revealed progressively and reluctantly.

Transparency leads to feedback, which in turn leads to mastery, and that progression is what unlocks autonomy. Anything less is low performance.

Aligned Autonomy

Alignment is the second ingredient of trusted autonomy. People need autonomy in order to reach their highest levels of creative performance,[63] but teams need *aligned autonomy* to effectively pursue mission. Without alignment, too much is left for interpretation. Even the most capable and well-intentioned teammates can differ on strategy and tactics, let alone problem definition.

Without aligned autonomy, teams tend to work on too many things, diluting impact over time—small impact in many directions rather than lots of impact in a critical direction. So even if some success is found, it will take longer to make a significant difference, which increases risk. The longer impact takes, the more likely it is to veer off target, if not become irrelevant[64]—and the more likely it is that a faster-moving competitor will replace you. Additionally, large, focused impact typically builds audience passion, while diluted micro impact builds forgettable utility. Aligned autonomy allows teams to work toward the one thing that matters the most next,[65] the thing most aligned with thriving or surviving. People need autonomy, but teams need aligned autonomy.

Alignment is also about more than effectiveness. Alignment doesn't just shape autonomy, it unlocks it—the more robust the alignment, the more everyone trusts that effort will be applied in the right general direction. Alignment is easy to get wrong, either by not explicitly pursuing it (underaligned) or by pursuing it with too heavy a hand (overconstrained). The former leads to inefficiency, and the latter constrains creativity. Let's explore how entrepreneurial teams align productively, starting with a look at the interplay between creativity and alignment.

Aligning Creatively

I once heard a CEO explain that we need to "make money any way possible." His inability to articulate a clear vision and mission was profoundly uninspiring, and it was obvious to me that the company would continue to work on too many disparate things. So I asked, "What about selling T-shirts?" He replied, "Exactly"—the wrong answer when talking about strategic revenue streams for an enterprise software company. (Aside: I've been called a jerk more than once.)

Now consider a different idea of creative alignment. At a private event (circa 2012), Reid Hoffman, cofounder and early executive chair of LinkedIn, described the "wall of not doing" where ideas that were interesting but not aligned with strategy were placed. It captured the idea for the future *and* made it clear that no energy was to apply in that direction right now. LinkedIn was acquired for more than twenty-six times the first company's worth, and it never sold T-shirts.

The crudest way to think about team culture is as a single arrow of collective force. When designing purely for progress in a specific direction, the goal of culture is to maximize the team's aggregate force in that direction—full alignment on what matters most next. This is the assembly line that produces five hundred thousand cars per quarter, all virtually identical except for color.

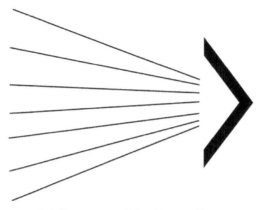

Full Alignment on What Matters Most

But for entrepreneurial teams—ones dominated by creativity, innovation, and problem-solving—this force arrow requires a bit more nuance. This is the startup that's building the first hundred cars by hand. These teams can't be so focused or so mentally tight that their creativity and problem-solving are stifled. Nor can teams be so mentally loose that contributors become demoralized by a systemic inability to focus—either for a period of time or on a specific scope of effort. This disrupts creative thinking and dilutes its impact across too broad an area.

Consider the diagram below that depicts this nuance of focus at varying degrees of certainty.

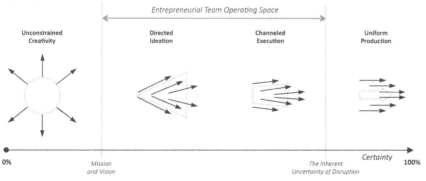

Creativity and Alignment

The horizontal axis is certainty, ranging from 0 percent on the left (full uncertainty) to 100 percent on the right (full certainty). Certainty here applies to everything that matters, including certainty in mission, audience, and strategy. It also includes certainty in the skills, people, and resources needed. And certainty is about risk—the form, degree, and timing of the challenges ahead.

Aside from the occasional wild pivot (YouTube started as a dating site), entrepreneurial teams live in a middle band of certainty, bound at the low end by the constraints of team mission and world vision, and at the high end by the uncertainty inherent in innovation. The arrow groupings in figure 3 represent the force distributions across individuals, with each arrow representing the direction toward which an individual is working—a specific goal, audience cohort, or business model. If all arrows point in the same direction, everyone is basically doing the same thing with minimal friction. And if all arrows point in different directions, no one is aligned on what they're doing, how they're doing it, or even why they're doing it.

The first group on the left is *unconstrained creativity*—the team is literally pushing in all directions at once. Once you constrain creativity by mission and vision, teams engage in *directed ideation*—creativity aligns toward purpose but remains wide to explore opportunities and risk. As ideation matures and strategy and goals are formulated, the funnel narrows further as teams engage in *channeled execution*. In this phase, creativity shifts to problem-solving (day-to-day execution) and the occasional creative disruption of plan ("We just learned something new that changes our core assumptions"). For entrepreneurial teams, the funnel never fully collapses to a single direction because certainty never reaches 100 percent.

Looking at teams through this lens explains what I simply stated in the introduction—the overarching goal of entrepreneurial culture is to amplify and align creative effort to convert novel ideas into audience impact. Amplification results from personal growth and increasing collective competence. Alignment is to mission, vision, and values, and ultimately to codeveloped strategy, goals, and metrics. Amplification mastery is creating the conditions for individuals and groups to pursue continuous improvement proactively, like elite athletes reaching for next-level performance. Alignment mastery is constructively constraining creativity enough to transform effort into impact, but not so much as to stifle creativity and problem-solving. Entrepreneurial teams must modulate between directed ideation and channeled execution, not just once as a team matures but repeatedly as new initiatives launch and new phases of growth unfold.

In my experience, amplification is easier for people to digest than alignment. There are two reasons for that. First, alignment inherently involves filtering out—saying no to ideas and to people who do not contribute to current mission or team. Filtering out ideas can shake people's confidence to contribute unless it is done constructively. And filtering out individuals can shake the team's sense of security unless it is done with decency and integrity. Unfortunately, filtering out is too often done carelessly, leaving people suspicious of alignment in general. The second reason for skepticism is that alignment for some leaders is just a euphemism for obedience. Constructive alignment is about transforming a group of well-meaning individuals into a coordinating team, not about getting people to follow commands. Culture is what you do, not what you say. So if you say "alignment" but act "obedience," you undermine intrinsic motivation and lead inauthentically, encouraging a culture of inauthenticity. The rest of this section explores how to align competently, first discussing what people align to and then how to align productively.

Aligning to What Matters

Alignment only improves team performance if people align to what matters. To that end, consider figure 4, which shows the three layers of alignment needed on entrepreneurial teams.

Foundationally, individuals must align to what it means to be productive on *this* team right *now*—not on a generic team or what the team once was or will be someday. It's this team right now. This alignment is ultimately created by who you hire, develop, and retain. And as we'll discuss in part II, this is about having a foundation of mission athletes tailored to your team.

Strategy	Goals	Metrics	Execution Alignment
Vision	Mission	Values	Core Alignment
A Foundation of Mission Athletes			Part II

Aligning to What Matters

The alignment needed beyond a foundation of mission athletes can be organized in two layers: a core alignment to mission, vision, and values, and an execution alignment to codeveloped strategy, goals, and metrics. Vision, mission, and values are the longer-term dimension. They are the team's "why" and "how," and thus the team's ultimate rudder. Strategy, goals, and metrics are the shorter-term dimension, reflecting the team's current objectives and approach.

Aligning to these elements improves the team's overall performance, focusing effort while unlocking autonomy teamwide. Because everyone has the same North Star (vision and mission), shared success strategies (values), and overall game plan (strategy, goals, and metrics), everyone can be trusted to operate with a high degree of autonomy. That trust also gives individuals the confidence and space to make decisions that matter—not just over task, time, technique, and team but over more consequential things such as course correcting and disruption. And the latter increases trust further, knowing that alignment is not blind to changing conditions.

Aligning Productively

Aligning the team from vision through execution unlocks effective autonomy, but how you align is the difference between creativity and brainless execution. To maintain intrinsic motivation, alignment must be a collective *pull*, not a centralized push. Without pull, you lack belief—belief that something should be done, belief that how you do it matters, and belief that the path forward is impactful and achievable. Without these beliefs, individuals do not internalize commitment and ownership. Pull starts with inspiring vision, mission, and values, but pull is ultimately achieved through engagement—giving capable people the opportunity to internalize ideas, question and improve them, and ultimately take ownership of them. Pull is the result of iterative dialog, not top-down mandate. Mandates and intrinsic motivation are mutually exclusive.

Aligning productively through team engagement is a balance between two forces: ensuring that people are sufficiently heard and ensuring that the team moves forward in a timely manner. Each of these forces produces dysfunction in isolation. It's impractical for everyone to be heard all the time—that's a recipe for stasis, not progress. And it's counterproductive to move so quickly that you miss critical debate and fail to inspire team ownership.

As teams transition from directed ideation to channeled execution (figure 3), productive alignment is a directed conversation with room for debate and disruption. It is directed through core alignment and strategic leadership. And it is open to debate, the source of collective wisdom and individual ownership. There are three principles that can help teams converge productively—time and scope boxing, a commitment to impact, and an appreciation of perspective. The more these are discussed openly, the healthier the alignment.

Time and scope boxing means transitioning from ideation to execution within a defined time and scope of work—"Over the next week, we need to plan the next three months of work on the feature set X, Y, Z." This gets easier with iteration, particularly with goal pipelining (strategically sequencing goals over multiple iterations).

Committing to impact, particularly within the spirit of iteration, means that the team does not seek the best overall approach—a never-ending task—but a very good next step. That mentality limits conversations, guiding individuals toward execution when enough certainty appears.

And finally, appreciating perspective means acknowledging that different roles have different natural insights. Those on the front lines of audience engagement, for example, often view things differently than those who see broadly across the entire team. There is no universally correct answer. Sometimes those on the front lines are most aligned with what needs to happen next, and sometimes those with the most strategic view have the best insights. Both have value, and which perspective wins the moment is not a cultural indictment unless it's an exclusive pattern.

Having a directed conversation with room for debate and disruption is another way to manage just-in-time structure. At any moment, spend the amount of time and effort needed to clarify and de-risk the next iterative step, and no more. Have vision to guide ideas and think long term, but invest in debate in proportion to the work ahead, and then trust in the iteration process (discussed in the next section) to appropriately steer and, if needed, disrupt.

Even if you do all of this well, there is no guarantee that everyone agrees with moving swiftly or is comfortable with the level of uncertainty inherent in entrepreneurial endeavors. Do leverage intellect across the team, but coach people who debate endlessly, cutting off input if warranted. And ultimately, exit people who can't level up in this way because they will define a culture of "think and rethink" rather than "think and do."

Iterative Autonomy

Iteration is the third ingredient of trusted autonomy. Iteration breaks large projects into a sequence of smaller, manageable projects that distribute risk over time rather than accrue and realize risk in a single win-or-lose project delivery. Project owners have room to fail, which unlocks autonomy—failing one iteration has isolated impact, so people can trust in the system to isolate errors. But the benefits of iteration to autonomy come not just from the act itself but also from the multiple touchpoints within each iteration that lets teams assess risk, steer tactics, disrupt the plan, and iteratively improve.

Iterating through milestones with feedback, steering, and disruption unlocks autonomy because people can trust that the system will improve, course correct, and respond to changes in fundamental assumptions. Without these touchpoints, team members up and down the operating stack are in the dark about progress and hoping for the best, which erodes the trust needed for autonomy. These touchpoints fall naturally into four themes: planning, steering, disruption, and retrospective. All of these can be formalized into dedicated meetings or be informal themes of daily stand-ups. Let's look at each of these in turn.

Planning: Create Alignment

Planning is the act of converging on the strategy, goals, and metrics for a block of work. The planning process creates alignment and is the bulk of the work needed to align productively. Because planning is *the* place where teams come together to identify the work that matters most next, how planning happens has a significant impact on culture. How fast teams converge defines speed and focus. How audience-driven, data-engaged, and outcome-oriented the participants defines mastery. And how productively teams can debate and converge unlocks autonomy.

Of the four types of iterative touchpoints, planning is the most prone to bloating and bureaucracy, and I have seen teams take six to eight weeks to plan a quarter's worth of work. It is critical in my experience to be as time-efficient as possible while not squashing critical debate. Here is my best practice: schedule a kickoff, propose goals, time-box the planning, ask individuals to think ahead and gather data, and then come together, focus, and get it done. It is far better for entrepreneurial teams to tweak a plan partway through its execution than to belabor planning. The former reinforces agility and speed, and the latter bolsters bureaucracy.

Steering: Tweak Alignment

Steering is the problem-solving needed in the face of unforeseen execution challenges and new learnings. Steering absorbs new data, tweaks actions and experiments, and realigns the team as needed to hit goals. Most software teams steer through *daily scrums*—short meetings where each person answers a few standard questions about yesterday and today, and detailed conversations are deferred to after the scrum. That builds trust among those on the front lines through accountability and transparency. To build trust more broadly, some teams also have *steering meetings* with key stakeholders on a longer cadence such as weekly, biweekly, or monthly.

Steering meetings hit many of the same goals as daily scrums—tactical tuning, coaching, and trust-building. Steering regularly gives everyone involved the chance to understand learnings and course correct, and those chances build trust in the system. Leaders sometimes bristle at the need for tactical steering ("Why do I need to course correct?"), but individual performance aside, tactical steering is normal. Misalignment happens when hypotheses meet reality and steering is needed to absorb, adjust, and realign. Steering meetings are also good places to "put a pin" in performance improvements for the next retrospective and to raise issues that can disrupt the entire iteration.

Disruption: Break Momentum

There must always be room for hypothesis-busting feedback from frontline execution to disrupt strategy and goals. Likewise, there must also be room for belief-busting feedback to update vision, mission, and values, although this happens less frequently. It is a fact that you cannot know everything knowable in advance of acting, particularly when the course ahead is uncertain. Hence the enormous value provided by iterating—taking an educated guess, doing, learning, and trying again. But for this process to work well, it must allow for disruption, or iteration is limited to tactical learning, not high-impact discoveries.

The balance between being too sensitive to feedback (and thrashing) and ignoring critical information (and crashing) is the classic "signal-to-noise" problem at the heart of many failures.[66] Getting this balance right is a podcast or two in and of itself, if not a book. Here's my rule of thumb: Pay attention to any signal that is not well understood; be less sensitive to noise that is understood; and codify the deviations in magnitude and frequency of noise that could indicate a new signal. A small, stable bounce rate (the rate at which people leave your site virtually immediately) from a website, for example, is noise, but a sudden rise in bounce rate or its significant deviation from a norm are likely signals that something fundamental has changed. Masterful teams build discipline around disruption and embrace it as a critical tool for trust—knowing the alarm will sound creates space for greater autonomy.

Retrospective: Improve Performance

Performance feedback improves mastery with each turn of the operational crank. It is the type of feedback built into software frameworks such as Scrum:67 Plan a two-week sprint of work, execute leveraging the team's current best practices, and finish with a *retrospective* to operate better in the next sprint. Each sprint is an iteration in the work done (output) *and* in how the work is done (input). Iterative improvement does not just apply to frontline work but to all aspects of an entrepreneurial endeavor—vision, mission, values, strategy, goals, and metrics.

At higher levels of operational alignment, retrospectives happen both formally and informally. Leadership access is key to informal feedback, and it is important to cultivate this access as a team grows—open-door policies, flatter organizations, random coffees, team lunches, and leader approachability. Formal feedback typically occurs in recurring meetings such as monthly planning, quarterly goal setting, and annual strategic reviews. Performance feedback through retrospectives builds trust in the system to iteratively improve the capacity, quality, and efficiency of its impact. Naturally, formally supporting multidirectional information flows takes some effort on larger teams. It's a given on smaller ones.

Autonomy in Execution

Most people on the front lines, me included, are generally accepting of a bit more top-down prescription when it comes to the team's overall vision, mission, values, and strategy—they want to buy into them and have a say, but they understand that not everyone develops these ideas together. But execution is where the rubber meets the road. This is where most people thrive when given the space, and bristle when overconstrained. As a consequence, frontline strategy, goals, and metrics—the elements of execution alignment—are typically codeveloped. And when done well, these elements not only fuel autonomy, they also align people effectively to what matters.

In this section, we briefly explore how execution alignment can unlock autonomy. Each topic below is too broad to cover in depth in this book. The focus here is instead on what they are and how they can be used to unlock autonomy.

Strategy

Strategy is a selected path to a long-term objective—a way to navigate a multidimensional decision space in order to seek a desired endpoint. There are typically many paths through this decision space, and strategy is choosing one, often with backup paths and trigger points for switching paths.

Consider, for example, a month-long objective of crossing a mountain range. Some paths are snowy, others are rainy, and others are temperate. Some encounter long rolling hills, and others have near-vertical slopes. There are many paths through the range that all end up on the other side. The rolling hills are lower risk, for example, but your particular team is composed of experienced climbers, so near-vertical climbs are not off-limits. The team's strategy is the selection of one path with a high likelihood of success, considering not just the conditions that will be encountered but also the team's strengths and weaknesses, as well as its time and resource constraints. The strategy also includes a handful of locations where the team can change course based on local conditions. And the strategy has contingency plans for emergencies.

Strategy is a big topic, and the right strategy for a particular team and mission is context-specific. Yes, there are broadly useful patterns. Sun Tzu's *The Art of War*, for example, is a popular business book for that very reason, as are books by business and military leaders. But while there are broad patterns, the right strategy for your team can only be determined in the context of the moment and the market. So aside from the shared success strategies codified in your values, expect to develop and refine your strategy regularly as you pursue mission.

Strategy is also not singular but rather an amalgam of complementary area-specific strategies, typically developed in tandem—this is particularly true of entrepreneurial strategy. This book, for example, is about team strategy, but entrepreneurial activities also require strategies for audience segmentation, customer development, product development, customer support, market differentiation, sales and marketing, fundraising, financing, and legal, among others. As teams move from directed ideation to channeled execution (figure 3), team members must operationally align to all these strategies in order to be effective—even if they don't fully agree with all of them, and they usually don't. This alignment unlocks autonomy (as we'll discuss below).

Strategy can also be understood in contrast to tactics. While strategy is a selection of a path to a long-term objective, tactics are choices in how best to achieve a near-term goal. In the above mountain range example, tactics would include shoe and equipment selection, as well as the attack plan for a specific slope. Given this distinction between long-term objective and short-term goal, it may seem that the difference between strategy and tactics is simply one of time frame—a two-year strategy is simply a tactic when viewed over thirty years. This is not the case. The key distinction is that strategy has vision beyond just task completion, and tactics do not.

Strategy is the means to achieve a mission in pursuit of a vision and thus imposes a constraint on near-term tactics. Tactics, by contrast, are mission-agnostic. Consider online advertising. Tactically speaking, if the goal is to maximize the number of ad clicks, then the ad copy and design will ultimately degenerate into clickbait ("You will never guess what so-and-so said"). A mission-oriented strategy might instead seek to build an enduring audience, one that believes in mission, finds value in the product, and ultimately stays. Clickbait is not aligned with such a strategy.

Teams are more effective with strategic alignment because everyone is on the same path (or at least close by) and can work together to accelerate their progress and manage risk. People who operate with strategic alignment complement each other's work, creating greater aggregate force. Returning to the mountain range example, if the objective also includes protecting a shared resource, then the mission is more at risk the more people diverge on their paths. And for success, it matters far more to walk a shared path than it does to choose the best one, catastrophically deadly paths aside. As long as people align productively and iterate, the strategic path can be adjusted or disrupted in the face of actual conditions.

Strategic alignment unlocks autonomy, particularly when coupled with iteration, because everyone can be trusted to be on the same path or at least close by, allowing for greater freedom of decision-making even beyond task, time, technique, and team. Additionally, the focus created by strategic alignment builds trust that the team can overcome challenges, precisely because the alignment channels horsepower and brainpower to face challenges as a group.

Goals

Goals unlock autonomy because they are codeveloped contracts for pursuing strategy. As teams go beyond directed ideation to channeled execution, goals and strategy define the execution channel and thus help build trust that execution is aligned. Goals are essential to impact because they focus effort, clarify success, and (the best ones) target outcomes. In simple terms, they answer two critical questions: What are we doing? And how do we know we've succeeded?

Entrepreneurial teams need goals more than plans. Plans outline anticipated activity for all involved, but they become irrelevant when hypotheses meet reality. Well-designed goals are robust to learning, allowing activities to respond to new information with agility. Plans tend to lock in predefined activities because it takes work to replan—goals are nimble.

The best goal framework I have used is Objectives and Key Results (OKRs), an approach used by Google and documented by John Doerr.[68] Objectives are goals, and key results are the quantification of goals (i.e., a measurable agreement on success). Objectives are meant to result in big, audacious, game-changing outcomes. As a consequence, they help teams go beyond the many important things facing them to the few that truly matter.

As a calibration of difficulty, each OKR owner (group or person) pursues about three objectives, each with about three key results and an average expected achievement rate of 70 percent. Consistently achieving higher suggests that the key results are too easy. Consistently achieving lower is more nuanced, suggesting that the key results are too hard, the objectives are irrelevant to actual operations (so people ignore them), or OKR owners are underperforming.

OKRs are typically defined for the entire team, with group OKRs cascading down from teamwide ones. OKRs lower in the organizational stack align to those higher in the stack. As a result of this synchronization, OKRs are generally developed on a cadence, such as quarterly, and the entire team iterates over multiple OKR cycles. The cadence size defines the challenge—an objective for a quarterly OKR is more substantive than a monthly one and less than an annual one. OKRs can also be nested (quarterly OKRs aligning to annual ones).

The rhythm of OKRs drives *macro flow*, the ability of a team to focus and rapidly iterate in a high-performance state for weeks or months (a topic explored in chapter 3). This cadence gives teams the opportunity to dive deep toward impact by experimenting, learning, failing, and trying again. Without that rhythm, there is no macro flow. Crises and ideation aside, if every day or week is like starting over, there is no real space for mastery.

There is a flip side, though, to the structured rhythm of OKRs—a loss of dynamism and agility. Teams lose dynamism when the OKR cadence is too long and progress is thus too slow, both killers for urgency and impact. Teams lose agility by the time-boxing nature of OKR cadences, which often cause groups to fill the time with the project, not end the project early. That happens not because people are laggards but because it's the system.

When OKRs were first introduced at Roblox in 2012, I was a big fan—I loved the boldness of audacious objectives and the clarity of measurable results. But eventually, I saw too many examples at too many companies of team pace being slowed down by OKRs, rather than accelerated. And the crux of the problem is this: The synchronization across multiple parallel activities that drives collective alignment also forces every team into the same cadence, which is not always the most efficient allocation of effort. Additionally, the cost of synchronization in terms of effort often outstrips the benefits in alignment as teams grow.

The best implementation of OKRs I've seen that addresses this bureaucratic tendency is to use the OKR goal structure in Kanban-style project management. A logical extension of agile project management, this approach stacks goals in sequence, defining each as an OKR; it then time-boxes each goal uniquely based on its needs. Smaller OKRs have shorter time frames, while larger OKRs have longer time frames. For parallel running teams, each team has its own Kanban work stream, and cross-team OKRs only end at the same time by accident. This approach requires additional sophistication in tools and mindset, as team alignment becomes continuous rather than cadenced. But the benefits in agility and dynamism are worth the cost.

The OKR framework—and goal setting in general—is a strong driver of culture. How you identify, define, track, steer, and evaluate OKRs, and how you respond to consistent hits and misses, defines culture. Objectives don't inspire? Then you aren't serious about mission or achievement, so why should anyone else be? The team doesn't monitor its progress transparently? Then no one is paying attention, so who cares? The team doesn't steer effectively, adjusting tactics or disrupting goals when needed? The team can't follow through on intentions, so why should anyone bother? The team doesn't address consistently missed goals? Then there's no accountability, so anything goes. Even if you haven't yet engineered your culture for high-performance autonomy, getting OKRs right is a big first step in that direction.

Metrics

Metrics are critical to entrepreneurial impact. They track goal progress, quantify audience experience, alert when performance norms are deviated, and become the ultimate unbiased arbiters of opinion and hierarchy. Metrics are both external (measuring audience-facing performance) and internal (measuring system performance). External metrics measure mission impact, while internal metrics provide diagnostic capabilities to understand changes in impact. Like values, the set of metrics define a system, with individual metrics complementing and balancing each other. The growth metric "user revenue," for example, should be balanced by "user lifetime value," or the former might be pursued to a counterproductive extreme.

Tracking and sharing metrics builds the trust needed for autonomy. If progress is transparent and deviations are monitored and addressed, everyone can trust *in the system* to track goals and critical performance. Without metrics and their alerting, those vested in outcomes (everyone) are left wondering how things are going and whether everything's okay, which undermines trust. The definition of metrics and the accountable ownership of them are key parts of the system that teams build for trusted autonomy.

There are five broad categories of metrics typically used by entrepreneurial teams. *A North Star* metric encapsulates a lot of complexity and represents the one thing that matters most to the overall mission at any given time. A North Star metric should measure impact, not input, and teams should have one and only one North Star for everyone. Not every individual or team can operate directly on the North Star, but everyone needs to be operating toward it nonetheless. In these cases, *Proxy North Stars* can be defined. Proxies are actionable metrics that are believed to align with the North Star, and believed is the key word—their validity must be proven.

Key Results track the progress of an OKR, and they often relate to the North Star or its proxies. They provide concrete feedback for steering, refining tactics, uncovering learnings, and disrupting incorrect strategies. *Key Performance Indicators* (KPIs) track an amalgam of strategic metrics, including North Star candidates, former and future Key Results, and other metrics that capture critical aspects of the entire endeavor. Teams do not commit to improve all KPIs all the time, but by definition, if any KPI performance degrades, the team disrupts other work to fix it. Lastly, *Diagnostic* measurements are used to understand changes to KPIs and are not necessarily operated on directly, either as a KPI interrupt or a North Star.

There is one more metric category that is not as commonly discussed as North Stars and KPIs—the unmeasurable metric. Automated concrete metrics are the gold standard, but metrics matter even when they can't be measured. Metrics shape creativity even before you have data. The simple act of defining a metric, even if you don't yet have the ability to measure it, influences ideas, priorities, and solutions. That leads to speed. You can develop the means to both measure and influence a metric in parallel, not waiting weeks or months to get a clean measurement. This was indeed one of the tactics Roblox employed during the revenue crisis described in the preface. So, define metrics even before you know whether they can be measured, and then measure what you can, either directly or through proxies. And even a qualitatively evaluated metric measured by the team's regular "high, medium, low" assessment has value.[69]

Special Cases

Below are a few special cases where autonomy may seem absent or not possible. On entrepreneurial teams, autonomy is always essential, but how it plays out in extremes is often different from what's effective for the normal course of creative effort.

Autonomy and Hard Turns

As I write this book, I have been watching the transformation of Warner Bros. Discovery under the leadership of David Zaslav. Over the past twenty-four months, Zaslav has killed CNN+ within a few weeks of its launch,[70] canceled the finished production of *Batgirl before its marketing push,*[71] rebranded its streaming service, exited a number of key executives, and questioned the economics of the company's production pipeline.[72] I don't know whether Zaslav's specific decisions will ultimately be successful in this transformation, but his approach is helpful to understand autonomy in the context of hard turns.

Hard turns often need significant internal disruption that can be upsetting and counterintuitive for those who have mastered the old system. Self-disruption is how Facebook rapidly shifted to mobile, how Roblox adjusted multiple times to changing conditions, and how I've operated in turnaround situations. But it does prompt the question: Is the hard tack needed for self-disruption counter to autonomy? The short answer is no.

The key word above is *transformation.* There are times when teams need to take hard turns in order to survive and thrive—either hard changes in strategic course or even harder changes in culture. Often, it's changes in both strategy and culture at the same time. There are three broad reasons why transformations are hard.

- *Organizational momentum:* Work invested in the current strategy and a team optimized for that strategy are both examples of the sunk cost fallacy.[73]

- *Vested interests in the status quo:* A new system creates new winners and losers in those who can and can't adapt, so those who are unwilling or unable to adapt resist.

- *Authentic belief in the status quo:* It is difficult for those committed to mission to depart from strategies they believe lead to success.

Overcoming these situations takes leadership fortitude and skill. You must have a clear vision for what needs to be done and why. You must relentlessly and unwaveringly focus on this transformation, highlighting misalignment every time a person or team is not aligned. You must exit anyone who cannot operate productively in the new paradigm. And you must be willing to look wrong and be unpopular.

As a result, transformations often look like micromanagement because there is little room for creative deviations from the transformative path, and dissenting opinions are typically not sustainable. But constraining creativity to rewire strategy or culture is not micromanagement. Rather, it is the force needed to free people of ingrained habits and beliefs, and to free teams of established operating practices.

Autonomy can exist during hard turns; it is just aligned along a much narrower channel. On an axis of certainty (see figure 3 earlier in this chapter), hard turns are closer to the upper limit of entrepreneurial activity than any other. Think of them as *extremely channeled execution*. To maintain a healthy entrepreneurial team during a hard turn, call out the moment. Let everyone know that the team needs to self-disrupt, and then explain why, inspire with vision, and instill confidence with competent strategy.

Hard turns are not about abandoning intrinsic motivation; they are about resetting the system. Low-mastery transformations are indeed micromanagement in execution, but high-mastery transformations shift people to a new system while maintaining intrinsic motivation. And once you're on the other side, remember to return to normal for all the benefits autonomy provides.

Autonomy and Efficiency

Autonomy and efficiency are sometimes at odds. If you know exactly what you need to do, it's more efficient to just tell people what to do and how to do it, but this undermines autonomy. Autonomy and efficiency, though, are not mutually exclusive. Autonomy is about long-term creative impact, both in inputs and output. Efficiency is about the level of waste in executing at any given moment. Together they form a healthy tension. For entrepreneurial teams, autonomy must be the norm, and any inefficiency can become a performance target if it matters.

The exception to this norm is an extreme emergency, something that's mission-critical and requires rapid and (generally) controlled triaging, response, and coordination. In these cases, autonomy is bestowed upon an individual or small team, sometimes called a *tiger team*, to lead the charge, with everyone else taking instructions. This sacrifices broad autonomy in the moment in favor of narrower high-impact mastery. When these situations arise, call it out explicitly, and get people comfortable with switching operating modes. Switch back when the crisis has resolved.

Autonomy and Authority

A product manager once asked me to review their work before a presentation they were about to give the CEO. They showed me three choices for a design. But when I asked which one they recommended and why, they didn't have an answer—on purpose.

Their plan was to show the CEO three options and then do what the CEO wanted. I hope you can see the problem here. The job of every leader is to have a perspective. Having a perspective requires work, and that work is fundamental to ownership and mastery. It doesn't matter whether you are overruled most of the time by someone with higher authority. The job is not to guess correctly; the job is to do the work. This person not only took a lazy approach to their job but also undermined the team's autonomy and its long-term capacity. That person received on-the-spot coaching from me, although "coaching" might be a bit generous in describing my response.

If you're lucky in your career, you'll work for someone with strong vision, high mental capacity, and innate urgency. Nothing sets your performance bar higher than doing something that matters alongside someone who thinks big and can solve big problems. But there is a challenge to working in these situations, and there is a critical decision for you to make. People with high intellectual capacity in an area can typically see and solve problems better and faster than most others. And when these people also wield authority, persuasion takes more work. Some people in these situations abdicate their autonomy and responsibility, and just play "decision divining rod" like the product manager above. These people do the mission and the team a great disservice.

By abdicating ownership, mastery, and autonomy, people rob the team of their own brainpower and horsepower, reduce the vetting of ideas, and lower the success rate of decisions. Even if a top-down decision is directionally correct, it can be improved with feedback, and sometimes that feedback is the difference between success and failure. So if you find yourself on the same playing field as an elite athlete, don't walk off the field and hand them a trophy. Play! Everyone's performance will be better for it. Do your homework. Align your ideas to mission, values, strategies, and goals. Get feedback. And then have a perspective that you're ready to defend.

Iterating the System

Autonomy is where engineering your culture can start to feel a bit overwhelming. It's easy to imagine spending a day on vision, mission, and values, and then iterating indefinitely as needed. But unlocking autonomy requires a bit more effort, not just in its practices but also in its mindset. Supporting autonomy *and* remaining aligned is beyond leadership 101 in my experience, and its systems are beyond the basics. But it is a mistake to conclude that a system for autonomy is inherently heavyweight and only warranted on larger teams. Autonomy is just as amenable to iteration as anything else.

For small teams, fewer than twenty for example, communication is a teamwide conversation happening every day. In this setting, unlocking autonomy is primarily about what leaders do in each interaction. They can be focused, opinionated, urgent, and frontline contributors, but as long as they are open to ideas, listen to feedback, codevelop goals, and encourage constructive dissent, autonomy will thrive. This is just good entrepreneurial leadership, and the benefits in personal ownership and initiative warrant the discipline.

Structurally, small teams also need to do a few other things to unlock autonomy. First, everyone should be able to answer three basic questions: What are we doing? Why are we doing it? How do we know we're making progress? Foundationally, this is served by vision, mission, strategy, goals, and metrics. On top of this foundation, small teams can further unlock autonomy through a lightweight project management framework such as Scrum.[74] Inherently iterative, Scrum and its equivalents break down the pursuit of mission into a series of time-boxed pushes. Each push is a chance not only to deliver new impact but also to improve the team's overall performance. The narrative of each iteration coupled with the goal setting and daily accountability unlock autonomy.

The heavier lift to unlock autonomy comes as the team grows beyond the "everyone's in the same conversation" size of thirty or so. At this point, autonomy requires additional structure, such as parallel streams of work, which in turn require coordination. This needs to be formalized as a system in order to thrive. But as long as the maintenance of that system is proportional to team size, the benefits in expanded brainpower and horsepower outweigh the costs of the formalization. We'll explore iterating autonomy further in chapter 5, "The Cascade."

CHAPTER SUMMARY

Humans have an innate need for autonomy—control over task, time, technique, and team. Generally, those most suited to entrepreneurial endeavors need high levels of autonomy.

Autonomy has three benefits for entrepreneurial teams. It maximizes brainpower and horsepower available to mission. It increases the team's ability to scale by distributing creativity and effort. And it attracts and retains the people you need the most.

Despite these benefits, leaders often approach autonomy hesitantly and inconsistently because it is not always clear to everyone involved what autonomy means or how to leverage it.

Autonomy on an entrepreneurial team is not unilateral, unaccountable action; it is pursuing mission, seeking input, answering questions, being open to feedback, and sharing information.

Competent leaders of intrinsically motivated people build systems optimized for team-based creativity, innovation, and problem-solving at increasing mastery and scale. They engineer the system and coach the participants to create a trusted environment that unlocks autonomy.

Leveraging autonomy requires trust—not trust in an individual to complete a project but trust in a teamwide system of peers and practices that guides distributed decision-making and self-corrects errors. The elements of this system are transparency, alignment, and iteration.

Transparency is the sharing of information to develop confidence in an outcome. The information shared must be sufficient (for evaluation) and necessary (focusing on what matters).

Alignment is not a euphemism for obedience but a team transition from *directed ideation* (minimally constrained creativity) to *channeled execution* (applied creativity). Entrepreneurial teams must align to what matters (vision, mission, values, strategy, goals, and metrics), and they must align productively to promote ownership (*pull* around a codeveloped plan).

Iterative autonomy unlocks self-improvement and self-correction. In practice, there are four areas of iteration: regular planning where learning is incorporated and alignment is created; steering meetings to incorporate tactical learning; explicit disruption when learnings break fundamental hypotheses; and retrospectives when performance is reviewed.

Most people on the front lines generally accept a bit more top-down prescription when it comes to the team's overall vision, mission, values, and strategy, but execution is where the rubber meets the road. As a result, frontline strategy, goals, and metrics—the elements of execution alignment—should be codeveloped. And when done well, these elements not only fuel autonomy, they also align people effectively to what matters.

CHAPTER 5

The Cascade

have developed an operational framework that captures the ideas discussed in part I—fueling by purpose, living by values, institutionalizing mastery, and unlocking autonomy. It was informed by the startup successes and failures I had previously experienced, and it was driven by the parallelism and speed we needed at Roblox. It was also developed with partners across the Roblox team, chief among them our CEO. I have continued to develop this framework, and I share it with the startups I work with because I believe it makes a difference.

I call this framework *The Cascade*. The term is not an acronym. Rather, The Cascade describes the flow of information and decisions from one set of elements to another, like the flow of purpose from vision to execution that focuses effort, or the flow of goals from the overall team to groups and individuals. The Cascade grew from my passion to ensure that everyone could answer these three simple questions for themselves and the team as we grew:

1. What are we doing?
2. Why are we doing it?
3. How do we know we're making progress?

While The Cascade is my foundation for trusted autonomy, it also cultivates mastery at the team leadership level. The more competently leaders can guide teams through the elements of The Cascade, the more mastery is role modeled at the highest levels for everyone. It is much more motivating, for example, to seek mastery when the leadership team has its act together. And it is this trait that establishes The Cascade as an element of entrepreneurial culture. It is the definition of collaborative *doing* that establishes focus and pace.

As we'll discuss, when the team is just a handful of people meeting daily, The Cascade is a simple form of the three questions above. It is lightweight and agile. But as the team grows beyond a single project all-hands, these questions require additional structure to align the missions and goals of multiple groups with the overall team. The amount of structure needed should strike a balance between the punching in all directions of too little structure and the speed-sapping bureaucracy of too much. I have seen firsthand the enormous benefits of focus and accountability as a team expands, but I have also seen the crushing bureaucracy of too much too soon.

Connecting the dots at key moments, such as annual planning or major strategic pivots, is tremendously helpful. This collectively aligns and inspires. But connecting the dots in formal documentation across the team on a weekly, monthly, or even quarterly basis can turn a nimble team into one that is harder to move.

The Cascade is about aligning autonomous action, much like rebalancing a portfolio or checking the compass on a long hike. It is critical to do this at key moments or collective effort will drift off course over time. But realigning too often is an overoptimization, a form of micromanagement that stifles creativity and reduces speed. Refreshing the entire cascade every time one group changes course, for example, slows everyone down without improving overall alignment—these changes are simply too small and volatile to capture often.

The antidote to overengineering The Cascade is twofold: a return to the three questions above (what, why, and how), and a reminder of just what all of this is about—unlocking aligned autonomy to maximize the effort applied to mission across the team. As long as your cascade is doing both of these without too much overhead, you're on the right track.

The Cascade

The Cascade connects the dots from vision through execution, and from the overall team to each small frontline group. By design, The Cascade does five things:

- Connects individual action to team purpose, fueling motivation.
- Defines a rudder for everyone to align to, unlocking effective autonomy.
- Defines feedback loops and touchpoints, unlocking trusted autonomy.
- Ensures teamwide initiatives are comprehensively supported.
- Realizes macro mastery, underpinning a culture of mastery.

Figure 5: The Cascade for a Team

Figure 5 is an overview of The Cascade as it relates to the elements of part I. It is composed of the two groupings previously discussed in "Aligning to What Matters" (from chapter 4, "Unlock Autonomy")—vision, mission, and values; and strategy, goals, and metrics.

Vision, mission, and values define *core alignment*. No matter how aligned someone is to a team's execution approach, if they are not aligned to the core, they will ultimately have dilutive and high-cost impact. They might get stuff done, but if they are unaligned with the team's purpose, they work off target. Or if they are unaligned with the team's standards of behavior, they cause friction. Core alignment is not easily coached, so first and foremost, find people who believe what you do about the world you want to see and the values by which you operate.

Strategy, goals, and metrics are the team's *realized culture*. The way a team executes reveals the actual rules for success, so how you execute must align with your core beliefs. Strategy, goals, and metrics also define *execution alignment*. Everyone must align to your execution approach, but this alignment is more coachable. Even so, exiting people matters as much as hiring and promoting. And remember, alignment cannot be a euphemism for top-down mandate. In order for alignment to pull and ownership to be embraced, The Cascade must be codeveloped.

The Cascade applies to every area of an organization, beyond core product, to include every role on the team—from product to marketing to sales to finance to general administration. If every team is aligned to the primary cascade, then each team acts in the same general direction, maximizing impact ("general" here means the *channeled execution* described in chapter 4, "Unlock Autonomy"). A teamwide cascade also ensures that initiatives are holistically and comprehensively supported. The launch of a new product segment, for example, is more likely to succeed with complementary support for audience engagement, operations, adjustments to legal and financial models, and (sometimes) longer-term team additions.

The natural implication of combining autonomy with multifunctional coordination is the grouping of people into cross-functional *autonomous pods*, much like the integrated assault teams developed by the U.S. military.[75] Cross-functional pods reduce communication cycle times and ensure that every required discipline is directly engaged in problem-solving. Holistic support from functionally siloed teams, by contrast, requires a management layer to facilitate communication and maintain critical alignment. That is slower, more bureaucratic, and more resistant to parallelization than cross-functional autonomous pods.

As stated throughout this book, culture should be iterated to provide just enough structure to overcome operating friction and unlock needed team growth. That includes The Cascade. The Cascade should be as threadbare or content-rich as the moment requires. It should start like a skyscraper's empty steel frame and flesh out over time as needed. The rest of this chapter explores how The Cascade evolves as a team and mission evolve.

Starting Out

In the beginning, there is one autonomous pod—the intimate team of cross-functional partners who embrace challenges and goals together. Barring dysfunction, the early team with a single project backlog solves problems holistically and efficiently. For quality, focus, and speed, this early team is a benchmark. And to the extent that this team can regularly improve its own productivity with tools and automation, it can and should remain small because its efficiency is so high (measured in impact per person, communication overhead, and administrative overhead). Complementing its size, early teams should have the leanest cascade possible to minimize bureaucracy.

There is one other reason to keep the team small when it's starting out, one that matters more than efficiency—agility. When the endeavor is new, the primary reason to keep teams small is to maximize the agility needed to find product market fit. Before a product has market fit, the team must be tenaciously focused on finding it because without fit, the team and its idea won't survive.[76] So until you have fit, keep The Cascade lean to ensure team agility.

For an early team, The Cascade can simply be the following table.

Element	Simple Version
Vision	What's the world we want to see?
Mission	What are we doing next to get there?
Values	Focus, urgency, and team health (see chapter 2, "Live by Values"). Solve high-friction issues immediately and in proportion to team size. Have a lunch every month or two to discuss what's working and what's not.
Strategy	Where do we need to be in a month, a quarter, or a year? Why?
Goals	What are we doing over the next six weeks? Who's doing what over the next one or two weeks?
Metrics	Daily fifteen-minute scrums with weekly or twice monthly resets. Metrics dashboards transparent to all.

Table 4: The Cascade for a Lean Startup

Early Parallelization

Product market fit is seldom a single transition. Even within the category of *early adopters*—people who embrace new products by definition—products often find fit within a subset of this group and then iterate toward greater segment depth. That iteration often involves growing the team. So whether it is to scale a robust product market fit or to seek greater throughput to solidify fit, teams typically grow over time. And when they do, several questions arise:

- How do we inspire people we don't know to join us?
- How do we identify the strangers most likely to succeed on this team?

- How do we keep the growing team focused, nimble, and quality-oriented?
- How do we promote, coach, and exit people to improve team mastery?
- How do we replicate the success strategies that matter most?
- How do we ensure that new leaders advance our culture?

Of course, all this wraps up into the big question we've been asking: How do we continue to create, innovate, and solve problems with greater mastery as we grow the team?

Answering the above questions ultimately fleshes out the lean cascade of table 4. Vision and mission statements are more formally developed, and values are more thoughtfully crafted. Likewise, more time is invested in strategy, goals, and metrics. These investments reap the benefits of inspiring, focusing, and aligning the growing team.

The other change that happens as teams grow is the parallelization of work, specifically the breaking apart of a single autonomous pod into multiple ones. This requires another leveling up. The Cascade goes beyond a cascade from vision to execution, to a cascade from team to pods—*a cascade of cascades*. Consider the first split of a single pod into two pods running in parallel.

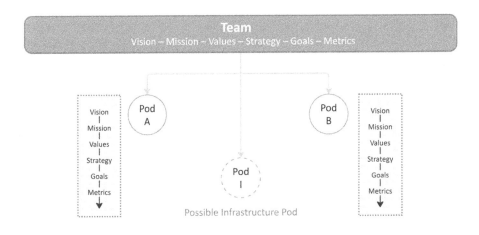

Figure 6: A Team of Two Pods

Figure 6 depicts a two-pod split with an optional infrastructure pod to build tools that unlock autonomy. As the figure depicts, there is a vision-to-metrics cascade for the overarching team, and one for each autonomous pod—and the latter must align to the former. This transition is where some teams struggle, either by overinvesting in pod cascades or by simply ignoring them.

Without its own cascade, a pod is not very autonomous: It must check in with some central resource every time execution reality upends planning assumptions. Some coordination is healthy, as in the *steering meetings* described in chapter 4, "Unlock Autonomy." But too much centralized coordination removes the autonomy of the pod to make decisions, which in turn diminishes ownership and reduces speed. Without its own cascade, a pod also pursues mastery to a lesser degree, lacking a vision that establishes a bar of excellence and a mission that focuses effort.

At the opposite extreme, overinvesting in pod cascades makes it harder to change course since every decision incurs a bureaucratic cost that exceeds the value of parallelization. As a result, the bar to change course gets higher over time, reducing agility. The investments in figure 6 must therefore be right-sized to unlock autonomy effectively—and no more.

In addition to developing a *cascade of cascades* to unlock distributed autonomy, two feedback loops must be institutionalized to cultivate the trust needed for autonomy—constructive feedback after execution and disruptive feedback during execution when underlying hypotheses get debunked. These loops were discussed in the section "Iterating the System" in chapter 4, "Unlock Autonomy." Figure 7 depicts this feedback in the context of the two overarching loops of The Cascade for small teams—a core beliefs loop of vision, mission, and values; and a rapid experimentation loop of strategy, goals, and metrics. Outside of a team's earliest phases, the core beliefs loop generally evolves at a slower cadence than the experimentation loop.

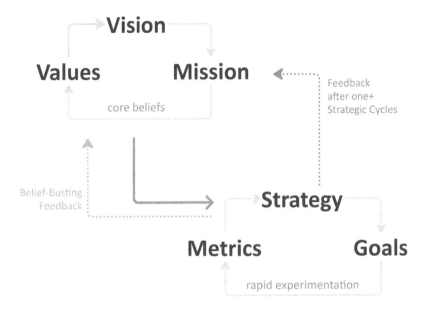

Figure 7: The Cascade Engagement Loops for Small Teams

Scaling Up

As endeavors grow further and pursuing opportunity requires broader impact, teams generally seek higher degrees of parallelization—the ability to pursue multiple substantive goals simultaneously. This is virtuous but also a significant level-up for the team. Well-executed, distributed autonomy is like a multithreaded computer performing instructions in parallel while periodically synchronizing effort. Failure to properly design and invest in parallelism achieves the opposite of what's desired—slower throughput and lower productivity. Even if you get most of the culture right for autonomy, it won't thrive if the communication and execution overheads are large.

My pursuit of distributed autonomy was inspired by Extreme Programming, a software engineering approach developed by Kent Beck, Martin Fowler, Ron Jeffries, and Chet Hendrickson.[77] The main tenet of Extreme Programming is that a long software delivery cycle has a significant risk of being irrelevant on launch. The market and audience conditions change so much between requirements-gathering and shipping that the solution provided is dead on arrival. To mitigate this risk, Extreme Programming espouses rapid iteration through holistic teams of engineers, designers, testers, support staff, product managers, marketers, and the customer. Extreme Programming is nothing if not a tight integration with the customer and the market.

We adopted this approach at Roblox, first breaking the original holistic team into game and web *autonomous pods* (split by technology stack) and ultimately into product-driven pods (split by feature areas). The approach allowed us to pursue multiple road maps in parallel and achieve deeper product depth faster than we otherwise would have. A similar approach was pursued by other companies at that time, most famously Spotify, which shared its experiences online.[78]

Autonomous pods have some great benefits for growing teams, including

- Increased parallelism through the pursuit of multiple simultaneous road maps
- Increased mastery in product depth and quality through specialization
- Increased audience value through increased mastery and attention
- Increased autonomy through cross-functional teams

Roblox achieved a bit of all these benefits, but the results were sometimes constrained by mistakes I made and dysfunctions I allowed to persist during my tenure. From what I've seen since, these mistakes are common in other companies and thus worth understanding. Mitigating these risks is the difference between engineered performance and managed bureaucracy. Here are the three main dysfunctions I've experienced:

- Overpodding—breaking teams into more pods than autonomy allows

- Underinvesting—failing to build sufficient infrastructure to facilitate autonomy
- Locking in—allowing structure and personnel assignments to take on lives of their own

Overpodding happens by intellectual enthusiasm and greed for speed. The main way this dysfunction materializes is high interdependency among pods. Too many pods rely on too many other pods for deliverables in order to hit their goals. This is not autonomy. The best solution is to reduce the number of pods and then interleave the smaller road maps into fewer larger integrated ones.[79] A similar solution is to create a "pod of pods" where autonomy is maintained at a mid-level team rollup.[80] That makes sense if the skills needed across the pod of pods have a high degree of overlap, but it is a more complex organizational structure.

Another way to think about overpodding is as an underinvestment in infrastructure—that the ideal pods don't have the tools and automation needed to operate without external dependencies. The solution is to reduce the pod count in the near term to ensure autonomy and then build the infrastructure needed to competently expand the team's parallelism over time. There is sometimes a strong desire to pod first and let friction drive investments (i.e., get the desired structure and then fix what's not working well). Indeed, there is some merit to this. But in general, it should be done sparingly and transparently because the team bears the brunt of the friction.

Allowing pod structure and personnel assignments to calcify causes a number of other problems. First and foremost, it creates siloed thinking, and you end up with a collection of competing fiefdoms rather than a team of teams. These fiefdoms may not just work at odds with each other but also at odds with the overarching mission, prioritizing siloed strategies over collective ones. This is a revenue pod prioritizing its road map over volunteering to help the onboarding pod fix a broken login screen. Entrepreneurial teams need shared not narrow ownership.

The second problem of calcified pods is hiring momentum. When every pod is rationally seeking greater throughput, the overall hiring plan becomes proportional to the number of pods instead of scaling with overall strategy. Another related problem is that pods—by design—drive product depth, but sometimes that depth goes beyond what is needed in the near term. This is the music app that has great search capabilities but can't consistently stream music.

The solution to the problems caused by organizational rigidity is a culture of dynamism—an a priori agreement embraced across the team of dynamically constituting pod structure and size to align with strategy. In essence, pods should be an output of The Cascade, not an input to it. The tension here is between the increased expertise of sustained involvement on a topic and the increased team dynamism that allows each macro iteration to meet the moment.

A Cascade of Cascades

As discussed earlier, The Cascade is not just a cascade of ideas from vision to execution but also a cascade from team to pod. The following diagram depicts this for a multipod team.

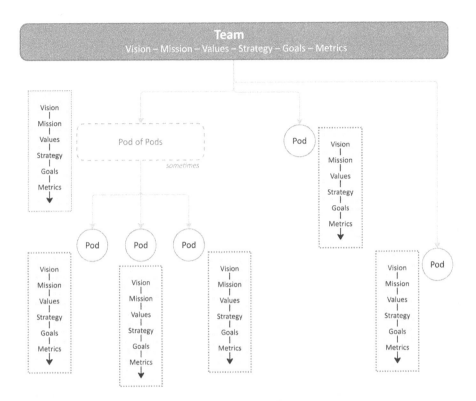

Figure 8: The Cascade of Cascades

Every pod has its own cascade from vision to execution, and all pod cascades must align to the team's overall cascade.

At sufficient team size, autonomous pods are an antidote to the loss of agency from command-and-control structures. But pods often lead to bureaucracy on larger teams if they are not implemented with care. The bureaucracy comes from two main forces: a desire to overregulate and premature optimization. If your team has the people and tools to support distributed pods, as well as the need for parallelized impact, then pod. But if too many people are feeling the bureaucratic overhead, then you are either spending too much time synchronizing cascades or you might not yet need the more sophisticated structure. In either case, the work feels artificial because it largely is. A *cascade of cascades* is necessary as you expand parallelism through pods, but it is also a key reason to delay parallelism until its benefits are clear.

Engagement Loops

In addition to codifying the structural elements that promote autonomy and mastery (vision, mission, values, strategy, goals, and metrics), The Cascade embraces the engagement that fuels trust and learning. On larger teams—ones with quarterly planning cycles, for example—this engagement is codified in three iterative loops: *core beliefs, planning, and steering.*

These three loops are connected in a forward pass of cascaded planning and a backward pass of feedback and disruption. These are depicted in figure 9, a more sophisticated version of figure 7. The loops are depicted with gray arrows. The blue reverse arrows on the right of the diagram are feedback loops from retrospectives, and the green arrows on the left are disruptive loops that break cadence. In practice, all activities in the diagram are conversations, informal in the early days and more formalized as a team grows.

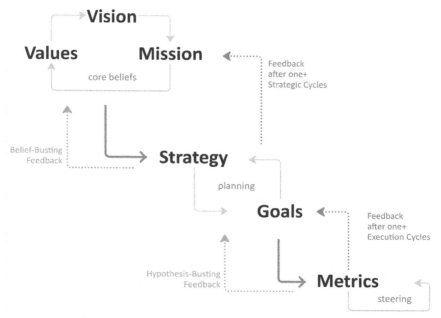

Figure 9: Cascade Engagement Loops for Scaled-Up Teams

Usually initiated by a team's founders or chief executive, the core beliefs loop iterates on vision, mission, and values to define core alignment for the entire team. That set of core beliefs cascades down to the planning loop, with information returning that refines core beliefs or disrupts them. The planning loop codifies the hypotheses that lead to strategy and the assumptions that convert strategy into goals. As learning occurs throughout execution, these hypotheses provide a clear benchmark against which disruptions can be evaluated. Additionally, goal setting and now/next team design in the planning loop can be calibrated against team capacity, and team capacity can be deliberately improved over time, either through additional people or improvements in operational mastery. The planning loop thus helps teams design flow for the next execution cycle, and its iterative cadence gives teams the ability to regularly raise the bar.

On paper, the diagram suggests that each loop is matured and then cascaded to the next loop as an input. This is not the case, nor should it be. That is a *waterfall method*, the antithesis of the Extreme Programming approach on which autonomous pods and The Cascade are based.

At early team stages, the three loops are often iterated together. It is not uncommon for customer validation, for example, to lead to tweaks to mission that improve clarity or focus. And the first few steps of execution can reveal a faulty strategy that requires immediate adjustment, if not full-on disruption. On larger teams, the three loops of figure 9 are also iterated in parallel, although each with its own cadence—longer for core beliefs and shorter for steering. As a team matures, these cadences do drift apart a bit. For every iteration of core beliefs, for example, there are multiple planning iterations, and for each planning iteration, there are multiple execution iterations.

Injecting Intuition

The Cascade is largely the product of analytical thinking. To maximize collective brainpower, The Cascade should be developed through top-down, bottoms-up, and lateral information flows all at the same time. This collaboration is generally fueled by analyses within each group. Analysis, though, is only part of the team's mental capacity. Creative teams must also leverage intuition.

Analysis is what people *assess should be done*, while intuition is what people *believe must be done*. Analytical thinking is also linear. Given situation X, what must effort Y be in order to achieve situation Z? As such, analysis is dependent on our capacity to understand the system in which we operate, but entrepreneurial teams operate in an environment they only partially understand. Intuition helps bridge that gap.

Intuition is nonlinear thinking—ideas that capture a lot of inputs and outputs in ways that are not obvious or understood. Such thinking often reveals opportunities that analytical thinking cannot. Intuition is sometimes underrated because it is believed to be biased. In my experience, though, analysis is no less biased than intuition, and biased intuition is simply low-mastery intuition. Just be sure to vet intuition against cognitive biases, and the best way to do that is to surround yourself with independent thinkers who seek mastery.

To balance the analytical thinking of The Cascade, teams should engage in exercises that explicitly leverage intuition. These involve fast, unstructured brainstorms with a mandate to think freely, allowing ideas that negate the standing plan (i.e., encourage spontaneity over structure). My exercise of choice is to ask each person involved to write down the top five things that must happen next with no judgment, no structure, no need for alignment, and no holds barred. You then merge the list into a single sort, which I like to do interactively, taking a page from Yammer's playbook.[81] Everyone gets X points per round to apply to ideas however they like, and the sort is curated over multiple rounds. Once completed, the sort is compared to analytically developed priorities. Does the latter capture the formal sort's top item? If not, it's worth discussing. Does it capture the top five items? It doesn't have to, but it's good for everyone to think through why.

Injecting Ideation

Ideation happens naturally in the cross-functional collaboration inherent in autonomous pods, particularly when product solutions are first explored. Consider, for example, the Extreme Programming model of the software engineer, test engineer, designer, and customer, all working together to define a new feature. Autonomous pods create opportunities for ideation by design, but these opportunities are easily destroyed by pipeline models of collaboration such as the delivery of requirements "over the transom" from product to engineering (a phrasing used in practice to describe the often-dysfunctional collaboration between the two groups).

Hack Week is another popular way for software companies to inject bursts of unconstrained creativity into their rhythms. Typically, Hack Week is a teamwide activity hosted every year or half-year, lasting from a couple of days to a full week. During Hack Week, people across the entire organization are free to create whatever product, tool, or process they want as long as it is relevant to the mission or team in some way. It does not have to be aligned with the current strategy, and the best ideas often aren't. To free people of constraint and de-risk the team's ability to return to normal afterward, all work is done in prototype form independent of the production product or service. Work is presented in a teamwide, party-like setting at the end of the week.

All my Hack Week experiences have been amazing. They have always reinforced the ingenuity of people if given the space to create, and I've always walked away feeling more excited to be working with the team than ever. Most Hack Week projects don't get directly released, but they inform future work and communicate ideas in powerful ways. The most inspiring ideas are added to team road maps, and the most impactful ideas disrupt the schedule and get shipped almost immediately. Hack Week is a great opportunity for many organizations across many fields. The exercise in autonomous creativity toward something that matters is inspiring, and the ideas are often mind-expanding. Hack Weeks can be slotted between macro iterations of The Cascade.

Iterating The Cascade

In a team's early phases, the primary reason to keep The Cascade lean is to maximize the agility available to find product market fit. But as a team grows, the primary reason to keep The Cascade lean is to minimize bureaucracy and friction. Because culture is what you do, not what you say, keeping The Cascade lean sends a strong signal to everyone on the team to do the same.

It bears repeating. While The Cascade has structure, it does not inherently have weight. The weight is what you add, and if you create a heavyweight process, that's the baggage you bring. At its core, The Cascade is simply a framework for (a) connecting the dots from vision to execution and from team to pod, (b) feeding back critical information that advances or disrupts the current track, and (c) deferring everything else that doesn't matter right now. That's it. How these things get done in practice varies from team to team. The only requirement of The Cascade is for teams to be clear on what they're doing, why they're doing it, and how they'll know they're making progress. And if you're not at least doing that, turning ideas into impact will be challenging.

CHAPTER SUMMARY

The Cascade describes the flow of information and decisions from one set of elements to another, like the flow of purpose from vision to execution, or the flow of goals from the overall team to groups and individuals.

In its simplest form, the goal of The Cascade is to enable each and every person on the team to answer three basic questions: What are we doing? Why are we doing it? How do we know we're making progress?

The Cascade cultivates mastery starting at the top: The more competently leaders guide teams through its elements, the more mastery is role modeled for everyone.

The Cascade also cultivates trusted autonomy. By aligning to what matters, everyone can be trusted to operate in the same general direction.

And by institutionalizing feedback loops for performance, alerting, and disruption, the system can be trusted to level up and course correct.

The Cascade ensures that the overall team connects the dots from vision, mission, and values to strategy, goals, and metrics—from core alignment to execution alignment.

The Cascade also ensures that each sub-team, or autonomous pod, connects the dots from the team's overall cascade to the cascade for that pod. And the cascade of each pod unlocks distributed brainpower and horsepower, giving each team an operating rudder and a vision to master.

For a handful of people, The Cascade is a few simple questions that can be answered quickly and then iterated regularly. As the team grows and requires additional structure, such as splitting into two parallel executing pods, The Cascade grows proportionally—each pod has its own cascade, and alignment and feedback loops are not only internal to each pod but across the team. And as the team scales larger to multiple parallel pods, The Cascade fleshes out again, proportional to what's needed to fuel speed and reduce friction.

The main challenge of The Cascade is the temptation to overbuild—to spend too much time in each cycle or to create too many pods. Both of these introduce bureaucracy. The Cascade is an overall framework that doesn't inherently carry weight, so leave your baggage at the door.

PART II
Mission Athletes

Aligned autonomy, covered in part I, is the system built for everyone. It is the foundation on which all individual growth rests because it is the common framework that everyone experiences. Together, a team's vision, mission, values, and the practices it employs to unlock autonomy and institutionalize mastery define its operating system. And to contribute effectively to that team, each person added must align with that operating system.

We now turn to *mission athletes*—how to find, develop, and retain those individuals most suited for both entrepreneurial endeavors and the team's operating system. If aligned autonomy is about building a collective innovation engine, the culture of mission athletes is about building a personal growth engine—another self-sustaining environment, but one focused on unlocking, coaching, and inspiring individuals to grow in personal mastery and autonomy.

The principal force driving mission athlete culture is the collection of peers who set tone, demonstrate values, inspire with impact, and hold each other accountable. Who a team hires, promotes, and retains is foundational to defining culture. But this is necessary, not sufficient. Organizational leaders must also, with equal conviction, exit those unable to contribute.

Even if you successfully build a team of mastery-seeking, owner-ship-oriented innovators, if the team has too many members who are unable to have material or constructive impact, the innovators will opt out one by one. Why? Because when too much time is spent by the productive compensating for the unproductive (which they will do), personal impact is hampered and collective success put at risk. This is not a recipe for retaining high performers. So equal to the job of building an environment for mission athletes is protecting it.

In a healthy system where the environment is developed and protected, the impact is positive for virtually everyone on the team. That means the bulk of a leader's time is spent finding new mission athletes, fostering their growth, and tuning the system in which they operate. And while exiting is only a small portion of a leader's effort in a healthy system, it is critical to team health that it be done and done well, with respect for those involved, transparent communication, reasonable investment in turnaround, decency in operation, and a sense of urgency.

What makes the system unhealthy—what causes turnarounds and exits to dominate a leader's time—is not staying on top of performance issues, not getting better at managing them over time, and not addressing upstream failures in recruiting. Fail to do these well, and your effort in these areas will mount. Do them well, and you'll spend most of your time on your mission and with the athletes driving its success.

Let's dive in.

CHAPTER 6
Define Success

The natural first step in building a system for individual success is to define what success looks like. For entrepreneurial teams, I define success for an individual as follows:

The ability to have impact toward the team's mission in a manner that aligns with the team's operating system and with increasing mastery and autonomy.

This definition starts with impact because impact matters. People don't have to have impact every day or even equally across the team, but people must have impact. And the way that their impact happens matters too. If people operate too far from a team's operating system, the gains will come at too high a cost—too many distractions, too much effort by others to extract value, too slow, or too little quality.

Individuals must also improve their performance over time in terms of both mastery and autonomy. They must seek feedback and leverage learning into realized competency gains. And they must improve their execution autonomy over time, increasing their capacity to take on more significant and complex projects with less oversight and greater communications savviness.

Unlike the definition of team success in part I, the above definition of individual success does not explicitly reference scale—the ability to increase one's impact over time, either through others or through increased skill. Broadly speaking, skill-based scale is a natural by-product of mastery. Some of the highest-impact people I have known, for example, have been quiet achievers who master critical domains to achieve exceptional impact. So skill-based scale is often redundant to mastery. However, some roles explicitly require impact scale as something to master, and in those cases, it should be called out explicitly. Organizational leaders, for example, work through the collective action of others, which means that scale for organizational leaders is a first order driver for success. These leaders should be held to account for scale explicitly.

Let's now dive into the criteria that define success on entrepreneurial teams, explore how these operate, and finish the chapter with a portrait of this success—the *mission athlete.*

Success Criteria

A definition of success like the above is necessary, but teams also need success criteria—concrete measurable standards that correlate to success and that can be assessed.

Success criteria are used to evaluate an individual's *probability of success*—a look-forward assessment of an individual's likelihood to contribute to *this* team and *this* mission in the near future. Evaluating an individual's probability of success happens throughout their life cycle on the team. It is central to hiring, core to crafting next-level growth challenges, and critical to differentiating between coaching a turnaround and an exit.

Some success criteria are always team- and role-specific. These criteria involve skills, domain knowledge, and operating expertise. As such, they are beyond the discussion here. The criteria discussed in this book are those I consider common to entrepreneurial endeavors. Consider them a baseline on which to build team- and role-specific criteria. Here's my baseline:

- Capacity to create, innovate, and solve problems
- Actioned alignment with the team's codified values
- Understanding of and commitment to the team's mission
- Adherence to the team's nonnegotiable operating principles
- Attainment of the team's minimum standards for mastery and autonomy

There is no implication intended that these are all in equal measure, and often they are not (we'll discuss this shortly). Let's now take a look at each of these criteria in turn.

Capacity to Create, Innovate, and Solve Problems

Entrepreneurial teams create, innovate, and solve problems repeatedly to realize the world they want to see. This naturally leads to the success criterion that matters most—an entrepreneurial team should only add or retain people who increase its overall capacity to create, innovate, and solve problems. This might seem obvious, but it isn't always in practice.

You cannot build a culture of innovation unless you hire people who can collectively innovate. You do not need everyone to be a unicorn visionary capable of boundless creativity and outsized problem-solving capacity, but you undermine your team's performance culture with people who lack innovative capacity in some way. And this applies to all areas of the team, from explicit creative endeavors such as design to those less imagined so, such as general and administrative roles. Innovative finance people, for example, automate routine work, build real-time data systems, and identify business opportunities, while routine thinkers expand the workforce for manual tasks. Requiring innovative capacity across the team creates a magical and inspiring atmosphere.

Alignment with Team Values

People must do more than know your values—they must live them. Assessing this well requires that leaders capture concrete examples of individuals demonstrating values, or demonstrating the opposite. Consider, for example, the engineer who consistently follows a software release they led by monitoring metrics, engaging with the community, and using the product. As a result, they address public-facing issues faster than any product leader on the team. This engineer is living the values of impact, integrity, ownership, mastery, and urgency. We typically notice value misses more than hits, so be sure to catch people succeeding like this.

Now consider the opposite engineering performance—the person who fires and forgets, who consistently has to be told by others of critical issues, and who thus has the slowest response to release issues. This engineer is not living any of the values demonstrated above. Give feedback in these moments to connect the dots from value to outcome, but also write things down for longer-cycle feedback, such as performance reviews and interventions.

The above suggests an important feedback loop from values assessment to design. Values had better be easy to demonstrate or it will be difficult to evaluate alignment. And values had better be strongly coupled to the team's success or it will be hard to motivate anyone to care.

Consider the time I got docked five points out of one hundred in a review because I didn't go to all the after-work team events and so fell short on a "camaraderie" value. The value proxy of "events attended" was incredibly measurable, but the ask was tough given we were already working eighty-plus-hour weeks. But more importantly, the camaraderie that matters most to me is the one developed through collaborative problem-solving in service of mission. As a result, my response to losing five points (idgaf) was likely not the one management had intended. Holding people accountable to vague or uncorrelated values does create culture, just not the one you want.

Alignment with Mission

Like innovative capacity and values alignment, aligning to mission matters too—not a token belief or one of blind exuberance, but an alignment that stems from true shared belief. What people actually believe is hard to know and certainly tricky to evaluate, but what matters is how that belief translates to decisions and actions.

People who believe in mission use it to make decisions, like adjusting a boat's rudder toward the North Star. The people most committed to mission operate toward it consistently, even when no one is around. By contrast, the people who don't believe in mission seem rudderless and often make decisions in counterservice to the mission. These are product leaders who build incremental features rather than getting curious about the audience or the vision. They are engineering leaders who don't know when to hack and when to craft, and who regularly choose incorrectly. And they are executives who embrace every marketing gimmick, lacking commitment to the long game.

Adherence to Nonnegotiable Principles

Many teams have at least one nonnegotiable operating principle. As a reminder, values are standards of behavior, and principles are standards of work. As such, principles are generally ever-evolving and a bit more flexible than values. But some principles have such shared commitment that they are close to being values.

An engineering team, for example, might have a testing culture, a documentation culture, or a no-documentation culture. These probably won't rise to the level of company values, but for some teams, working against these principles can cause too much friction and distraction. For these nonnegotiable principles, people will be evaluated by them as if they were values, not through structured process but informally—the team will organically reject members who don't embrace nonnegotiable principles. So it helps to make them explicit requirements.

There is one pitfall to nonnegotiable principles: alienating the outside-the-box champion who shows up at just the right moment to upgrade an outdated mindset. To mitigate this, openly embrace the tension of challenging principles, even seemingly nonnegotiable ones. Make it permissible as part of the pursuit of mastery, but also get comfortable limiting conversations that stop being useful. As a good friend used to say whenever a novice engineer endlessly challenged our engineering design requirements: "We are not all doing this for the first time."[82]

Attainment of Minimum Standards of Autonomy and Mastery

Like nonnegotiable operating principles, the team also has minimum standards for mastery and autonomy, often unspoken or informal but existing, nonetheless. And like nonnegotiable principles, these standards will be assessed organically, as in a teamwide rejection of a new member, if they are not evaluated formally. Once again, it helps to define these standards explicitly.

There is another reason to do this beyond reducing friction and confusion. The informal enforcement of autonomy and mastery by the team is all too often just in the near term. In the longer term, without intentional reinforcement, teams tend to *lower* the bars on these criteria, succumbing to the stressors of recruiting urgency and organizational size.

To counter this, use autonomy and mastery explicitly when evaluating people's success. And use team discussions to refine, clarify, and reinforce standards. If you do this well and hold the line, the team's standards for mastery and autonomy should increase over time as the team and everyone on it matures.

Creativity, Innovation, and Problem-Solving

An individual's capacity to create, innovate, and solve problems is core to their entrepreneurial impact—and therefore core to who you hire, promote, and retain on your entrepreneurial team. The following is a brutally short summary of these concepts, tailored specifically to traits in individuals. The summaries are intended to complement the ideas explored in part I.

Creativity

My go-to example for creativity is John Shedletsky, Roblox's first employee. John is classically creative in the arts, from painting to music, but his creativity extends to virtually any intellectual topic, from game design to human behavior. Among his friends and colleagues, John is renowned as a rare creative thinker, and there is absolutely no way I can contribute creatively at John's level in the areas in which he excels. There is no effort I could invest or learning I could pursue that could transform me into John. But I am a creative problem solver, regularly tasked with leading teams to do things none of us have done before. We get curious, learn, develop vision, experiment, and adjust to ultimately solve new problems in new ways.

Creativity is making something new from an internal vision. It is imagining something that doesn't exist and bringing it to life. Creativity often has external influences, but true creativity is something unique to the creator, driven by an expressive desire, not an attempt to copy. And each creation is a window into the creator's larger vision.

We often think of creativity through the arts—music, paintings, stories, characters, illustrations, humor. But creativity exists in all fields. In science, for example, creativity starts with a desire to understand a system, which leads to a set of hypotheses, which leads in turn to experiments and ultimately an academic paper. Academic papers certainly don't exist without analytical thinking, but they flow from creativity.

Creativity can also be a connecting of dots that most others don't see. It is seeing an unrecognized pattern or association, or it is the synthesis of seemingly disparate information into a new idea or understanding.[83] As a result, its expression often looks crazy or impossible. But truly creative people are not irrational; they are just operating in a larger dimensional space—like operating in three dimensions when the world only understands two. Some scientific and technological advancements, for example, result from creatively applying one discipline to another, like bringing a niche mathematical framework to an experimental field science.[84]

It's also been my experience that creativity is not exclusively innate but arises out of innate characteristics and developed habits such as being curious, becoming well-informed in breadth and depth, thinking abstractly, thinking dynamically, and mentally modeling systems. Putting that together leads some to see where the "puck is going"[85] over large time frames, not just the near term, which can lead to sea changes in human experience if applied toward impact.

While I don't believe that creativity is exclusively innate, it has been my experience that creativity is much more innate than innovation and problem-solving. Problem-solving is very much a discipline, though some are more attracted to it than others. And innovation, by my definition below, is also a discipline. As such, you generally can help an individual improve their abilities to innovate and problem solve to a greater degree than you can improve their ability to create.

The difference between John and me described above reflects my broader experience that creativity is not evenly applied across a subject area. But it has also been my experience that creativity is not evenly applied in depth either. Some people are simply not sufficiently creative for entrepreneurial endeavors because they lack one thing that John and I share: a mental freedom that rejects rules, constraints, and the status quo. Practical considerations certainly matter downstream when teams navigate the current world, but they hamper upstream creativity, channeling vision too early into iterative improvements rather than bold departures.

Problem-Solving

Problem-solving is repeatedly overcoming challenges through the application of principles, creativity, systems thinking, and feedback loops. As humans, we solve problems every day, so we each have a pretty good sense of what problem-solving is. What matters for developing success criteria, though, is what capable problem solvers look like. Here is my simple rubric.

Good problem solvers

- view the system—the entire relevant mechanics, from micro to macro
- understand what should happen—know both the inputs and outputs
- understand the gap between what should happen and what does
- have the relevant skills to fix the problem

Great problem solvers also

- run toward problems, if not charge toward them
- break down big problems into a series of smaller ones
- investigate root cause, expanding the system view as needed
- operate by a set of principles, defining the system and its solution
- question what ultimately needs to be fixed, open to both product and usage
- explore ways to obviate the problem without fixing it, such as removing a constraint

And masterful problem solvers do all the above through others, leading teams of problem solvers to solve the seemingly impossible.

There is one overuse of problem-solving worth noting—solving all problems at once. Successful entrepreneurial teams—ones that survive early risks to ultimately thrive—require competent strategy, including a strategy for *sequencing*. You don't solve all your problems all at once. Instead, you focus on the one innovation that matters most next, leaving other areas of your product to more mundane solutions. Roblox's sequencing, for example, started with a physically simulated virtual environment (as in a video game), but ultimately expanded to innovations in community, marketplaces, collaborative experiences, and creator tools.

Innovation

Innovation is commonly defined as creating something entirely new to the world, not just new to you.[86] This is a helpful definition, particularly when thinking about how an idea or product fits into a larger strategic landscape. But in the context of building entrepreneurial teams, I use a more specific definition—innovation is not about *having* a new idea; it is about *bringing* that idea to the world. Impact matters.

Innovation is the application of creativity and problem-solving skills in a coherent direction to realize substantive change. It is the transformation of creative ideas into external impact, and it almost always involves a great deal of persistence and problem-solving. And because innovation is typically disruptive, it often involves starting a movement, inspiring with purpose, and assembling a team of believers. If creativity is an exercise, then innovation is a discipline. Unfocused creative thinkers don't change the world around them. Those who harness creativity do, and that harnessing is innovation.

Innovation is a skill that can be developed. And while some are more naturally inclined to take risks, be open to new ideas, and assemble teams, the principles and practices of innovation can be learned. Anyone who has gained experience working on entrepreneurial teams knows there's a difference between the first-time founder working intuitively and the seasoned entrepreneur well-versed in team building, product development, and a host of other innovation-critical ideas. Both of these founders can have high impact, but the experience of the latter reduces idea churn, team friction, and general inefficiency. Whether it's technologists, scientists, artists, philosophers, or social advocates, innovators develop mastery not only in their subject disciplines but also in the idea-to-impact transformation process.

Innovation is ideating, solving problems, executing tactics, developing strategy, inspiring action, assembling great people, keeping teams aligned, and engineering an environment that unlocks intrinsic motivation. Innovation is doing what matters, not just what's important. And it's getting stuff done even on the hardest days. Innovation is thus a journey—a multiround effort of think-do-learn loops that drive toward increasing impact with increasing mastery. Innovation is not solitary creation but team-based transformation. And even when the full-time staff is just you, the innovation team includes your audience because innovation requires shared belief.

Probability of Success

Now that we have defined success criteria for entrepreneurial teams, let's take a closer look at probability of success, a term we have only briefly defined previously. Here's my definition:

Probability of success is a look-forward assessment of an individual's likeliness to contribute to mission, based on the team's success criteria and a current understanding of the person's operating characteristics.

Probability of success is an actual assessment, defined either qualitatively (high, medium, low) or quantitatively (a probability from 0 to 1 or equivalent percentage). The current understanding of a person's operating characteristics comes from interview sessions (for candidates) or from lived team experience. In practice, assessments to hire, promote, and exit are made with a mix of data (scores on evaluations, performance statistics, peer assessments) and personal experience (interactions and collaborations). And on larger teams, ones with more people to assess and resources to invest, data is being incorporated increasingly into assessment models.

In my experience, probability of success, while sometimes implicitly part of the conversation, is often not explicitly talked about, leaving conversations unnecessarily squishy. For recruiting assessments, for example, I have seen the following ratings for post-interview candidate evaluations: "want to work with," "do not want to work with," "will quit if we hire." This is way off the mark because the assessment becomes abstract (harder to define and compare) and personal in the wrong way, as in what makes the interviewer comfortable or happy.

A candidate's assessment should instead be a probability of success based on stated team and role success criteria, with interview sessions focusing on those criteria. Even if this probability is sometimes hard to assess with precision (and it can be), it is far better for everyone involved to focus on what matters—an individual's *impact* on *this* team for *this* mission right *now*.

Probability of Success vs. Fit

Earlier in my career, the term used most often in assessments was "fit." The term had the benefit of simplicity—"Does this person *fit* on the team?" But the term is also incredibly imprecise, leading to overly subjective evaluations that don't advance the mission.

Consider, for example, the advice I received many years ago when asking others for hiring tips: "Hire someone you want to have a beer with." First, I don't generally drink beer. Second, and embracing the analogy, my "beer" is hard work and gallows humor. These are the traits that click with me—and that's the point. My "fit" is not yours, and neither definition likely lines up with performance.

Thinking about "fit" derails your mental performance model (from crisp to hand wavy), narrows your hiring pool (hiring is hard enough), and reduces your team's intellectual diversity (sustained creativity and problem-solving thrive on such diversity).

Defining success criteria, on the other hand, establishes a mental model that helps you focus on performance, opening your recruiting efforts to the broadest possible talent pool. Should you enjoy working with your teammates? Absolutely. But for an endeavor of belief and impact, the enjoyment that matters most derives from creating and problem-solving with good humans toward shared purpose and with shared operational values.

Assessing probability of success has one other benefit over "fit"—it is a continuum, not a discrete evaluation. Yes, a continuum is more complicated, but helpfully so. It allows you to coach the moment, driving toward elevated mastery as the success probability increases and moving toward broader life coaching beyond the team as the probability decreases.

Success Criteria in Practice

Defining success goes a long way toward relevant and impactful people assessments. And codifying success criteria helps ensure those evaluations are consistent across the team. But there is one more piece to the puzzle. In practice, assessing a person's probability of success from multiple criteria is not always straightforward and can lead to some unintended consequences.

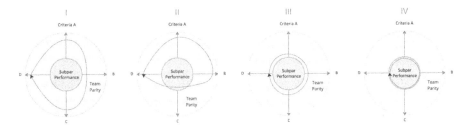

Figure 10: Success Criteria in Practice

Figure 10 depicts a multicriteria evaluation of four people, be they candidates or active team members. Each arrow represents a different criterion. They can be values, values and principles, or a mix of any of the success criteria developed for the team or a role. The inner circle represents a minimum standard, the outer circle is a theoretical maximum standard, and the curve is an individual assessment. Assessments that land within the inner circle are subpar, while those outside it are acceptable. Person I is the typical successful candidate or team member—someone with relative strengths and areas needing improvement but is operating universally above your minimum standard. Person IV does not belong on the team, and it is obvious to everyone. The two middle cases can be difficult to manage and significantly impact culture.

Person II has just one area that falls below your norm, and all the others are exceptional. A common example of this is the hyper-talented jerk. Person II poses the question: Is it okay to lower your standards in one area for an all-star? Making a hire/exit decision for Person II can be challenging and involves more coaching (if they are on the team) or more discussion (if they're being recruited) than Person I or Person IV. The decision is hard because the practical answer is "it depends," meaning context matters.

Hiring Person II is not a question of should you make an exception because the reality is that at some point you probably will. The question is: So now what? Everyone else is living by a value that defines your culture, and is Person II exempt? If culture is what you do, not what you say, this seems like a problem. There is an answer to this conundrum, however, and it is twofold: (1) no, the person is not exempt; and (2) the broader team must make the decision, not have one imposed on it. And that decision is to take a calculated and managed risk to accept the outsized talent at the higher cost of increased coaching and the distinct possibility of failure. Person II must accept that improvement is needed and be open to feedback. Person II's exceptional talent makes them an exception, and for norms to matter, exceptions must be rare and openly managed.

Person III is the classic okay contributor—no areas of exceptionalism, just barely meeting the standard across the board. Like Person II, Person III often involves more discussion or coaching than others. Person III poses the question: Is it okay to have okay people on the team? In my experience, it is not. It is hard to create a culture of mastery if someone is just all around okay (no area of exceptionalism). If you identify Person III during recruiting, you should pass because culture is what you do. Hiring okay people reinforces a culture of mediocrity, not mastery.

If Person III is already on the team, then they are likely a mis-hire and should be asked to leave for the same reason. If they are well intentioned and mission-oriented, experiment with a different role if one is available, but make the call if the experiment doesn't reveal exceptionalism in some way. And note: If the new role is too similar, then the experiment is not sufficient to find exceptionalism somewhere else. One experiment teams often make is simply to change the organizational manager, but if the role is not sufficiently different, this just shifts the problem to someone else.

The diagram suggests that the criteria are measurable enough to create a plot. This is not the intent. Concrete measurement is not always needed in decision-making. It's the mental model that matters and the conversations that result. If you happen to have criteria that are easily measured, great, but be careful of overreaching. Quantitative proxy measurements are often worse than direct qualitative assessments because they suggest a certainty that doesn't exist. In those cases, go with the qualitative assessments, and work on evaluation consistency as a team.

The Mission Athlete

I have developed a shorthand for the success criteria defined in this chapter—the *mission athlete*. As the words imply, mission athletes pursue a shared mission as athletes, seeking continuous improvement in personal and team performance based on feedback. This represents entrepreneurial team members much better than the terms "talent" or "employee."

As in sports, mission athletes pursue mastery as part of their daily routine, and that pursuit is their overarching strategy to tactical refinement. It is also through mastery that athletes achieve social status—the veteran, the play maker, the force multiplier, the work horse, the high-impact contributor. Beyond mastery, athletes are driven by belief, including the advancement of human performance (purpose) and the pure love of their sport (connection).

Athletes leverage principles, or standards of work, to fuel performance, such as the host of principles that guide athletic training programs.[87] And the best athletes live by values, particularly the ones articulated under "Performance Values" in chapter 2.[88] For proof of this, just check out the training programs of Steph Curry, LeBron James, and other elite NBA players.

Athletes don't materialize from thin air—they have natural talents but only mature to high performance through hard work, persistence, and coaching. Good coaching can help an athlete improve, and elite coaching unlocks an athlete's full potential. And because coaches are not on the field, athletes have ultimate performance autonomy. Coaches must therefore become adept at achieving impact through others.

Athletes require feedback in order to improve, and the great athletes seek it out. To achieve high impact, entrepreneurial teams must thus get as comfortable with feedback as sports teams. This is not always easy. To push through discomfort, teams must shift their thinking from mistakes to performance. They must embrace feedback as a symbol of excellence, linking feedback to success and focusing on mastery over short-term results.

Finally, and critically, not everyone wants to be an athlete. Some people just don't want to compete against a standard, or they don't connect enough with the effort to master it. These people can contribute to amateur teams, but they will not last in the pros. And even among those who do want to become elite athletes, not everyone reaches the pinnacle of achievement, though many can still contribute and be successful in some way.

There's one more thing before we conclude this chapter. There has been a lot of discussion in recent years about the characteristics of Gen Z in the workplace and how they differ from prior generations. Aside from the pitfall of judging individuals by the reputation of their generation, this discussion is simply the latest in a recurring theme—that the latest generation seems different. In other words, Gen Z, Millennials, Gen X, and Boomers are all a bit different on average.

Is this true, and could knowing these differences help you be a more effective leader? Sure. But this is at most tactically important. What matters is strategy—to recruit, develop, and retain mission athletes, those pulled by mission, committed to growth, and seeking ownership. Every generation has mission athletes, and I don't need a large sample size to know that—it has always been shockingly easy to get ahead if you just commit and contribute. So go find mission athletes for your team. Create an environment that inspires and helps them grow. And then exit those who are unwilling or unable to become mission athletes.

CHAPTER SUMMARY

An individual's success on entrepreneurial teams is defined as the ability to have impact toward the team's mission in a manner that aligns with the team's operating culture and with increasing mastery and autonomy.

Teams must define concrete *success criteria* aligned with this definition to evaluate an individual's *probability of success* in contributing to the team and mission moving forward.

While success criteria are ultimately context-specific, there is a baseline set of criteria for entrepreneurial teams:

- Capacity to create, innovate, and solve problems

- Actioned alignment with the team's codified values
- Understanding of and commitment to the team's mission
- Adherence to the team's nonnegotiable operating principles
- Attainment of the team's minimum standards for mastery and autonomy

In the context of entrepreneurial teams, creativity is defined as making something new from an internal vision. Problem-solving is repeatedly overcoming challenges through the application of principles, creativity, systems thinking, and feedback loops. Innovation is the application of creativity and problem-solving skills in a coherent direction in order to realize substantive change.

An individual's probability of success is not always easy to assess in practice, and care must be taken when considering a person who operates completely out of your norm, such as the exceptional person who is outstanding in some criteria and subpar in others.

The term mission athlete will be used in part II as shorthand for the success criteria described in this chapter and the characteristics of team-based performance discussed in part I.

CHAPTER 7

Recruit Mission Athletes

There are many motivations for expanding a team—it is understaffed and overworked, or it's going after a new market and missing key expertise, or someone just left. These motivations don't operate in isolation, but live in the context of pressure—internal timelines, external deadlines, mounting opportunity costs, and the growing stress of team members running too lean.

Together, these motivations and pressures create many ways to hire the wrong people instead of doing what matters—adding people who increase the team's capacity to create, innovate, and solve problems. Yes, you often need to hire for a particular expertise, and time always matters, but *while you recruit tactically, you must hire strategically.*

Tactical recruiting is about operational tasks such as searching for skills, managing job posts, and marshaling candidates. It is also about writing job descriptions, reaching out to expert communities, and crafting interview funnels to assess pertinent skills. These are all important, so go do them, and do them well. But tactical recruiting is only part of the story.

Strategic hiring, by contrast, is about finding mission athletes who align with your team's vision, mission, values, and its other success criteria. It is about finding mission-driven people committed to personal and

162

collective growth who amplify team success, not just add to it. To find these people, you must break out of the interview and get to know the person. What motivates them? How do they operate? Why do they get out of bed in the morning? What do they believe as it relates to your mission and values?

If you overestimate someone's skills but find a person who aligns with your success criteria, the worst outcome is that you've added a great contributor and still need the skill set. But if you hire someone with a great skill set who does not align with your mission or team, you haven't solved for skill because the person will not last. So hold the line until you find a mission athlete. There are many great resources on tactical recruiting—this chapter is about hiring strategically.

You Don't Have to Hire

Hiring is often akin to crisis management, and if it doesn't feel that way, just give it some time. The process might start with a need or desire, but the longer a search takes, the more the pressure to compromise mounts as need becomes pain and desire becomes necessity—hence the crisis. The first rule of crisis management in my experience is this: End the crisis, and then fix the problem. In other words, act tactically to create the space needed to act strategically. The best way to create that space in recruiting is to remember that you don't have to hire.

Consider this common scenario. You need to hire an expert to lead a new initiative because the current team is focused on existing priorities and insufficiently experienced in the new area. Unless the new project is existential, performance-minded leaders don't disrupt the team early on, instead deferring new projects and structure until a candidate is hired. These leaders then work hard for a quick recruiting win, focusing on tactical efforts to find qualified candidates. As the process endures, though, the pressure to "just pick someone" mounts with the rising opportunity cost of not launching the initiative. This temptation generally leads to mis-hires.

In response to the pressure to "just pick someone" and to keep the search strategic, effective leaders prompt a collective decision—hold the line or disrupt. A choice to hold the line *reasserts* the current priorities, maintaining the original plan. Disrupting the plan, on the other hand, *adapts* the current team to the recruiting need and launches the new project before the expert arrives. Both decisions create the space needed to find the mission athlete with the needed expertise. And in both decisions, the recruiting pipeline is reexamined from acquisition to offer, tweaking the system to improve performance. Disruption ultimately wins if the process takes too long.

Disrupting the team to take on a new project when it lacks critical expertise or is already operating at capacity can cause stress if it's not done well. It can feel to everyone involved like wanting more for less. But this is easily avoided if project leaders operate with mastery to disrupt productively. Here's my pattern for doing so.

- Deprioritize some current projects to release team bandwidth.
- Assemble a kickoff team with a project lead to launch the effort.
- Set realistic goals, and define success as establishing critical momentum.
- Build relevant subject matter expertise among the kickoff team.
- Redouble efforts on recruiting those needed for the longer term.

Note that the answer is explicitly *not* that everyone just does more. Mastery in entrepreneurial endeavors is about focus, and focus means choosing. Instead, the approach reprioritizes and refocuses the team at large on what matters most now. A key lever of internal disruption is prioritization, so use it as a tool to create the space needed to recruit strategically.

Disruption has several benefits aside from creating space. First, mission athletes like challenges, personal growth, and doing things that matter. Refactoring the current team creates opportunities for learning, advancement, and leadership, and it puts participants on the mission's frontier where athletes like to live. Second, any expansion of the team's scope requires it to build in-house expertise beyond a few subject matter experts anyway. Learning by doing is a great path for knowledge acquisition. And finally, because culture is what you do, working with the current team now to launch a critical project instead of waiting sends these three strong signals:

- We do not wait to do things that matter.
- We are flexible and reorganize as needed to have impact.
- We have what it takes to move ahead.

Of course, expertise matters, as does hiring a leader with experience in an area new to the team. Go find those people. Just don't hold impact hostage by waiting for the expert to arrive, and don't hire an expert who fails to meet your team's success criteria. Instead, create the space to expand the team strategically toward its evolving structure.

The above approach holds even when the problem is that the team is understaffed because the flip side of being understaffed is being insufficiently focused. Critically overworking yourself and others, while a badge of honor for some, does not an athlete make. Cyclists have recovery days and take turns creating *draft* for each other.[89]

There are real costs to hiring someone under pressure who does not align with your mission and success criteria—the near-term friction of having that person on your team, the opportunity cost of not hiring someone else, the stress and effort of exiting them, and the inefficiencies of restarting your recruiting pipeline. So when hiring to alleviate staffing shortages, create the space to endure a bit longer. Narrow the focus, reorder priorities, and build tools to reduce manual effort. Then go hire strategically.

You Don't Hire the Best Person for the Job

There is a recurring theme I've heard throughout my career—"We only hire the best." Sometimes that means "We only hire the best, so let's see if you measure up." This is the fastest way for me to hand back their measuring tape and leave. And other times it means "We only hire the best, so let's be super picky until the best person walks through the door." That humble brag typically masks a slower-than-average operating pace. And sometimes it means "We only hire the best, so our exiting rate is far below everyone else's." This is another humble brag that can mask broad misalignment and low accountability. On a positive note, "We only hire the best" is better than the low mastery "Let's just find someone" (a.k.a. one of a million fungible candidates).

"We only hire the best" is problematic even beyond dysfunctions like these. Even if you embrace the assertion of hiring "the best," what you actually mean is that "We only hire the people we *think* are the best"—if you don't accept the inherent uncertainty of hiring people, then good luck identifying and exiting the mis-hires. "We only hire the best" also encourages low-urgency recruiting, one in which the default instinct is rejection. This typically happens when everyone involved has veto power and candidates are evaluated against an imaginary ideal.

But more than any of these concerns, the framing of "We only hire the best" misses the point. What fuels both recruiting urgency and mastery, rather than hiring "the best," is adding a team member who has a high probability of success in doing the job (a skills assessment) and a high probability of success on your team (a culture assessment). If you're lucky, you hire the person with the highest assessed probabilities, but this is a difference without distinction.

No matter how you attempt to quantify assessments (and it is good to do so), your ability to distinguish the highest-probability candidate from the merely high is suspect at best. But your ability to identify a group of candidates with high probabilities of success is achievable, and the work you put in to do so yields long-term benefits. And even if you could assess it reliably, the distinction between highest and high washes out over time because, as we'll discuss in the next chapter, mastery is an uneven progression—the highest probability of success candidate today might be outperformed a year from now by a mere high-probability candidate.

It may seem that I am advocating for speed over substance. I am not. I am advocating for both. You should absolutely have masterful standards.

And you should only add team members who increase the team's collective capacity to create, innovate, and solve problems. But remember that there is not just one person capable of fulfilling your criteria. The job of recruiting is not to find a needle in a haystack but rather to build a compelling pipeline of high probability of success candidates—the mission athletes. Go build that quality pipeline and act with urgency.

Start with Vision

When hiring for a new role, I no longer start with a job description. A job description is really a marketing document that should inspire, excite, and filter. When hiring mission athletes, starting with a job description does not get to the substance of the search, and relying on it principally renders the search tactical and checklist-oriented. So all my searches now begin with a *vision document*, one that encapsulates virtually all the elements discussed in part I.

A vision document includes the following:

- Vision—the long-term vision for the role (two-to-five-year window)
- Mission—the next step in achieving that vision (one-year window)
- Values—team values plus one or two role-specific values (e.g., responsiveness)
- Strategy—strategic options and recommendations, and sometimes requirements
- Goals—very near-term Objectives and Key Results (three-month window)
- Scope—the role's areas of responsibility
- Priorities—a stack ranking of daily and weekly focus (from most to least critical)
- Expertise—the ideal skills and knowledge needed

The above is a personalized version of *The Cascade* discussed in chapter 5, so the elements align with the team's overall vision, mission, strategy, and goals. To foster autonomy, the document is presented to candidates as one they will own moving forward, with the expectation that it will be revised after a few months by them to reflect their learnings and emergent vision. Mechanically, the job description is externally facing, while the vision document is presented to candidates at some point during the interview process to elevate the conversation.

Starting with a vision document has a number of benefits. First, it is much easier to write a job description once you have a vision document, and the job description can more easily be delegated to someone with marketing expertise rather than being owned by a hiring leader. Second, a vision document fuels engagement by inviting a candidate's questions and ideas, and thus it helps evaluate a candidate's connection to the mission and the team. Third, it sets the tone of purpose, mastery, and autonomy—purpose by the vision and mission for the role, mastery through the articulation of the document itself in crafting a role, and autonomy through the ownership the new team member has in the document moving forward. Fourth, a vision document focuses everyone, including the candidate, on strategic hiring, not tactical recruiting. The very elements of being a mission athlete are articulated in the document. And finally, the document helps the new team member hit the ground running with a clear vision of their role and mandate to act. More than one person I've recruited using a vision document has subsequently shared their appreciation of the approach and credited it for their smooth onboarding.

Topic	Articulation
Vision	A creative engineering team engaged in its work, aligned with mission, and operating with increasing mastery and throughput over time
Mission	Leverage tools and other efficiencies to increase the team's collective bandwidth by 2x over the next two years without increasing team size by 2x and while strengthening creative culture.
Values	Team values + responsiveness + service to team
Strategy	Options to be Discussed and Finalized • Team expansion and restructuring • Roles and responsibilities review • Tools and automation development • Monitoring, system self-correction, and issue response improvements
Goals	**O**: Establish concrete mission momentum (three months) **KR**: Quantify a baseline of system health, throughput, and team health **KR**: Expand the engineering team by two mission athletes **KR**: Mitigate the top three team-reported operating frictions **KR**: Revise this document with additional OKR recommendations
Scope	Backend services and application programming interfaces Engineering, testing, deployment, scaling, and operational response
Priorities	1. Site uptime (breaks team flow) 2. Critical site health against KPIs (breaks team flow) 3. Team health and alignment (creates team flow) 4. Pipelined initiatives (leverages team flow)
Expertise	Prior experience leading an engineering team of similar size for a product similar in technical complexity and characteristics. Bonus for having worked in an organization two times larger in size. Bonus for breadth of experience across a few teams, both high and low-performing. Bonus for expertise in areas X and Y.

Table 5: Vision Document Example for an Engineering Lead

Get to Know the Person

Building teams that create, innovate, and solve problems requires that you hire people geared for these things. And to do that, you need to get to know the person you're evaluating—human to human. What is their drive to create, innovate, and solve problems? Do they have the patience and dedication for mastery, the inner confidence and personal vision for autonomy, and a true shared belief in your mission? What makes them tick? What motivates them broadly?

There is no better way to "unlock" someone for your mission than to align the team's success with who they are and who they want to become.

Find Their Stories

The best way I've learned to get to know someone through a conversation is to find the formative stories of their life or career—stories that resonate with their purpose and potential. Mechanically, I try to uncover two things: something the person has done that truly excites them, and something relevant they'd rather not talk about such as a professional challenge or failure. Respectively, these two stories help you understand the person when they are unlocked and thriving, and when they are shut down and struggling.

The story of excitement is your avenue to a candidate's creativity, innovation, problem-solving, and intrinsic motivation. And the issue they'd rather not discuss provides a window into their character—how they frame a failure or misstep, their capacity to learn on reflection, and their ability to accept ownership. Be careful not to evaluate these stories through your own emotional lens or you'll bias your assessment. Excitement, for example, doesn't require animation, and constructive reflection doesn't negate frustration.

So how do you get to these stories? First and foremost, be authentically curious and human. Start with a true desire to get to know the person, and because what you believe is what you communicate, that curiosity will generally open up the person. Conversely, any signal from you that this is a test will close the person down, and the savvier the person, the faster they'll retreat to pure interview speak. I always start with a sincere compliment of something they've accomplished, particularly something formative that I connect with. I then follow the person where they lead. I don't care about the minutia until I get to a key story, and then I dive deep.

Here are a few examples of key stories:

- Leading a project that initially pushed them beyond their comfort zone
- Taking over a struggling or failing project and turning it around
- Failing multiple times at something and ultimately succeeding
- A situation they handled in a way that still creates unease and regret
- A time they were exited from a project or team
- An unconventional or difficult career turn, typically involving saying no to comfort
- A conflict with a colleague that never resolved and had personal consequences
- Something outside the norm of applicants such as being an Olympian, serving in the military, or building houses for a few years in a nonprofit

One caveat: The legality of what is and what is not off-limits is ever-evolving, so be sure to align your story investigation with what's permitted.

In addition to curiosity, empathy also opens the conversation. Understanding how you would feel in their shoes and expressing that typically encourages the person to add context or correct your impression. You can learn a lot about how to do this well by listening to great interviewers who take authentic interest in each subject. Hint: They also do their homework.

Understand Personal Motivation

Adding people to the team who connect with your mission and values matters, but what they believe for themselves matters just as much. Are they hungry for a win? Do they seek formal leadership? Do they want to do something they believe in? Or maybe they want to work on cutting-edge technology or provide for their family. Know what drives someone, and you can motivate them to achieve great things. Don't know this, and you are just a boss.

Personal motivation is critical to coaching people on your team but equally critical in evaluating whether a person should be on your team in the first place. And the evaluation should be mutual. Asking the person whether this is the right mission, team, and role for them matters as much as asking the reverse. If your team and your mission align with the person's journey, then they will find fulfillment on your team and will perform at their highest potential. I have found joy and success in my career, for example, when what I am doing aligns with who I am, allowing me to deliver impact unique to me. It feels electric.

You can glean personal motivation indirectly through the stories the person tells and through answers to follow-up questions that just happen to reveal something deeper. But you can also just be direct, learning enough about them to ask the question that cuts through the noise. You can only be direct if you establish trust, and you only establish trust by being authentically curious and empathetic—by being human more than being an interviewer. Get to know what motivates someone, and you can help them identify the best situation for them, on your team or beyond. And if they do join your team, you've already started collaboratively unlocking their potential.

Finding Signals

Evaluating someone's intrinsic motivation and capacity for entrepreneurial teamwork is an acquired skill that gets better with investment—but you must make improving that skill a priority, and you have to put in the work. I am not an academic expert in the definitions and signals of creativity, innovation, and problem-solving. As I've said elsewhere, there are countless books, papers, and careers dedicated to these concepts. The following table summarizes what signals I look for when assessing these qualities. Consider it a data point, and then build your own.

And remember, the signals are just that—signals. Once you get a signal, dive deep to grok how that person values, understands, and demonstrates the high-level quality and the extent to which they are driven toward it. My strong preference is for concrete examples of these qualities, not just conversations about them. Talking about mastery is great, for example, but it's a lot better when someone tells you about the time they decided to change careers and then took courses at night to develop skills, participated in technical challenges (and won one), and ultimately got a new job in a dream role. That story says mastery and a whole lot more.

Quality	Definition	Signals
Creativity	Making something new from an internal vision; connecting the dots most others don't see	• Develop talent in the arts • Unconventional problem solver • Deep dives on interests; highly informed • Identifies patterns from little data • Thinks nonlinearly and dynamically • Unencumbered by contraints
Problem Solving	Effectively identifying, triaging, and solving problems	• Analytical systems thinker • Curiosity in how things work • Ability to rapidly organize and prioritize • Unintimidated by complexity; pursues simplicity • Speed despite complexity • Runs toward challenges
Innovation	Transforming idea into action through creativity, problem-solving, and team	• Persists through challenges; has grit • Inspires action through belief and mission • Inspires alignment through strategy and values • Builds teams that create and problem solve • Focuses on what matters over the important • Synthesizes multiple disciplines in new ways
Mastery	Continuous pursuit and attainment of higher performance	• Elite achievement in skill-based activity • Deep dive learning that leads to impact • Can talk deeply on a topic years later • Interested in details; inquisitive • Frustrated with poor performance
Autonomy	Ability to deliver while owning the conditions of execution	• Solo achievement in substantive project • Progressive leadership scale and role • Interested in how people work • Opinionated in how to execute • 360-degree project ownership
Purpose	Capacity to be inspired by, commit to, and focus on purpose	• Inquisitive about your team's purpose • Discusses the rationale of past projects • Consistently asks "why" and expects an answer • Failed at something and still believes in it • Did something hard, fueled by purpose

Table 6: Signals of Creativity and Intrinsic Motivation

Break Out of the Interview

Hiring mission athletes using a traditional skills-testing interview approach is not optimal. You might be able to get someone in the door, and you might learn that you want to work with them, but will they want to work with you? They need to be inspired by the mission, but they also need to be inspired by you, the team, and the environment. It's not about excitement or gimmicks but rather consistency and substance—having a process that genuinely involves team-based creativity and problem-solving[90] and reveals who you are and what you believe. You are not putting together a series of tests. You are engineering an end-to-end experience that exemplifies your values and gives everyone the context to assess shared probability of success.

Culture is what you do, not what you say, and your recruiting pipeline is a candidate's primary view into your team's culture. Are there late responses to emails, confusing instructions, and inconsistent messaging from team members? Give them team swag that says "get stuff done" all you want, but they won't be convinced. Is there a streamlined, effective, and collaborative experience where they learn something from good humans? You don't have to say anything more.

One practical consideration is that your team and the candidate will ultimately make a significant investment in time and effort by the end of the process. To that end:

- Engineer the process to reduce time spent on low-probability candidates.
- Inspire candidates in proportion to the investment they'll make next in the process.

To optimize team investment, engineer the process as a funnel with multiple stages, explicit go/no-go decisions, and fall-off in participants at each stage. Good funnels hold the line and only progress candidates who inspire. When in doubt, pass. And to inspire candidates, ensure that each phase is accompanied by relevant and right-sized engagement and materials. For example, asking a candidate to deliver a thirty-/sixty-/ninety-day plan before they've met the hiring manager will not entice candidates with multiple active opportunities. So engineer your funnel to minimize your team's investment and maximize the candidate's motivation at each stage.

The Offer Is Still the Interview

Most candidates who sail through the recruiting pipeline negotiate their offer in good faith and quickly join the team. Occasionally, though, something else happens.

Consider one candidate I interviewed a while back. They believed in the mission, excited everyone throughout their interviews, and ultimately yielded a high probability of success assessment. It was a no-brainer hire. The offer was made, and then things shifted. The person had compensation requirements that didn't seem well researched. We agreed on one condition, only to learn that there was another and another after that. The candidate became intermittently responsive. And after a few more rounds, there was another curveball—their current team made a counteroffer. It was a mess, and the temptation was to push through. They were a great candidate, so we just needed to get them over the line, right? And if we passed now, we'd have to continue the search. Ugh! So keep going, right? Absolutely not.

The temptation to push through is wrong because it fails to realize that the offer is still the interview. Agreeing to join a team is always a life-impacting decision that necessarily triggers emotions and creates stress. You learn a lot about a person in this final phase such as how they make decisions when the stakes are high. You learn about their values, humility, integrity, decency, gratitude, and transparency. And you discover their ability to embrace the big picture, which speaks to vision and strategy. Most of the time you don't learn that much—people are appreciative, ask a few questions, negotiate in good faith, and are excited to join the team. But sometimes you learn a lot. The offer is still the interview. You are still evaluating the person's probability of success after the offer is made. If that probability falls below a critical threshold, you should pass. You will save everyone involved a lot of time and pain.

The reality in these situations is that something was missed along the way to the offer—a legitimate requirement that was overlooked or a character trait that was not uncovered. The temptation is to identify and close this gap for the next candidate. Certainly, do this if the gap is tactical such as forgetting to ask for compensation or location requirements. But beyond that, don't let every exception create a rule because that's a fast track to bureaucracy.

Instead, know that this scenario exists, and be ready to manage the situation effectively—consider it a mis-hire that just hasn't happened yet. This makes the situation analogous to exiting a team member whose probability of success is rapidly diminishing. As discussed in chapter 9, give the person honest feedback and the opportunity to turn things around, and then exit them from the process as needed. Your offer is not immutable. It is contingent on the process closing in a way that positively reinforces what you've already learned.

Hire for Success

I was asked to hire a marketing associate within the first month of my joining Roblox. The process yielded two viable candidates. The hiring decision should have been easy, but it wasn't at the time because I did not yet have the right mindset.

The first candidate would have valued the job—they were qualified, and the role would have helped them demonstrate a potential we both believed they had. I believed that given the opportunity, the candidate would be inspired to dig in. The second candidate was also qualified, although less experienced. But they were highly engaged with what we were doing, enthusiastic and curious about our space, asked great questions, and had a trajectory that demonstrated grit and hard work. I never really thought about how the job would help this candidate because I was too busy thinking about how she would help us. I correctly hired the second candidate, Christina McGrath, whose hiring I count among my greatest career achievements. Christina became a serial entrepreneur at Roblox, leading multiple initiatives across a wide range of disciplines with significant impact. Christina is also one of the core contributors to Roblox's early success.

The distinction between these two candidates matters. The first candidate had a potential I hoped to unlock, fueled (I hoped) by their inspiration for the opportunity. But the second candidate showed signs of the very success patterns we already had at Roblox, putting me in a position of amplification. The second pattern wins.

The role of a people leader is to hire the candidates with the highest probability of success for the mission and the team. By choosing the second candidate, I hired for success. Hiring with the hopes of unlocking potential generally correlates to mis-hires, while hiring with the expectation of amplifying success correlates to outsized performance. Understand what drives success on your team, create an interview experience that uncovers and explores signals of those drivers, and then hire the candidate with the highest probability of success for your mission and team.

CHAPTER SUMMARY

While you recruit tactically, you must hire strategically.

Strategic hiring is about finding *mission athletes* who align with vision, mission, values, and other *success criteria* that are critical to elevating the team's capacity and impact.

You do not have to hire. Whether your goal is to expand capacity to do new things or alleviate an overworked team, do not let pressure drive you tactically to just grab someone to fill a seat. Instead, create the space to hire strategically by focusing, reprioritizing, and building tools. And remember, the flip side of being understaffed is being insufficiently focused.

You also don't hire the best person for the job. Given the imprecision of human assessment, you can't distinguish between the highest probability of success candidate from the high. Instead, hire someone with a high probability of success in doing the job (a skills assessment) and a high probability of success on your team (a culture assessment).

Don't try to find a needle in a haystack, but instead build a compelling pipeline of high probability of success candidates—the mission athletes. The mastery goal here is not speed over substance, but speed and substance.

Start with a vision document, not a job description. Job descriptions drive tactical recruiting. Vision documents drive strategic recruiting through the role's vision, mission, values, strategy, goals, scope, and priorities. Job descriptions flow from vision documents.

Get to know the person—human to human. Find their stories through authentic curiosity and empathy. But even more so, find what motivates them personally. Know what makes someone tick and you can motivate them to achieve great things. Otherwise, you're just the boss.

Break out of the interview through direct collaborative engagement on real issues.

The offer is still the interview. Exit people whose probability of success dips too low.

Hire for success—not in your success of coaching a person to greatness but in an individual's demonstrated high probability of success to contribute to your mission and your team right now. Don't hire to find and unlock greatness; instead hire to amplify it.

CHAPTER 8

Develop Mission Athletes

D eveloping mission athletes is the core blocking and tackling of indi- vidual success. It is an investment in the growth of individuals across the team toward greater personal mastery and autonomy. If done well, this effort creates a flywheel for personal development—a system that increasingly runs on its own fueled by the team, allowing leaders to focus on high-impact interventions (socializing mission, reinforcing cul- ture, and responding to crises).

Developing mission athletes is not a continuous act of micro adjust- ments—like someone posing a mannequin—but rather a partnering with an individual to pursue their growth. They own it, and you assist. Devel- oping mission athletes goes beyond the systems engineering of teamwide influence, the approach of part I, to engaging with each individual. And for this engagement to be effective, both coach and athlete alike must buy into a foundational growth mindset. *By inviting someone to join your team, you are not just asking them to contribute to mission; you are also calling them to pursue personal growth and committing to support that pursuit.*

Operating together, the ideas in parts I and II constitute a system for entrepreneurial culture—fuel by purpose, live by values, institution- alize mastery, unlock autonomy, define success, recruit mission athletes, develop mission athletes, and coach out (the next chapter). These are mapped below in figure 11, a visual representation of the aligned autonomy of mission athletes. This figure also represents the entire system each individual encounters on a thriving team, and it is profoundly impactful to their experience—*by design*. It is thus critical to appreciate this system in full when thinking about the growth journey of those on your team.

The bottom layer in figure 11 contains the foundational elements of the team's operating system—the principles and practices that apply to everyone. The top layer is the system for finding, developing, and retaining mission athletes. The activities of this layer rest on a foundation of success criteria, which represent both the team's operating system and role-specific criteria.

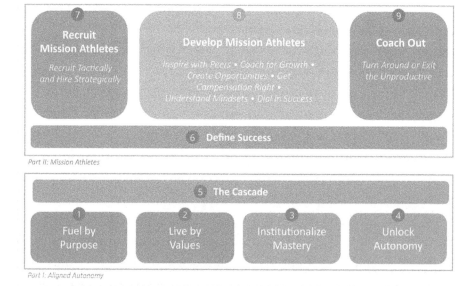

Figure 11: The Aligned Autonomy of Mission Athletes

Together, the elements depicted in figure 11 constitute a holistic system for unlocking intrinsically motivated contributors in a common cause. It is the innovation engine that entrepreneurial leaders must build and protect for enduring, scalable, and regularly improving performance.

And if done well, leaders achieve the two overarching goals of culture previously stated in the introductions to part I and part II, respectively.

- The team's enduring ability to advance mission with increasing creativity, mastery, and scale (part I's definition of success)
- The individual's ability to have mission impact in a manner that aligns with the team's operating culture and with increasing mastery and autonomy (part II's definition)

There is yet one more way to think about figure 11, one that sheds additional light on the dynamics at play. Acting together, the elements in figure 11 also constitute an economic system for intrinsically motivated individuals where the product is personal growth and the currency is effort. And like other economic systems, this one includes incentives (growth opportunities, social stature, financial rewards) and signals (who gets hired, promoted, and exited). Extending the analogy further, part I is the overarching governance model that guides aggregate behavior—inspired by a greater good, living by a code, aligning yet distributing action, and continuously improving collectively. If the incentives, signals, and governance are designed well, both individually and collectively, the system is self-actualizing, self-organizing, and self-improving. Intrinsically motivated people can plug in, have impact, and share ownership.

An economic system analogy has one other benefit—thinking systematically about market failures. The two most relevant market failures to entrepreneurial teams are the tragedy of the commons (degradation of shared resources)[91] and externalities (costs borne by those not receiving benefits).[92] A typical tragedy of the commons is broken infrastructure used for day-to-day operations, such as monitoring systems, software development systems, and internet availability. And a typical externality is a development team shipping bad product, leaving it to operations and customer service teams to fix problems and help the audience.

Market failures, by definition, require intervention beyond the individual to resolve. The market failures associated with individuals include the inability to meet baseline performance standards; the inability or unwillingness to live by values; the inability or unwillingness to grow in mastery or autonomy; actively resisting vision, mission, values, the team's operating system, or the team itself; and actively disrupting the team, breaking individuals out of micro flow (hours and days) or groups out of macro flow (weeks and months). Economic systems break down if market failures are not addressed, and the system described in this book is no different. Addressing these failure modes is the focus of chapter 9, "Coach Out."

We now turn to the specifics of developing mission athletes, first with a look at team member retention and then exploring the strategies listed in figure 11.

Team Retention

As a precursor to exploring how to fuel individual growth, let's first consider retention—keeping people on the team. The reason is simple: The team's overall goal is not just to enhance the mastery and autonomy of its members but also to *retain* its highest contributors. It is therefore critical to understand individual retention when thinking about personal development.

Retaining team members can be tactical such as "We'd better not lose Jess who's critical to the next phase of our growth." Tactical retention can work, so go be tactical. But what matters more is strategic retention, the overall retention caused by teamwide forces and investments in individual growth. To that end, let's explore the retention calculus individuals compute regularly and then turn to strategic retention levers—levers we've already been discussing.

Personal Success Criteria

Borrowing from Maslow's hierarchy of needs, my simple model for why people stay on entrepreneurial teams is twofold: The position satisfies the basic needs of having a job, and the experience satisfies a multitude of reasons for being on an entrepreneurial team (see figure 12).

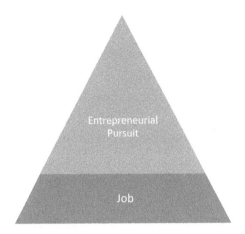

Figure 12: Tactical Retention Considerations

In the simplest of terms, the decision to stay or leave a job boils down to three questions:

- Is this the best thing I can do right now to provide for myself and my loved ones?
- Does this job help me have the life I want to live right now?
- Is this the best path for me to have a better life tomorrow?

The first is a statement of basic needs. The second is an individual's unique mix of work and life experiences. And the last statement is about growth and future opportunity. This assessment is foundational—no matter how inspiring the team and its mission, individuals cannot work at odds with these fundamentals for long. And while people typically don't consider these daily, they do think about them more often when any part of their lives gets disrupted, on or off the team.

Moving beyond the basics of having a job, the decision to remain on an entrepreneurial team is a mix of mission alignment, personal and team growth, and the team's collective probability of success. I call these considerations *personal success criteria*, and everyone has them whether or not they explicitly craft them. Here are my personal criteria:

- The people on the team inspire and drive me—I want to be on *this* team.
- The project, role, and subject matter connect with me—I'm excited by *this* work.
- Who I am matters—I am contributing based on my talents, skills, and intuition.
- The project's mission matters—I am doing good work.
- The project is set up for success—the project has champions.
- I am set up for success—I have champions.
- I am growing—I am investing in my future.

Even if people haven't codified their criteria like I have, they are evaluating every day the value of the mission, the team's probability of success in pursuing it, their probability of success on the team and in life, and what influence they have on all of these. To the extent the team is collectively advancing mission, individuals can grow and have impact, and the team's operating friction is not too high, people will generally remain.

When coaching someone one-on-one, it's critical to understand their personal success criteria because that's what they are using to evaluate their place on the team. More broadly, a generalized model of personal success criteria, one representing the aggregate, can help you understand the incentives at work across the team. Meet these criteria sufficiently, and your team will retain more than it attrits. Fail to meet them, and expect the opposite.

Strategic Retention Levers

It turns out that the very things you do to enhance performance on entrepreneurial teams are also your best levers for strategic retention. Unsurprisingly, an environment where intrinsically motivated people thrive is also an environment that retains those who are most able to create, innovate, and solve problems.

Strategic retention levers for entrepreneurial teams can be organized into two distinct sets: *team levers* that impact the team in aggregate, and *individual levers* that impact individuals as a cohort. The following two tables show how these pieces fit together. Not every lever needs to be at 100 percent, and some are natural tensions of others.

Team Lever	Description
Purpose	• Shared belief; collective purpose • Source of energy and resilience to challenges
People	• The caliber and humanity of teammates • Relationships matter, team friendships fuel stability, and inspiring peers retain similarly valued and operating team members
Values	• The social contract of behavior • Your codified values are a statement of what you believe, but your realized values define who opts into the long term and who opts out
Impact	• The sum total of everyone's contribution to mission • Belief without impact does not sustain intrinsic motivation
Efficiency	• The ability to transform effort into impact • Minimal friction and bureaucracy in tools, practices, and policies
Competence	• The mastery of overall leadership and team execution • Another source of resiliency via collective probability of success
Transparency	• The visibility of the full cascade (chapter 5) from belief to impact • Transparency removes distraction and increases trust
Growth	• Growth in impact or mastery toward mission • There are always reasons to stay when vision is big and progress is real

Table 7: Team Levers of Strategic Retention

Individual Lever	Description
Purpose	• An individual's set of motivations • Resilience to internal and external distractions when personal purpose aligns with mission and role
Autonomy	• Ownership of execution conditions • Owning inputs personalizes impact, associating mission and team with self
Mastery	• Pursuit and attainment of higher performance • Mastery creates long-term opportunities on and off the team, increasing retention while progress is substantive
Values	• An individual's operating system • Sustainability increases with the alignment of team and personal values, as both a standard of and formula for success
Impact	• Personal impact is the reward for effort • Effort without reward is not sustainable
Gratitude	• Recognition of personal contributions • Impact must be recognized to be truly sustainable
Head Space	• Elimination or reduction of destabilizing distractions • Examples: low compensation, bad behavior, confusion, bureaucracy

Table 8: Individual Levers of Strategic Retention

Doing Your Job Matters

As we've discussed throughout, if you want to innovate toward a mission that matters, the best thing you can do is build an environment where creative problem solvers thrive. But sometimes crises arise such as a sudden downturn or existential threat. In these times, leaders tend to forget about strategic retention and overindex on tactical retention, pursuing a bunch of short-term ideas to keep people happy and positive.

Under stress, tactical retention can lead to gimmickry—parties, team swag, hiding bad news, rampant huzzahs, opportunistic raises. These fly in the face of competence, further undermining confidence. So double down on what matters more than anything else—*doing your job*. As a leader, that job, first and foremost, is to execute through teamwork—to solve real problems for and with the team, and to contribute directly to mission success. Execution is your best strategic retention lever, particularly in crisis. Good execution breeds confidence, and bad execution creates fear. So when the doubt and fear of crisis opens the door to mass exodus, do your job.

Inspire with Peers

Fueling personal growth with inspiring peers is fundamental to developing mission athletes. Assembling a critical mass of peers who exhibit the team's success criteria goes a very long way to building a self-sustaining growth environment. But doing so requires you to make a critical choice: You must add people to your team who elevate everyone's performance, rather than add people who reinforce the status quo or throttle collective growth. The same thing goes for who you promote, who you retain, and who you exit. Nothing raises the bar more naturally than increasing the visibility of a team member with leveled up skills, expanded capacity, and a desire for growth.

Consider my experiences at Stanford University and Roblox, for example. Both were inspiring and stimulating, and in each case, I simul-taneously ran toward making my own contributions while wondering how I could hold my own alongside incredibly talented individuals. As a result, I grew on two levels—in personal capacity fueled by effort and peer learning, and in the maturity to work with confidence alongside oth-ers more talented than I was in one area or another. The people around me made me better and more confident, even though the journey was sometimes humbling. And the experiences showed me what true mastery looks like, not just through my accomplishments but through the habits of those around me—the work ethic, the curiosity, the focus, the vision, and the commitment.

Inspiring peers set the tone of collective and personal impact. They demonstrate values and inspire with effort. And they hold each other to account, demanding of each other a commitment to mission and mastery. That is the team you can have. Imagine what it can do. Without inspiring peers, mastery and growth seekers ultimately leave because they don't see the one crucial resource that is hard to beat—peers who elevate the game. Having peers who inspire does not guarantee success, but having a team that underwhelms throttles success at best.

The right entrepreneurial culture attracts and retains inspiring peers *by design*, not merely as a by-product. So build a team of inspiring peers who fuel personal growth, but also build an entrepreneurial environment that amplifies and retains them. Codify the team's success strategies ("Live by Values," "Define Success"). Hire people who elevate the game ("Recruit Mission Athletes"). Build an environment for creativity and problem-solving ("Fuel by Purpose," "Unlock Autonomy," "Institutionalize Mastery"). Develop those who do the same (this chapter), and exit those who diminish the team's capacity and disrupt flow ("Coach Out").

Coach for Growth

Assembling a critical mass of peers who personify your team's success criteria is necessary for entrepreneurial growth, but it is not sufficient. It is also essential that each individual grows toward greater mastery. As a reminder, mastery is defined in this book broadly, beyond subject matter to all areas of entrepreneurial activity, including leadership, collaboration, execution, and audience engagement.

Coaching for growth encapsulates the practices that encourage and support the pursuit of such mastery by individuals. And because improved personal mastery generally leads to greater collective mastery (not always, but mostly), this coaching must be a core competency of all entrepreneurial leaders, both those formally charged with guiding others' growth and those informally charged with setting the tone through influence and example.

Coaching for growth is only possible if everyone involved has a growth mindset, coach and coached alike. To quote Carol Dweck, one of the authors who coined the term:

> Individuals who believe their talents can be developed (through hard work, good strategies, and input from others) have a growth mindset. They tend

to achieve more than those with a more fixed mindset (those who believe their talents are innate gifts). This is because they worry less about looking smart and put more energy into learning.[93]

In my experience, you cannot instill a growth mindset in a person, but you can cultivate it. So first and foremost, hire and retain those with a growth mindset by including it in your team's success criteria. This is captured by the mastery criterion described in chapter 6, though you can also name it explicitly. Beyond this foundation, coaching for growth involves the following:

- Align purpose to connect team and personal growth.
- Understand mastery to appreciate its sometimes-uneven progression.
- Associate learning with feedback so learners don't just appreciate it but seek it.
- Expect ownership, reinforcing the reality that mastery is earned, not given.
- Define masterful goals to propel performance without demoralizing.
- Ensure quality feedback that is relevant, constructive, and actionable.

Let's consider each of these in turn.

Align Purpose

At one point in my career, I hit a hard performance ceiling of my own making. I was easily frustrated with operational roadblocks and anyone who created them. I was organized, supportive, focused, and mission-driven. I got stuff done, helped teams get their stuff done, and consistently solved problems. I believed in what we were doing, loved my job, and put in long hours toward our collective success. But my tendency to become frustrated with operational friction (mistakes, low urgency, low ownership) demotivated people and I'm sure caused some not to seek out help when they needed it most. I am eternally grateful to my then boss, Dave Baszucki, who suggested I get coached, and to the coach we found, Keith Merron, who helped me level up.

There were three ingredients to Keith's remedy: voice dialog, motivation mapping, and purpose alignment. Through voice dialog, I learned that there is a part of me that is, in isolation, rationally frustrated by inaction. I can accept those feelings without judgment, understand them, and then choose how to respond. Second, by mapping my motivation across community, achievement, and power, I learned that I am driven by achievement most of all, which explains why roadblocks trigger me. But the great unlock for me was purpose alignment.

Deep in my being, I really wanted to be a good leader—someone who unlocked greatness in others, not just someone who organized others. Keith positioned my tendency to get frustrated as a roadblock to that deep-seated goal, firing up my outsized achievement drive in the process. As a result, my personal drive became aligned with what I needed to do most at that moment as a leader—to positively coach the team toward higher performance. This was a masterful approach by Keith, and it worked, measured directly in the feedback I received from others and indirectly in the growth I subsequently saw in myself and the team.

Here's the moral of the story. To coach someone through performance roadblocks, you sometimes need to help them drive through personal stumbling blocks. That is what I mean when I say elsewhere in this book that who you are matters and that leadership ultimately requires all of you—not all your time, but your full being as a contributor.

To intrinsically motivate a person to bust through a performance plateau, try aligning their personal purpose with their role. Alignment to the company mission is entry stakes. That shared belief is critical to creativity and resilience, but it does not alone unlock greatness in an individual. You also need to tap into personal purpose, and that means getting to know the person, a process that starts during recruitment.

In my breakthrough above, there was a singular connection between what I needed to do and what I wanted to become. In general, though, personal purpose is more multifaceted—a mix of career achievement, team mission, family well-being, social standing, financial security, and a core sense of being. The more you connect what matters to an individual to their mission and role, the more capacity you unlock in that person to reach higher mastery.

One critical caveat: The win here only comes authentically, as in truly getting to know a person enough to help them clarify what matters for them, and then aligning that to mission, team, and role. Inauthentic manipulation, one not simultaneously seeking team and individual growth, is not deep enough to transform long term. And as we'll explore in the next chapter, "Coach Out," an authentic attempt to align purpose is the basis of mutually deciding whether the mission, team, and role continue to make sense for the person, not just the other way around.

Understand Mastery

Coaching for growth is coaching for mastery. We explored mastery in part I from the perspective of team success, covering mastery's benefits, the importance of flow, and how to measure culture. There is one additional idea that helps all involved pursue higher levels of performance with greater resilience—*mastery is an uneven progression.*

Mastery is the never-ending pursuit and attainment of higher performance. According to IDEO, a well-known product design firm accredited with coining the term *design thinking*, "The arc of mastery is long and the end point can move just as you near it."[94] In addition to mastery being perpetually out of reach, its pursuit is also not monotonic—people don't just get exclusively better. Rather, when pushing through to higher performance, people sometimes take a step backward, sometimes they temporarily plateau, and almost everyone surprises you. How well and how quickly an individual progresses are indeed key indicators of their future success, and not everyone's progression will work for *your* mission on *your* team in *this* moment. But it is a mistake to assume that all progressions are continuously upward.

Figure 13 depicts the theoretical performance progressions of three people pursuing mastery in the same area (three salespeople, three engineering managers, three pianists, etc.). The solid s-curve is the idealized asymptotic approach to mastery, and the arrows are individual progressions. These curves are not analytically derived but just mental models, and the picture is provided merely to help you visualize the ideas.

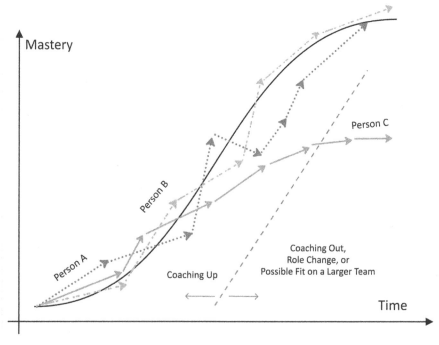

Figure 13: Mastery Progression in Practice

The figure illustrates a few key points about mastery's progression.

- Some people start out as "stars" (Person A), reaching higher levels of early mastery faster than their peers, but they don't necessarily stay that way—mastery is uneven.

- Others are slow and steady achievers (Person B), gradually getting better, but even they do so in fits and starts—everyone plateaus now and again.
- Sometimes even the best performers take a step backward (Person A), only then to excel beyond momentary expectation—it's best not to write people off quickly.
- Sometimes people just plateau for all practical purposes (Person C)—not everyone plays at Carnegie Hall, and that may or may not be a problem.

Figure 13 also depicts a diagonal line parallel to the idealized mastery progression. The line conceptually represents a dividing line between those who are progressing upward and those who have reached plateaus. For the latter group, you have several options that depend in part on organizational size, from exiting (when small) to experimenting with different roles (at medium size) to simply allowing a person to settle in to a mid-level role (on a larger team). The latter, though, has negative cultural side effects—namely, the entrenchment of people no longer growing in mastery. We'll explore these further in the next chapter, "Coach Out."

The observations illustrated by figure 13 have two consequences for coaching. First, personal mastery is a personal journey, one that spans beyond this moment and this team. You can coach toward it, like a guide on a mountain climb, but you cannot ensure it. Everyone owns their own climb and will do so in their own time. Second, given the uneven trajectory people generally have toward mastery, you are well served by first assuming greatness and then learning otherwise. This is a safe assumption if the other two elements of part II—hiring mission athletes and coaching out—are working well. If not, fix them. By engaging with someone through a challenge or milestone with a learning mindset, you are best positioned to understand how they operate today, where they might go tomorrow, and what's in the way of them getting there.

In my experience and absent externalities, a person's pursuit of mastery at each moment is defined by three things—a growth mindset, relevant capacity (skill), and relevant instinct (intuition). All these are mutable and coachable, though not infinitely so and not always on a timetable that matters to your team. Additionally, capacity and instinct are often role-dependent, even within the same subject matter. A random group of information security experts, for example, have capacity and instinct variations that empower some to create, others to scale, and still others to execute. This latter association of role with capacity and instincts suggests the ability to "dial in" each individual to a role that best unlocks their potential. This is indeed the case, but yet again, your ability to do so is often limited in practice—you just may not have another role available.

Finally, because success is defined in the context of mission and team, the mastery that matters in practice goes beyond role expertise. It includes mastery in leadership, alignment, execution, values, and the team's operating system. That's at the heart of being a mission athlete—mastering position and mastering team play. Each person progresses differently within each of these areas, achieving veteran status in a skill, for example, while remaining a novice in leadership. Unevenness is the norm. Failure to grow cannot be.

Associate Feedback with Success

To pursue mastery, individuals must be open to learning. And to be open to learning, people must associate feedback with growth, and growth with success. To foster this association, leaders must value near-term learning more than they shun near-term failure. And to value that, they must play for enduring impact, not a quick win.

It also helps to talk about failure analytically and openly, before and after the fact such as how doctors review a surgical procedure. Before a procedure, they consider what can go wrong and how to mitigate risk, and afterward they review what did go wrong and how to avoid that failure next time. If you coach with a mindset of continuous improvement, your team will have the same mindset. But if you coach in fear of mistakes, the team will fear the same. A team that doesn't embrace risk has a hard time innovating, let alone disrupting. Value learning, coach people to embrace risk, and continuously improve.

The other way to reinforce the association between learning and success is to institutionalize this relationship in how the team operates. A great example of this is the principle of *proportional response*, which I learned from executives at IMVU around 2010.[95] After any outage or software bug, the IMVU team made an investment in infrastructure proportional to the cost of the issue—a new alert, an automated test, an architectural change, or an automation system. Not only does that reinforce ownership and accountability, but it also connects learning to success. You can't make the proportional investment if you don't understand what happened and why, and the investment improves the mastery of your system, enhancing future success.

Having a learning mindset raises an interesting question. If you value learning more than you shun failure, doesn't that undermine the drive to succeed in the short term? In other words, are you making it okay to fail if you just learn afterward. In short, *you are making it okay to fail but not okay to fail to try.*

In my experience, successful outcomes are not driven by fear of failure but achieved through the pursuit of mastery—putting in the work that leads to success. When releasing new product features, for example, putting in the work means understanding user needs and aspirations through direct engagement; creating solutions that align with vision; assessing user experience with a high bar; cataloging and mitigating risk; thinking through rollout and user onboarding; communicating with users in advance; and ultimately holding the line on poor quality. I've seen high-risk features roll out very smoothly and low-risk features crash and burn.

There is a clear pattern to all of this. The people who put in the work consistently have better outcomes. Success is not guaranteed in any single project, but it tends to follow those with the right habits. So build habits that lead to success and learn from failure. There is no tension between learning and success when mastery guides.

Expect Ownership

Ownership is fundamental to growth. On entrepreneurial teams, growth typically follows the pursuit of mastery, and mastery is earned, not given.

Fostering growth requires that you expect ownership in each person. When someone leads a project, for example, they own all of it—all the work, risks, complexity, scope, and implications. This is not to say that owners perform each task themselves or work without seeking advice. Rather, ownership in this context means that project leads accept full responsibility for their inputs *and* their outcomes. I call this working without a net. In practice, on effective teams, no one really works without a net, and teams are most successful when people have each other's backs. But true ownership assumes there is no net and works accordingly.

Expecting ownership asks people for their plans, assessments, timelines, and trade-offs. You, of course, have input—you just start with their leadership. The more you support ownership, the more you support mastery, growth, and distributed action. And the more you undermine ownership, the more you create a culture that throttles on your specific instructions.

Expecting ownership also shifts your leadership away from managing toward coaching, and the difference between these matters. Mechanically, coaching is pulling. It's providing vision and mission, offering guidance, and then asking for strategies, goals, metrics, and key tactics. Managing by contrast is pushing. It's developing virtually all aspects of a project, from goals to plans, and tracking execution tightly. Coaching builds entrepreneurial capacity, while managing undermines intrinsic motivation and team-based innovation.

Coaching amplifies ownership, while managing diminishes it. As such, managing tends to alienate the intrinsically motivated people you need most for entrepreneurial endeavors, while retaining those who need or want real-time direction. That means managing leads to bureaucracy in the playbooks, documentation, and processes needed to ensure that directed doers stay on track. By contrast, coaching leads the way to less heavy and streamlined distributed action.

In this light and thinking again about intrinsic motivation, managing often leads to programmatic work styles (repeatable, high certainty, and task based), while coaching leads to creativity and systems thinking. When one senior leader was asked to leave Roblox, for example, I asked a board member for the rationale, not having worked closely enough with the person to know. The board member replied that the leader was too programmatic, creating too many manual, people-heavy processes. And instead, we needed systematic leaders who would leverage incentives, software, and community to create self-sustaining systems.

Define Masterful Goals

Masterful goals play a key role in coaching for growth. And in this book, we discuss three ways to think about goal-setting mastery. In chapter 4, "Unlock Autonomy," we discussed how clear and well-designed goals can increase autonomy and ownership by building trust in execution alignment. In chapter 3, "Institutionalize Mastery," we discussed how to set goals to optimize flow—supporting near-term flow with goals that are balanced between being challenging and achievable, and supporting longer-term flow with iterative goals that allow individuals and small groups to focus for days and weeks at a time. And finally, in the next section, "Create Opportunities," we will discuss how to use goals to give individuals multiple ways to experiment, learn, and grow. Together, these ideas encapsulate the types of goal setting needed to coach for growth.

Ensure Quality Feedback

I learned C++ on the job at Knowledge Revolution (KR), fresh off my PhD in computational fluid dynamics. I was a seasoned scientific programmer, but I did not have a formal computer science background, nor did I have any experience with object-oriented programming. I could have learned C++ on my own, but I probably would have flailed a bit, mired in hackery. Instead, KR assigned me the best technical mentor I have come across— Paul Mitiguy, physics engine colead at KR and now a beloved teaching professor at Stanford University.

At the start of his day, Paul and I would sit side by side, looking at my code from the day before and planning the work ahead. Paul was excruciatingly detailed and coached on all levels of programming, from the formatting of whitespace to performance tuning to designing class libraries. It was not always easy for someone like me who liked to do good work, but Paul was always constructive and thankfully never pulled punches. As a result, I reached higher levels of mastery than I would have otherwise attained and at a much faster pace. I am ever indebted to Paul, not just for instilling in me a love for C++ but also for giving me a life lesson in mentoring.

Coaching for growth starts by cultivating a growth mindset that is open to feedback, but it then requires that individuals receive *quality feedback*, just like athletes need subjective and objective performance measurements. To be productive, feedback must be improvement-oriented, not problem-oriented, and it must focus as much on what's working as on what's not.

Feedback must also be relevant, specific, timely, and useful. That means the person giving the feedback must be close enough to the work to understand it—analogous to a craftsperson (Paul) working with an apprentice (me). And because each person on an entrepreneurial team pursues mastery in multiple dimensions (subject area, leadership, problem-solving, creativity, execution), they ultimately need competent feedback in multiple dimensions over time. At a minimum, each person should have a mentor most closely associated with their role. For individual contributors, this mentor can be a more senior individual contributor or a skill-based technical lead. For leaders, formal and informal, mentoring must embrace both the skill area they lead and the discipline of leadership itself. This usually expands one's mentoring circle beyond the team.

There are three typical blockers to delivering quality feedback: Leaders don't embrace coaching, leaders are unable to provide insight, or leaders are afraid to be honest. I've already addressed the importance of coaching, and the second issue is ostensibly solved by having mentors closely related to the work. Let's talk about honesty. Hesitancy to give direct feedback is likely caused by having the wrong mindset, one that associates feedback with failure rather than personal growth. Giving feedback is being in service to others in their pursuit of mastery. It is how you show true support. If you find yourself hesitating, align yourself to mastery, and commit to giving growth-oriented quality feedback. Like all things that matter, if difficulty makes you want to give feedback less often, that means you need to do it a lot more often.

Create Opportunities

Every athletic competition is an opportunity for greater mastery. So is every artistic performance, every operation by a surgeon, and each item built by a craftsperson. Likewise, coaching individuals toward greater entrepreneurial mastery requires opportunities for growth, and the more varied the better. Here are a few ways to craft growth opportunities, sorted roughly by those available on smaller teams to those more relevant to larger teams with established cadences.

Projects

There is a natural growth opportunity built into team-based creative endeavors—the project, a time- or objective-scoped effort. Each project is an opportunity for participants to improve, individually and collectively.

On Scrum software teams, for example, each *sprint* (a time-boxed effort) is not only a collection of deliverables but also a new opportunity to improve, a philosophy codified by the retrospective that follows each sprint (teams assess how well they performed and identify one area for improvement in the next sprint). Sprints and retrospectives are great for teamwide improvement, but unless individuals are coached as part of the process, individual performance will come along for the ride at best. If you want to use projects for individual mastery, then build personal retrospectives into the process on some cadence that aligns with project completion.

Personal retrospectives should line up with a project's completion but not necessarily happen after every project, particularly if projects are short in duration. I would not, for example, have individual retrospectives after each sprint. That would balloon bureaucracy and is an unnecessary cadence for personal growth conversations. Personal retrospectives can be used even when the team doesn't practice Scrum.

Challenges and Quests

Opportunities for mastery can also be provided through challenges and quests, which are used in game design to drive player engagement and retention through mastery.

In gaming, a *challenge* is a small achievement-based objective relevant to game play—a player completes the challenge to level up. Challenges start and end, and performance can be easily measured. In addition to the benefits of the skills mastered, completed challenges deliver rewards such as badges that signify success. Rewards don't have to be significant, and badges don't have to be public for impact. The achievement and recognition are what matter. A quest in gaming is a series of challenges that lead to even greater rewards. Quests require alignment around a narrative in order to be compelling, such as a hero's journey or other adventure.

On entrepreneurial teams, challenges and quests can drive people toward greater mastery, provided they are created authentically to level up and not simply to manipulate work hours. I'm not suggesting gimmicks for skills development—explicit badges, challenges, and quests—although that would be authentic to a gaming company. Rather, it's the ideas that matter. Challenges and quests are useful mental models for planning growth opportunities, as are the ideas of rewards, recognition, and a progression fueled by a compelling narrative.

Consider an individual contributor on a small team at their first job. Their first quest might be to master the skills needed to own a solo project as a lead, with a narrative that speaks to their personal ambitions or contributions to the mission. To complete that quest, the individual must complete three challenges, each corresponding to a different skill. The individual pursues those challenges during their normal project work, and regular retrospectives are used to provide quality feedback. Ultimately, the person completes those challenges, unlocking the "solo lead" capability. As with all things that involve extrinsic rewards (like badges), they are effective on entrepreneurial teams only as tactical complements to the strategic forces of intrinsic motivation.

In practice, small teams don't have the bandwidth to design challenges and quests explicitly, and larger teams often develop a "leveling matrix" to rationally guide skill mastery and promotions. Furthermore, capable people leaders create challenges and quests intuitively, organically, and without the nomenclature. But ideas and nomenclature can amplify the benefits of intuition, and that is the intended spirit. Whether or not you codify challenges and quests, remember their mechanics and how they can be used to drive individual mastery, engagement, and retention.[96]

OKRs

The Objectives and Key Results (OKR) framework is a popular planning tool that aligns and focuses teams on near-term goals. Objectives are compelling achievements toward mission, and key results are concrete measurable outcomes that indicate objective success. OKRs were discussed in detail in the section "Autonomy in Execution," in chapter 4.

In the context of growth, OKRs can be used to create natural opportunities for individual mastery and its coaching. They are typically set quarterly but can also be set more frequently. Weave mastery into the OKR process by working with individuals to identify next-level personal mastery goals, establish check-ins throughout the OKR cycle, and review growth in a retrospective.

One Thousand Opportunities

If people grow through opportunities and if everyone leads in some way (see chapter 2, "Live by Values"), then everyone should have as many leadership opportunities as possible—formal and informal, big and small, crisis response and long-term investment, hyper-tactical and high-quality. You don't want a few leadership opportunities a year across your growing team. You want thousands of opportunities, particularly on larger teams.

Opportunities get limited if roles become entrenched, so the best way to unlock opportunity is to have a *dynamic organization*. Here are a few examples.

- Distribute ad hoc project leadership as broadly as possible, resisting the urge to reuse a handful of go-to achievers. Also resist the urge to codify project ownership into standing roles until there is demonstrable value in sustained effort, preferring instead dynamic assignment by project. Involve ad hoc leaders directly in high-level conversations, giving them experience operating up and down the people stack. Nothing says ownership and opportunity more to a new team member than collaborating directly with the CEO. Dissociating project leadership from formal roles maximizes opportunity.

- Title people as broadly as possible, focusing on skill, and assign scope independent of title—product manager, not product manager for feature X. That creates a cohort at each skill level, keeping the focus on mastery and away from silos. It also normalizes the fluid movement of scope across the cohort and keeps leaders creatively fresh by solving problems across domains. This can be done with both individual contributors (software engineer I) and leadership roles (director of Engineering, VP of Finance). This approach hits a wall at the C-level where positions map to external expectations (CEO, CFO).

- Challenge the team to reorganize regularly, encouraging people to experiment with subject, skill, partners, and scope. Don't just reorganize in response to individual or team performance issues. Instead, reorganize when natural opportunities occur such as going after a new audience segment or as part of an OKR cadence. And just like high performers need to associate feedback with mastery, they also need to associate organizational change with opportunity.

The more everyone gets comfortable with scope volatility (how many people or projects they manage), the more room there is to create opportunities for new leaders without replacing existing ones. Don't force people to give up a role they truly love or someone they enjoy working with just for the sake of change. But do create growth opportunities by resisting structural entrenchment.

Get Compensation Right

Compensation is often misunderstood. While compensation can demonstrate value and convey appreciation, it is not, in my experience, the biggest lever for attracting and retaining mission athletes. Rather, compensation is at best a nonissue and at worst an energy-sapping distraction. When people are well compensated, they put energy into the reasons they joined the team such as impacting a mission that matters and contributing to a team that inspires. But if they are undercompensated, their energy gets sapped. It's not the money—it's feeling underappreciated.

Consider this real-world example. An extremely hardworking person, universally admired as a "can't lose" team member by senior staff, didn't get a substantive raise after two years because the market salary charts indicated she had hit the limit for her role. The company was cash-conscious, a good thing, but not existentially cash-strapped. There was no financial mandate to keep salaries flat. In describing the situation to me, the person remained committed in the near term but was not feeling appreciated and was no longer confident she'd be around in a year.

Culture is what you do, not what you say, so what does this tell the team member? It says loudly that the company values rules and process more than it values her, and it is willing to have outcomes that undermine its own success as long as the rules are followed. Individuals are *the* means of a team's impact, and a team is defined more than anything else by who it hires, promotes, and retains. Good luck with a strategy of demoralizing a "can't lose" team member.

The failure here is strict adherence to a system. But no matter how well intentioned, *the system is not the mission; the system is in service of the mission and the team.* So consider an alternative to the approach. Let the teammate know that the market has plateaued, but because they are so valuable, you are breaking the rules and giving them a raise in recognition of their impact, current and future. People will fight for this team because they are seen.

So how do you get compensation right? In short, develop a data-driven, flexible approach, and then evaluate the outcomes in the shoes of the recipients. If the outcomes don't make sense, change the approach. The more flexible you are, the more ad hoc the compensation and the less fair the outcomes across the team. And in the opposite extreme, the more rigid you are, the more you get cases like the above where everyone lives at the mercy of a spreadsheet. Let's now take a look at getting compensation right in a bit more detail.

Building Blocks

Here are my building blocks for getting compensation right:

- Third-party benchmark data for specific roles, industries, location, and team size
- A leveling matrix that maps external roles to laddered success criteria
- Band percentile targets that define default compensation on this team (e.g., 75th)
- Band-busting language for true exceptions to break through salary bands
- Regular sanity checks to make sure the system's output makes sense

These building blocks operate together toward a single goal—an accurate and up-to-date model that guides team compensation and codifies the treatment of exceptionalism. A detailed description of these is beyond the scope of this book, but the following is a brief summary.

Third-party benchmark data is fairly accessible these days as a subscription, just be aware that they are typically a few months behind the actual market—so also use data from candidates' competing offers to update your internal model. A leveling matrix maps an external role from one of these datasets, say software eng II, to your team's success criteria, such as appropriately leveled descriptions of leadership, project management, self-sufficiency, and expertise. Band percentiles, also found in external datasets, define compensation at each level for a role by a distribution, as in "50 percent of all people in role X have compensation Y."

Band busting allows an exceptional contributor to exceed all reported compensation without leveling up. This is critical because leveling should be about mastery, not compensation—it is far better to pay someone above a salary band because of their value to the team, than it is to artificially inflate their mastery. The former rewards exceptionalism (the point), and the latter undermines mastery. Explicitly naming someone an exception is key to systemizing band busting—even on a high-performing team, not everyone can be an outlier. And using sanity checks, such as regular reviews of compensation up and down the people stack, ensures that the overall outcomes—including band busters—align with common sense.

Do Give People a Win

Compensation negotiations are part of a long-term relationship that also includes coaching an individual toward greater mastery. So whatever happens in any single negotiation impacts the long-term coaching relationship, both for the better and for the worse.

Show appreciation, act with generosity, and champion a vision of growth, and individuals will understand that you are partnering in their success. But be combative, play to win the moment, or fail to yield on any requests, and you become just the boss.

If you are truly hiring and retaining high-impact mission athletes, give them a win when they negotiate. Keep it grounded, keep it data-driven, and keep it rational (band busting included), but give them a win. I have personally seen the lingering ill effects of people never getting anything beyond the initial offer, as hiring managers rigidly stick to salary bands or bad models of power. Some candidates are never satisfied, so don't bother trying. But for the high-impact contributor who asks for a bit more? Give this person something and let them know you're happy to do it.

Giving people a win is among the highest bang-for-buck things you can do for individual engagement and retention. And to be clear, a win matters because of the appreciation it shows, not simply the compensation it delivers. For larger or compensation-constrained or regulated teams, there are other types of wins beyond annual compensation, such as bonuses, "star awards," and accelerated promotions. The point is less the value of the win than the appreciation it shows.

Don't Offer Cash-Stock Trade-Offs

During negotiations, teams sometimes offer a trade-off between stock and cash compensation, as in "We can give you more cash, but you get less stock." The rationale is fairness—two equally leveled peers should get the same total compensation even if one prefers one form over another. This approach is fine for contractors who are short-term by definition, but the practice is generally problematic for full-time team members.

The trade-off can be viewed as a proxy for the individual's confidence in the team's success. In reality, the trade-off decision is typically about personal finances, but the appearance can linger. I would avoid putting team members in this position. Additionally, the trade-off can be complicated to calculate and linked to the uncertainty of private company valuation, for example. That can, in turn, lead to difficult conversations one and two years later when people question their overall compensation package.

Avoid the trade-off, and negotiate instead on the compensation band percentile (25th, 50th, or 75th). If you still need a lever, commit to considering an accelerated promotion after six months or a year, commensurate with performance. If the candidate considers a delayed promotion an excessive risk, they are either too title-oriented or you have failed to build trust during the recruiting process that you honor your word. And if you consider this too much of a risk, then you are probably more unsure about the candidate than you are willing to admit.

Don't Pay to Retain

Above all else, do not try to pay people to join a team they don't believe in or to stay in roles they don't want. The reason to avoid this is because sometimes it actually works. The people most willing to work for cash over purpose and growth generally don't pattern match to the creativity, innovation, and perseverance you need to do new and great things. Focus instead on building a compelling environment for mission athletes and eliminating compensation distractions. That will attract the people you need the most and turn off the rest.

Competing with Market Makers

Your team may sometimes be at the mercy of large market makers, particularly in tight labor markets of specialized skill. Even in looser markets with wider compensation ranges, other teams might be able to pay more. So how do you compete in these environments? You have two levers.

- Pick a strategically critical role on your team, and then compete head-to-head for talent to accelerate your progress and punch above your weight.
- For all other roles, find people who believe what you believe, ignoring the market makers.

The first lever is a clear win, given an important caveat. The person can't be an industry shaper who fails to meet your team's success criteria. Rather, they must have a high probability of success on your team for your mission right now. The person who wants to work at Big Co Dream Machine, for example, might not love building teams as much as building high-profile technology for well-known brands to boost their personal brand. This person won't be successful even if you can land them. And that leads directly to the second lever—ultimately finding people who believe what you do about the mission, the team's values, and the opportunities for growth and impact.

Consider figure 14 that depicts the benefits offered by two different teams. I have selected four criteria as an example, but others matter, too, such as autonomy and mastery. The two teams depicted are not the same. Team I doesn't offer as much cash as Team II, but it offers more ownership in the company, a greater impact on mission, and an easier ability to have impact.

Teams I and II generally pattern match to small and big companies, respectively, but not exclusively. Smaller companies generally pay less and offer more equity per role than larger ones because they have less cash and higher risk. And in general, the impact of one person is harder to understand on a mega team than on an intimate one. But effectiveness is not a given.

Teams big and small are capable of effectiveness and susceptible to bureaucracy. So to attract high performers, your team must be high performing and then play to its other strengths. This will attract people who find meaning not only in your purpose but also in the shape of what your team offers (as illustrated, for example, by figure 14). It is difficult on a small team to lure people who want Big Co comforts, but it is also thrilling to find mission athletes excited to build your team.

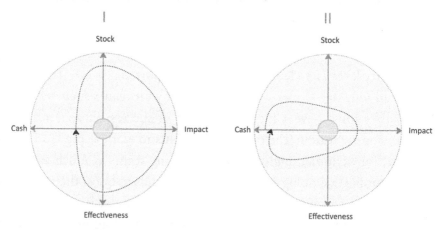

Figure 14: The Benefits Structure of Two Different Teams

Note that I did not include purpose as a dimension. That is because every team needs clear and compelling purpose to inspire, regardless of team size. Every creative team has to get this right, or it won't attract and retain the people it needs the most.

Understand Mindsets

In addition to everything we've discussed, there are a few additional considerations particular to certain mindsets. Here are a few of the more common ones I've experienced.

Imposter Syndrome

Imposter syndrome is feeling ill-equipped for the role you have or the situation you're in. You feel as if you are faking it without necessarily making it, and people who feel this way generally discount their competence and wins.[97] It seems to happen when a transition in roles and responsibilities goes beyond the incremental and crosses some self-imposed artificial boundary, allowing insecurities to emerge. While imposter syndrome is not an official diagnosis, it does exist, and I believe the feeling is more common than people are comfortable admitting.

I felt imposter syndrome acutely as a first-year Stanford graduate student taking rocket propulsion. This was Stanford after all, and surely no one was struggling like I was. I felt like I did not belong, particularly when my first midterm grade was 16 out of 100—even though I also knew the highest grade was only 20! It turned out that everyone felt the same way, but no one would admit it until we all passed the course (barely).

So here's my general rule: Unless you actually cheated to get your role, assume you belong where you are, and then go make your role your own. It may not always be easy or fair, but don't let others, real or imagined, suggest you don't belong. Let insecurity fuel your effort, but otherwise ignore it and just get busy having impact. Focus on mission, seek mastery, and put wins on the board. These always matter, regardless of the confidence of the contributor.

People with imposter syndrome often land a new role for good reason, usually a mix of hard work, talent, and grit. They can make exceptional contributions if coached through this moment of doubt. It's a transition, not a description, so help people get comfortable in their new shoes in order to unlock their growth.

The Newly Arrived

At the other end of the spectrum from imposter syndrome are the newly arrived. They are the team equivalent of the nouveau riche of the early nineteenth century—people with newfound status and authority who seem to equate talent, effort, and luck with just talent. Left unattended and without self-realization, these people produce a host of dysfunctions on their way to authoring their personal Greek tragedies.

At a minimum, the newly arrived plateau in their performance and opt out of a further pursuit of mastery. Beyond that, they can disrupt those around them with hubris and self-granted special privileges. They tend to strengthen silos, build fiefdoms, and otherwise solidify their positions. None of this is good for any organization, let alone one trying to create and innovate.

The antidote is to double down on what matters—mastery in pursuit of mission. On the road to mastery, everyone is a student, no one has arrived, and what you have done pales in comparison to your achievements ahead. And in the pursuit of mission, everyone must lead and have impact. These ideas can help people burst through understandable moments of self-indulgence. Exit those who don't push through because they will ultimately undermine the team.

Growth-Hungry People

Growth-*oriented* people stay on your team and seek to excel to the extent they see growth opportunity such as growth in self, skills, role, impact, community, and stature. This is healthy, and everything you do to help mission athletes reach higher levels of mastery also helps you retain growth-oriented people—the challenges, the feedback, the opportunities, and the rewards. But there is a big difference between growth-oriented people and growth-*hungry* people.

You want a team of growth-oriented individuals, but you must guard against people who are too hungry, either temporarily or as a matter of character. Growth-hungry people are never satisfied, and indulging them leads to several dysfunctions, from role and salary inflation to the team's oversensitivity to momentary speed bumps. Belief fuels resilience, and growth-minded people can deliver exceptional impact. But indulging personal growth for its own sake reduces resiliency. To avoid these pitfalls, always return to substance—to mission and mastery, and the growth-seeking that works in service of them, not the other way around.

Comfort Seekers

Comfort seekers stay on the team to the extent they can achieve stability, and they generally excel to the extent needed in order to stay on the team.

Seeking comfort is not the same has having a healthy work-life balance. Plenty of people I know have meaningful family lives, fulfilling volunteer pursuits, and energizing hobbies—and then they come to work with intensity, urgency, and a desire to have impact. Having other equal or higher life priorities does not make someone a comfort seeker. Comfort-seeking makes them a comfort seeker. There is no role for comfort seekers on an entrepreneurial team. You simply cannot innovate without a desire to disrupt the status quo, and disruption is often uncomfortable.

The retention problem with comfort-oriented people is not failing to retain them but inadvertently retaining them, particularly when you retain so many that it defines culture. People whose tendencies gravitate toward comfort over growth will undermine the team's performance through a siren song that "okay is good enough." And teams that gravitate toward comfort will ultimately be outperformed.

A dominantly growth-oriented team will cause comfort seekers to self-select out, either during recruiting or once on the team. If your team does gravitate toward comfort, look no further than your realized culture, the totality of what you do and allow to be done—the unproductive meetings, the easy goals set, the unaddressed hiring mistakes, the unsolved problems, and the belabored critical decisions. Sharpen your success criteria for recruiting and hiring, and eliminate the practices that rank comfort over growth.

Dial In Success

Toward the tail end of my PhD, I had a conversation with my advisor. We were talking about a fluid dynamic phenomenon, and he enthusiastically shared with me a related realization he recently had while watching water flow down the tub drain. I thought this was remarkable, but not for the obvious reasons. I did not think about fluid dynamics outside of my work, but he clearly did. That was an important difference between us—a lesson I've kept with me the rest of my life.

Success is very much tied to connection, and the best sign of connection is what you do when you don't have to do anything. My advisor was dialed into his role, and I was not. I decided that day to finish my PhD as fast as possible so I could move on and find my connection. That drive pushed me to working ninety-plus hours per week, and I finished within the next eighteen months.

No one, including the most versatile, skilled, and hardworking people, can excel in every role. I certainly admire those who can capably take on a broad set of challenges, but sustained high impact only happens when a person's mission and role align with their skills, intuition, and purpose. A big part of coaching for growth is helping mission athletes "dial in" success.

Dialing in success has two core elements: identifying and refining a role that aligns with a person's strengths and complementing that person with the people, tools, and mentoring needed to augment their weaknesses. In this context, the progression toward mastery is not just a series of challenges to advance skills but also a series of experiments that reveal personal operating systems, outsized strengths, and growth-blocking blind spots.

The learning from these experiments can help dial a person into the right role—one they connect with, can accel at, and will invest in. But there is one critical caveat for team building: Because mastery matters, dialing in success has limits. You can help a person seek an aligned role, but the person must ultimately have substantive impact in a time frame and manner that work for your mission and team. To build a culture of mastery, *you must dial in success, not mediocrity.*

Helping a person dial in involves understanding them more deeply—how they engage with the world, what motivates them, and what skills they are most capable of mastering. There are people who are innate teachers, caregivers, healers, counselors, thrill seekers, and storytellers—people who bring their essence to their roles regardless of subject matter or title. And when people complement their essence with mastery in their field, they make a role their own, bringing a unique approach to something that might otherwise be mundane. This is the CEO with extreme operating abilities who builds an execution machine. Or it is the head of Engineering with innate teaching abilities who builds a masterfully skilled team. Or it is the marketing lead with the elite storytelling instincts who connects the mission to fundamental human aspirations.

There are some helpful questions to uncover how a person naturally operates. My favorite is "What work-related things do you think about when you are not working?" Or similarly, "If you could only do one thing to contribute to our mission, what would that be?" When I've asked this, some people have answered that they'd fix bugs. Others say they'd build more features. And still others say they'd get the team organized and streamlined. These tell me a lot about the person. Understanding what people do freely helps uncover what instinctively attracts them.

Dialing in success can be a bit of the chicken or the egg—it's hard to get to significant levels of mastery without tapping into natural skills and curiosity, yet some level of mastery is needed to explore different roles. The path through this is experimentation and effort; that is, trying lots of things and putting in the work to do each thing well. Experiments where people don't try, don't inform. In this pursuit, you are looking for a few concrete things to align.

- A role that leverages existing skills, to provide immediate impact
- A subject that resonates, to leverage natural curiosity and intuition
- A craft that engages, to inspire the effort needed to develop expertise
- A team that aligns, to inspire mastery and highlight the value of contribution
- A mission that connects, to fuel for the work needed for mastery and impact

When people find these things, work feels like swimming with the current, not against it. Entrepreneurial work should energize people—not every day but on enough days and especially on average. Crises aside, if people too often go home feeling drained and can't reset for the next day, they might not be dialed in to the right role, the right team, or the right mission. How someone feels in their craft, on your team, and with your mission are all good indicators of how well they are dialed in. But here is another caveat worth exploring.

Taking on a significant challenge is often hard, particularly challenges that push people outside their comfort zone. This often feels like swimming upstream until suddenly it doesn't. So how do you know whether you're persevering toward a challenge worth pursuing or are just not dialed in properly? My best advice is to put in the work, learn, and give it some time.

As a distinction, you persevere through a single challenge, and you dial in success over multiple challenges. You need to push through a few challenges in good faith to create the learning needed to dial in your success over time. Pushing through helps you rule out hard work and lack of mastery when you initially feel discouraged. Without a few successful challenges under your belt, you can't really know whether the role feels wrong because you haven't yet succeeded or because it's not right for you. Go get some wins, and then evaluate the fit.

Coach What Matters

In part I, I suggested that asking team members about their ability to be productive—remain in flow, work without friction, and have impact—is acting more in their interest than asking about their happiness. Additionally, in part II, I have emphasized the importance of getting to know the person and aligning individual purpose with mission, team, and role. Surely for many, if not all, happiness is a component of one's overarching purpose. So then what's wrong with asking about happiness? In short, nothing. Teammates should support each other's happiness, particularly as time together leads to friendships. But the pursuit of happiness should not be at the *center* of entrepreneurial team culture for a few reasons.

First, an individual's happiness is holistic to their lives and deeply personal, so what they experience on your team is simply one component of happiness. Happiness is thus beyond the capacity of any single team to deliver. Second, the true value of entrepreneurial teamwork for individuals is *fulfillment*, a critical component of happiness but not its equal. This fulfillment is pursuing a compelling mission alongside inspiring peers while growing in personal mastery. This kind of fulfillment is actually quite a profound contribution to each team member. Focusing on happiness, something a team does not control, instead of on entrepreneurial teamwork, something it does control, ultimately reduces the positive impact that a team can have on its members.

Finally, entrepreneurial fulfillment is fueled by personal growth, and growth is by definition uncomfortable. The best of our leaders—business, religious, civil rights, and political—have all called believers to uncomfortable action in the name of disrupting the status quo. Getting your mindset challenged, learning new skills, and working through crises are uncomfortable. They lead to growth and fulfillment but don't always leave people feeling happy in the moment. So coach what matters—a fulfillment achieved by working with purpose alongside inspiring peers while growing in mastery. Do this well, and everyone is on their way to their own personal happiness.

CHAPTER SUMMARY

By inviting someone to join your team, you are not just asking them to contribute to mission. You are also calling them to pursue personal growth and committing to support that pursuit.

Developing mission athletes is a collection of complementary activities designed to inspire and support the pursuit of mastery—inspiring with peers, coaching for growth, creating opportunities, getting compensation right, understanding mindsets, and dialing in success.

Inspire with peers by adding and promoting people who elevate everyone's performance—individuals who seek mastery, are committed to mission, and expect the same in others.

Coach for growth by cultivating a *growth mindset*—a belief that increasing mastery can be achieved through effort and feedback. Then build on that mindset. Align an individual's purpose with their role. Understand that mastery is an uneven progression. Associate feedback with success. Expect ownership. Define masterful goals. And ensure quality feedback.

Create opportunities for growth through project selection, challenges and quests, and formal goal setting. Create additional opportunities by leveraging dynamic organizational structures and generic titling, among other approaches.

Get compensation right by ensuring that regardless of the system you create to map performance to compensation, the results make sense in the simplest terms, avoiding the pitfalls of blindly adhering to a set of rules. The system must serve the mission and team, not the converse.

Understand mindsets in order to navigate common culture-damaging patterns—the diminishment of imposter syndrome, the indulgence of the newly arrived, the extremes of the growth-hungry, and the drag of the comfort-seeking.

Dial in success by getting to know the person you're coaching, identifying their personal operating systems, outsized strengths, and growth-blocking blind spots. Use this knowledge to match the person to the role and enhance the team by assembling complementary skill sets.

CHAPTER 9
Coach Out

T he elements of culture described in this book work together to unlock intrinsically motivated contributors in common cause. In the last chapter, we discussed how these elements can also be viewed collectively as an economic system with incentives (opportunities, stature, rewards), signals (hires, promotions, exits), and governance (part I). This latter mental model also offers a helpful framing for people issues—market failures in an otherwise self-correcting system.

In the course of normal events, failures in individual behavior occur that require intervention to correct, and making those interventions swiftly is critical to the health of the overall system. Put simply, some people, wittingly or unwittingly, undermine both performance and performance culture. They must swiftly be coached to turn around or exit—*the productive must be protected from the disruptive in order for the team to thrive.* I refer to these people issues as market failures because intervention is required by the leaders responsible for building culture. Peers and direct reports cannot exit a struggling individual, though the more adept can coach upward.

While the mental model of market failure is helpful in understanding disruption and motivating a response, it lacks an idea critical to entrepreneurial culture—that how you treat those who are struggling and how you exit those unable to course correct matter just as much as taking action to protect the environment. That how is the subject of this chapter, coaching out.

Coaching out is not a euphemism for firing someone but rather an approach that transitions organically from coaching growth to coaching a turnaround to asking an individual to leave. It applies the same set of principles throughout someone's progression regardless of trajectory. It includes honest feedback, human encouragement, objective assessment, and true opportunity for growth. Coaching out also helps conversations progress iteratively and thus without surprise, from athletic coaching to suggesting that someone does not belong on the team. And finally, coaching out instills confidence throughout the team that everyone is treated fairly, gets honest and clear feedback, and has authentic opportunity to respond.

The realization that unlocks effective coaching out is this: Coaching up (to greater mastery) and coaching out (turnarounds and exits) are on the same continuum. You do not cross a discrete boundary when transitioning from one to the other. Rather, you flow with the individual, following their progression to higher levels of mastery or to lower probabilities of future success. Along the way, you assess probability and coach, meeting each moment with what's needed—from coaching mastery, to coaching performance, to helping identify the right mission, role, and team for the individual beyond your team. At some point along the progression toward lower probabilities, you cross a threshold where the probability of success has diverged sufficiently from the possibility of it, and the transition of the person off the team becomes inevitable.

We'll begin this chapter with the building blocks of coaching out— key concepts to understand and frame actions. We'll then move on to the mechanics I developed at Roblox and have used ever since—a progression of conversations from athletic coaching to exiting. And finally, we'll discuss coaching out in practice, first covering some common mistakes and then reviewing some of the market failures common to entrepreneurial teams.

Building Blocks

The following ideas are foundational to the mechanics that follow in the next section, and they inform the practical discussions later in this chapter.

Understand Disruption

The impact on your team of someone who does not meet your success criteria is both real and nontrivial, and the person doesn't even have to be overtly distracting in order to disrupt. Consider figure 15, the example I use to explain this impact.

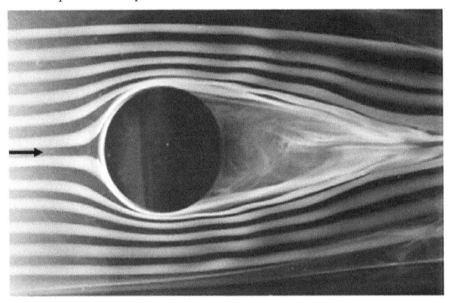

Figure 15: The Disruption of Flow Around a Cylinder[98]

Figure 15 shows fluid flowing left to right around a cylinder. The cylinder is perpendicular to the image, and the dark circle is its cross section. The white lines are smoke trails emitted from the left. In this analogy, the cylinder represents someone not meeting the team's success criteria, and the smoke lines represent everyone else. There are three relevant observations.

1. The upstream flow has uniformly spaced smoke trails.
2. The smoke trails bend around the cylinder, compressing along the way.

3. The cylinder leaves turbulence in its wake.

The upstream flow represents the flow states that a high-performing team achieves in the absence of disruptors. The smoke is literally flowing smoothly like my creativity does when I'm "in a zone." These flow states include both micro flow (the flow of an individual over a day or week) and macro flow (the flow of a team over weeks and months).

When an individual does not meet baseline performance standards, others on the team route around the person, taking on their job—not out of malice but because the jobs need to get done. People who care route around issues, whether they are external or internal. That stresses the team because it compresses people's time and leads to collective lower performance—you cannot create, innovate, and solve problems well with disruption and stress. Adding to that stress, the disruptor leaves turbulence in their operating wake, leaving it to others to navigate and repair.

Most of the time, your team acts faster than you and routes around the disruptor. This routing is often your best canary in the coal mine, as it was for me repeatedly. And because culture is what you do, not what you say, the speed and mastery with which you remove this disruptor, either through coaching up or coaching out, will define the culture for everyone else. Have the challenging conversations, act with urgency, and protect the environment, and everyone else will do the same. Fail to do those things, and everyone will do that too.

Coach the Continuum

In this chapter's introduction, I asserted that coaching up and coaching out are on the same continuum. Figure 16 below presents a picture of that continuum. The left vertical axis is the look-forward assessment of an individual's *probability of success*, and the banded rows are annotated zones of the continuum. The dashed arrows depict various paths through the continuum, highlighting the coaching expectations and approaches that follow the individual's journey.

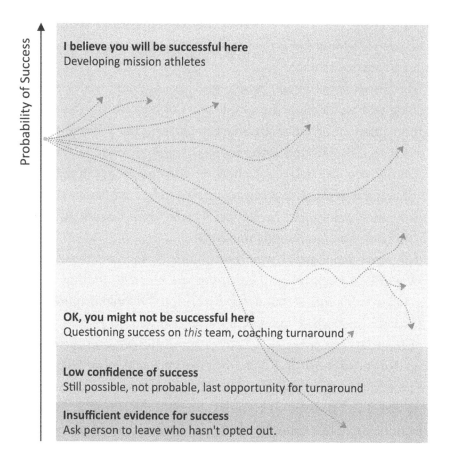

Figure 16: Coaching the Continuum

Let's start with the assumption that most people on your team are performing well and in the Green zone. People in this zone are coached toward greater mastery, as discussed in chapter 8, "Develop Mission Athletes." This coaching includes responding productively to both exciting wins and discouraging losses, and setting goals and tuning performance to ever higher mastery.

Assuming most people are in the Green is a good assumption if you're actively pursuing mastery in all three coaching jobs—recruiting, developing, and exiting. And the size of the Green band relative to the others is a rough benchmark of how well you are doing these jobs. To the extent this zone is big, the system is healthy. But if your Green zone is relatively small, you are adding too many people or exiting too few who fail to meet the team's success criteria.

The Yellow zone contains people who have not improved with athletic coaching or have developed multiple areas of concern. In this zone you begin to question the individual's success on the team, shifting your effort to coaching a turnaround since mastery is not currently in the picture. Necessarily, you dive deeper into how the person operates in the hopes of identifying a root cause. It is always helpful to be transparent and direct, but here these values take on heavier weight. Both become increasingly difficult while also increasingly impactful.

For some individuals, their probability of success assessment dips below a critical level, beyond which you are mentally shifting to asking them to leave. My rule of thumb for this critical threshold is approximately 50 percent—somewhere between a 60 percent and 40 percent probability of future success it becomes hard to authentically claim there is still a chance for turnaround. This is the Orange zone, and most people do not turn around from here, though some will still surprise you. You must have a very direct and transparent conversation with the person at this critical moment or you risk increased surprise and friction down the road.

If your conversations have been sufficiently transparent, direct, and inquisitive, then there is a nontrivial chance that the individual will leave of their own accord, having also concluded that their probability of future success is too low. This is preferable for all involved because it means the individual has taken ownership of their path forward, hopefully as part of constructive growth. A voluntary exit also means a lower-stress transition for the team. Anyone who does not voluntarily leave enters the Red zone, and you are actively managing their exit to be as constructive as possible and to minimize a negative impact on the team.

It's an Assessment, Not an Indictment

More than a few people I've exited went on to outsized success somewhere else, working at marquee companies, joining hot startups that had terrific success, becoming serial founders, and branching off successfully into entirely different industries. This never surprised me, even in my early days. I was lucky to intuitively understand that not being able to contribute to *my* team was a lot different from not being able to contribute to *any* team. That intuition became a foundational mindset in my approach to coaching turnarounds and exits.

While coaching someone through the continuum, you are making repeated assessments of an individual's probability of success and then talking with them about these assessments. This can be difficult, but it is less so if you remember that *you are making an objective assessment, not a personal indictment.* And because you tend to communicate what you believe, if you focus on assessment, the person receiving the feedback will generally understand that distinction as well.

It also helps both parties to remember that your assessment is very specific. Explicitly, your assessment is about a person's performance measured against the team's success criteria. But more specifically, it is an assessment for *this* team, *this* mission, right *now.* You are not making a statement about forever everywhere.

An assessment mindset shifts the focus from personal failure to the right mission, role, and environment for this person at this point in their career, even if that is off this team. It also shifts the focus from work performance to the individual's broader success. The reality you face when adding people to your team is this: What you pursue and how you operate will excite people who believe what you believe and operate how you operate, but it will stress and confound everyone else. Who that is will be an assessment you make, not a personal indictment.

As an example of the specificity of your assessment, consider figure 17 below.

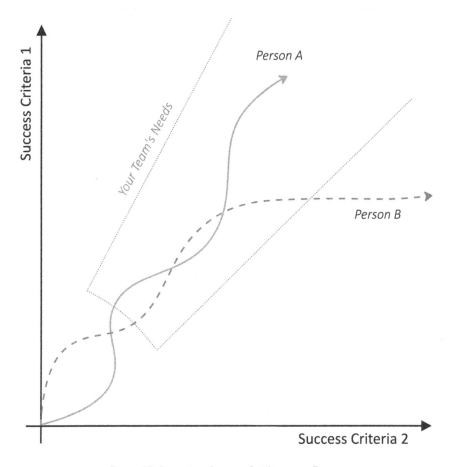

Figure 17: Operating System Settling over Time

This figure depicts two people's personal operating approaches over time with respect to two success criteria. The dotted space in the middle of the diagram represents your team's operating needs. Early in their careers, Persons A and B experiment broadly, discovering through experience not just their strengths and weaknesses but also the types of environments that best unlock their respective potentials. Both people join your team when they are aligned with its criteria.

Person A evolves to a performance profile that remains aligned with your team, maturing in both criteria over time. Person B exits your range, continually growing in one success criteria but plateauing in another. As discussed elsewhere in this book, the path of Person B may not be a problem, particularly if their mastery in one area is so outsized as to become a team advantage. In this example, though, let's assume they exit the team.

Both individuals ultimately grow in personal performance to have significant mastery and career contributions, but one simply no longer aligns with your team's needs. Indictments are thus not just counterproductive; they are not even relevant or necessary. The only thing that matters is *this team, this mission, right now.*

It's Not About Being Nice

I met Jeannie Kahwajy[99] in graduate school while she was researching interpersonal interactions. Her thesis was that effective interactions require us to be both open and modifiable. To the extent we're closed and rigid, we shut down engagement, but to the extent we are open to another's perspective and willing to be changed by it, we can unlock collaboration while remaining committed to our principles.

Jeannie also cautioned against a common misconception: interpreting being open and modifiable as simply being nice. To Jeannie, it mattered far less how you engage with another (extremes aside) and much more about what you believe because people know what you believe without your saying it. In Jeannie's words, "it's not about being nice"; it's about hearing the principles and ideas of another while sharing your own.

The same phrase is valid for the people ideas in this book, particularly when faced with coaching someone out. It is not about being nice. It is about building an environment where mission athletes can create, innovate, and solve problems. And then it's about being decent to anyone who is unable to contribute. People are not on your team to play, but neither are they on your team just to work. For innovative endeavors, people are on your team to create and solve problems with purpose, and that requires you to uphold the people environment first and foremost.

Succeeding over the long haul will sometimes require you to do things that won't feel nice, like coaching someone out who works hard, believes in the mission, is well loved, but is underperforming in too many areas.

You need to coach them out, and you can be decent while doing it, but it still won't feel nice.

If you misinterpret decency as being nice, you will pull your punches, putting the team and mission at risk. Creating an environment that fuels intrinsic motivation is not about making people happy; it is about leading people to fulfillment by connecting purpose to impact. And building a high-performing team is not about forever coaching everyone but about coaching those who believe in the mission and meet the team's success criteria.

Require Ownership

Ownership is critical to the type of growth you want at all levels of the continuum. Ownership is key to mastery, and mastery is key to developing a high-performing team. Those operating in the Green zone likely do not need you to reinforce ownership, but they might occasionally need encouragement to embrace it outside their comfort zones. For everyone else, ownership must be fundamental to your coaching and explicit in your feedback and expectations.

When coaching serious performance improvements and turnarounds, like for those in the Yellow and Orange zones, ownership requires that you coach, not coddle.

- Give people a clear picture of where they are and where they need to be.
- Connect their performance to the success of the mission and the team.
- Advise, encourage, inspire, direct them to resources, and be available.
- Be clear on your obligations to the mission and the team.
- And then STOP.

Going beyond this shifts ownership from the individual to you. And because culture is what you do, not what you say, owning the performance of an individual or a team will not build a team of owners. Instead, you will cultivate dependents, and true owners will leave the team. The only way to build a team of owners is to require it by your actions and then transition those who can't own their performance off the team. The job is not to make anyone into anything but to build an environment that unlocks mastery and autonomy. Ownership is essential to that.

Removing ownership from performance coaching and turnarounds also creates another problem—outcome ambiguity. Consider the typical performance improvement plan (PIP), a checklist of tasks to be completed in order to remain on the team. What happens if someone meets the criteria to the letter but not the spirit? Do you have to keep them? You might be at legal risk if you don't. And what about the person who comes close but doesn't meet the PIP? Do you have to let them go? If you don't, your plans don't mean much.

PIPs muddy the water. And because the team leader ultimately makes the final decision anyway, incorporating data beyond a plan's criteria, suggesting otherwise to team members is inauthentic and boxes you in. In my experience, nothing good has ever come out of a PIP.

Example: PIPageddon

One of my earliest experiences with a PIP was with a senior engineer who was not contributing as expected. He had been hired for a specific role and had been vetted for all relevant skills. It certainly seemed that he could do the job, but week after week very little got done.

Initially, the coaching he received was increased to help him push through. His direct manager and the chief technology officer (CTO) both spent time with him daily to review progress and the work ahead, but to little avail. The situation soon became tense, veering into the combative. Ultimately, the senior engineer's manager put him on a PIP that prescribed detailed daily and weekly milestones. He continued to receive coaching from his manager and the CTO. Suddenly, his energy picked up, and he delivered on those milestones, though just barely. He was then promptly exited from the team.

There were two issues that led to his exit despite his meeting the PIP. First, the experience during the PIP was not positive for anyone involved and increased the universal opinion that his values did not align with the team's. Second, he did the bare minimum and only under duress, leading all involved to conclude that the uptick in productivity would be short-lived. The final decision was correct, but it was harder to execute because the PIP was met on paper.

The decision was not the problem, nor was the feedback or the opportunity to turn things around. The problem was the PIP because PIPs work against ongoing learning by defining turnaround as a sequence of events, not a series of experiments. Don't PIP. Coach Out.

Probability vs. Possibility

One of the harder failure modes you'll find yourself in as a people leader is coaching someone through a turnaround when you've already decided to exit them. I am against any sort of theater like this. It wastes everyone's time, it's stressful for all involved, and it is often humiliating for the person being exited—if you know how it will end, so do they, and so does everyone else.

If you find yourself in this situation, you have already made a critical mistake, such as missing a key moment of candor earlier in the process. That mistake is not made better by walking through a turnaround that will not succeed. Instead, take the action needed, exit the person quickly, and commit to doing better next time around.

What happens in these situations is that the probability of success goes to zero before you effectively communicate the seriousness of the issue. As someone progresses away from mastery toward lower performance, your assessment of their turnaround probability progresses toward exit, diverging noticeably from an "anything is possible" ideal.

While it is always possible to turn things around—and that ideal allows you to coach with an open mind—you coach probability, not possibility. You follow the person where they lead and adjust your coaching as you progress. To avoid the above failure, you must have the Yellow and

Orange conversations while probability is still high, and you have not yet decided. Once you cross that threshold, it is too late, and whatever conversations have been missed remain missed.

Coaching while probability of success is high allows you to remain authentic as you discuss the person's potential future on the team. The gap size between possibility (ideal) and probability (reality) helps you dial in the right kind of encouragement, from strong belief (both are aligned) to hopeful encouragement (widening gap) and ultimately career coaching (critical gap).

Probability also guides time and effort. The lower the probability, the less time and effort remain for the turnaround. As with your assessment of success criteria, be transparent with the person involved about the possibility of turnaround and your assessment of its probability.

Green, Yellow, Orange, and Red (GYOR)

All the above building blocks lead to a practice I developed called Green, Yellow, Orange, and Red (GYOR). The practice codifies a few things.

- An assumption of greatness, learning otherwise
- A coaching mindset that drives toward mastery
- The progression from coaching up to out when those situations arise
- A process that is decent to those involved, despite tough situations

Getting these right matters, not just for the person involved but also for the team. Having a transparent and repeatable process for exiting people is critical to the sense of security for all who remain—that there is a process, that people receive coaching and clear feedback, that attempts were made to reduce surprise, and that everyone has an opportunity to turn things around.

I developed this approach early in my tenure at Roblox after making mistakes that did not sit well with me. My primary goal was to develop an approach that allowed me and other leaders to fulfill our obligations to the mission and the team while being decent to anyone exiting the company.

My other goal was competent speed—having a structure that aligned with our values and operating approach allowed all of us to move efficiently. Lack of structure is slower in this case.

Figure 18 shows the coaching continuum again, rotated 90 degrees counterclockwise. The continuum is again overlaid with Green, Yellow, Orange, and Red bands. The curve is the assessed probability of success throughout a progression that leads to exit.

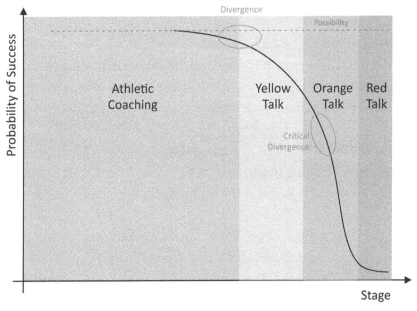

Figure 18: Green, Yellow, Orange, and Red Progression for an Individual

Green Talks

Green is the standing assumption—if you hire for success, coach for mastery, and exit people who cannot sufficiently contribute, you should robustly assume that everyone on the team is in the Green. This is not a passive state. Rather, you coach these individuals toward greater mastery (chapter 8, "Develop Mission Athletes"). And you continuously improve your environment for creativity, innovation, and problem-solving (part I), while regularly assessing everyone's day-to-day experience as feedback to this environment (realized culture).

Because this is the athletic coaching zone, expect to provide feedback regularly to people across the team. These are quick fire-and-forget conversations consisting of clear micro feedback with a focus on mastery. It is about leveling up, not falling short. If you remember that feedback is the path to mastery, you'll be much more inclined to give feedback in a helpful way.

Example: Green Talks

Here are some examples of Green feedback:

> *That was a very productive meeting. One piece of feedback: I think people would have engaged more if you presented less and asked more questions. And you'll get more buy-in that way for your project. (Leadership Mastery)*

> *I really appreciate how you "act like an owner" all the time, but I wasn't feeling it as much today when you handled that user issue. What's up? (Value Mastery)*

For more examples of similar feedback, check out *The New One Minute Manager* by Ken Blanchard and Spencer Johnson. It includes one-minute goals, one-minute praising, and one-minute redirects.[100] It's been around a while, with good reason.

Yellow Talks

Green Talks are not demerits that accrue against you, and coaches should generally "fire and forget." But Green Talks can progress to Yellow Talks as performance degrades. Having a Yellow Talk about the need for repeated feedback on the same issue, for example, is more serious than a quick course correction.

Yellow Talks are still about coaching, but the coaching progressively becomes more about turnaround than mastery. And because of that trajectory, your coaching should broaden to identify the right role, mission, and environment for the person in general, not just the here and now. Possibility and probability of success have started to diverge, which means your encouragement should change as well, from optimistic to hopeful, or you risk sending mixed signals.

In these talks, it is imperative that you communicate your concerns about the person's diminished probability of success so they have the information needed to act. You should also start documenting your feedback and interactions when Green Talks escalate to Yellow. There is a nontrivial chance that this person will leave the team, and that requires you to prepare for more serious conversations ahead and for defending your decision.

Example: Yellow Talk

One of the most common Yellow Talk topics I've seen is about improving output quality or being more detail-oriented. This is particularly true of a cohort of software engineers who have a higher bug rate than average (a bug is code that does not work as intended). Everyone ships bugs, and every piece of software contains bugs. But accepting that reality is not the same as embracing it.

Software engineering mastery means creating a sequence of testing and monitoring that spans prerelease and postrelease. It also means tracking bugs and fixing critical ones as defined by a team-developed rubric. An engineer's first bugs are usually the topic of Green Talks and team retrospectives, with a focus on iterative improvement in shipping quality. However, if the engineer ultimately ships enough poor-quality code to become an outlier (in quantity or impact), a Yellow Talk ensues. Here's an example of a Yellow Talk in this context:

> I've noticed that you have shipped bugs twice as often as most others on the team over the past few weeks. This is concerning because it impacts our users, and it diminishes the quality that the team is used to delivering. Have you noticed this too? What do you think is causing it? And what have you tried to do to reduce your bug count?

Notice that this starts with the concrete observation—in this case, a data-driven one. The conversation also identifies concern, which is the shift from the fire-and-forget tone of Green to the turnaround tone of Yellow. The phrasing also ties the concern directly to audience impact, first and foremost, and then to the mastery of the team, the other value not being met. The conversation then shifts to ownership. Does the person see it, too, and have they been thinking about what's causing the situation and how to correct it?

If the response is ownership (that there has been awareness and effort), then the conversation shifts to coaching assistance—improving the person's plan, identifying ideas and tools to fill in gaps in the plan, and, where appropriate, assigning a mentor. But if the response is not about ownership, either lack of knowledge or lack of self-correction, then the conversation must (a) reinforce core values affected, in this case impact, mastery, and ownership, (b) reemphasize the concern, and (c) set a follow-up to hear the person's plan.

To reinforce ownership, do not overspecify all that can be done to reduce bugs but instead point the person to resources and people who can help, leaving it to them to own the follow-up.

Orange Talk

The Orange Talk is serious. It is the last stop before asking someone to leave. A person enters this talk in one of two ways: (1) a progression of Yellow Talks escalates beyond a critical threshold, or (2) some singular event is in significant but not fatal violation of a value or norm.
There are three critical pieces to an effective Orange Talk:

- The issue must be absolutely clear.
- You must be clear that the person's place on the team is at risk.
- The individual, not you, must own the turnaround.

You must be clear about the problem so the person has an opportunity to turn things around. I heard a great piece of advice relevant to this many years ago: Whatever conversation you expect to have on someone's last day, have that conversation beforehand. That is the Orange Talk.

You also must be clear that the person's place on the team is in jeopardy so they understand the severity of the situation. Communicating this clearly is also the best way to reduce surprise if you ultimately exit the person. Reality check: Some people are surprised no matter what, but it still matters that you put in the work, both for the team and to reinforce mastery. For reference, here is my go-to line: "Your performance is not compatible with working here long term" or "The situation is not tenable long term," and then I provide concrete examples of the issues.

Most people managers understand the need to clearly communicate the issue and severity, although some have trouble executing the ownership piece. But it is critical (see "Require Ownership" earlier in this chapter). While the person must own their turnaround, you remain the coach. Be available to help as invited, and provide initial guidance. Just remember the person must own their mastery, or success will be blunted and muddled.

Red Talk

If you've done everything well so far, one of two things happens. First, after the Orange Talk, the person may leave of their own accord, based in part on your helping them identify the right role, mission, and environment for them. That person walks away with greater potential for future success and a preferable exit path, and it happens more often than you might think.

Alternatively, you progress to the Red Talk, which, while still intimidating, is more straightforward because of the Orange Talk. The Red Talk goes something like this:

As you know, we have been discussing the issue of X for some time. A few weeks back we met, and I told you that the situation was not tenable. Unfortunately, we have not seen sufficient progress, and I have made a tough decision. Today is your last day on the team.

If you can say that honestly, then you've had the appropriate conversations previously. And if you can't say that, then you missed a step. If the Red Talk has resulted directly from a fatal violation of a value or norm (e.g., harassment or altercation), then no prior warning is possible. But if this is the last stop in a well-executed coaching progression, it should not surprise anyone.

Be it a flagrant violation or the end of a journey, the meeting should be short. Long Red Talks serve no one. Do not engage in back-and-forth debate, not because someone doesn't deserve to understand but because the decision has been made and the debate they probably want to have is fueled by emotion—understandable but not helpful. In my experience, any back-and-forth to go over the details just makes people feel worse. The details should already have been covered in previous talks. And here is a must: Always have someone in the room with you for the Red Talk.

Finally, please note: This book is about enduring values, principles, and practices, but laws change; use the above suggestions as fodder for your own approach, and coordinate with appropriate legal and human resource professionals when exiting someone from your team.

Example: Red Talk

Here are two real-world examples from my personal background.

- Person A thanked me during a Red Talk. After I said it was their last day, they cited the thoughtfulness and honesty with which I discussed their strengths *and* weaknesses, not just the latter. They used our discussions to help identify the job they wanted next.
- Person B got very angry, claiming complete surprise, and threatened to sue, all despite not having logged into Salesforce for the past few weeks—a job necessity.

Person A had received the full GYOR approach, and it did not take much time or effort. As a result, things went smoothly, and I left feeling I had helped both individual and team.

Person B had not received the full GYOR approach, despite my already having codified it (good habits are easy to break for everyone). The person had not heard previously that we believed they weren't working (a claim we could substantiate). Under the stress of the situation, I and the other executive involved moved quickly, assuming it was obvious. It is never obvious, so put in the work. And after putting in the work, just know that some people are still surprised.

After the Red

What do you do next? Does the person serve their two weeks, leave at the end of the day, or leave immediately? The answer is incredibly personal to you and also context-dependent. I'll share what I have come to believe and why.

I am strongly in the "leave immediately" camp. Give the person severance, be generous, but then shut down their access and walk them out of the building. I completely understand that some find this harsh. But when the decision is between an individual's near-term feelings and the team's ongoing well-being, I feel a stronger obligation to the latter.

There are a number of significant downsides to letting a person linger after they've been exited, and I've seen them firsthand. They air their grievances, overindex on the elation of "finally getting out," get agitated, scare people, undermine the mission, or try to convince others to quit, just to name a few. I don't blame people for any of this—getting fired can be traumatic. Instead, I blame myself for creating the space for people to negatively impact the team. I empathize with the embarrassment people feel when being walked out, but extending their time does not reduce the embarrassment. What does help is how you handle the entire process. If the process is fair and transparent with opportunity for turnaround, most people understand.

The better you get at the entire process and the more you frame the decision around probability of success on this team at this time, the more likely that people will leave voluntarily. There is certainly room for flexibility in these situations. A person who says, "I love this place, but I don't think it's right for me anymore" does not need to be escorted out as soon as they finish that sentence. But even in these circumstances, I encourage swiftness. The person should leave at the end of the day or the end of the week. Pay them whatever you want, but separate the money from their professional engagement with the team.

GYOR in Practice

The following are some of the common mistakes people make when implementing GYOR.

Bypassing the Yellow Talk

Going from a minor performance tweak to "Your job is on the line." This creates an abrupt transition that surprises people and leaves no real opportunity to improve. While it does move quickly, it does so in a way that smacks of unfairness and undermines team belief in transparency. Root cause: being impatient or (typically) avoiding a hard feedback conversation.

Bypassing the Orange Talk

Going from "I have some concerns" to "You're fired." This fails to clearly communicate that the person's place on the team is in jeopardy. As such, it creates a surprising and sloppy experience that undermines the team's sense of safety and security. Root cause: waiting too long, so it would be inauthentic to coach turnaround.

Forever Yellow

Allowing someone to remain in Yellow (serious concern) indefinitely. This normalizes a culture of mediocrity and subpar performance, and it causes ramifications beyond people to product and tools. Root cause: failing to uphold mastery as a core value.

Forever Orange

Taking no action after telling someone their place on the team is in jeopardy, such as holding multiple Orange Talks if a person's probability of success is critically low. This sets a culture of moving slowly, not solving problems, and tolerating team stress. Root cause: confusing niceness with decency, underprioritizing team and mission.

Effort and Time

People new to GYOR can assume it takes a lot of effort and time—too much actually, with too much focus on those exiting than remaining. It is an understandable perception, but here is my experience. If you embrace mastery in coaching both up and out, you will put in the right effort at the right time, and you can move with speed. Speed is essential because the people you exit are, by definition, not compatible with your success criteria and are disrupting the team.

In reality, most of your effort and time is spent with those in the Green, as it should be. The time spent with individuals in Yellow, Orange, and Red can feel longer because it is more intense, but those zones should consist of relatively short, direct, and high-information conversations on an energetic cadence toward turnaround or departure.

But how long should it take? In practice, the time it takes to progress from Yellow to Red is context-dependent, but there are some patterns. Figure 19 maps what I have found to be the two most important parameters to speed: how fast the person is eroding culture, and how much of their work is routing to others.

The diagram contains four cells, one for each combination of the two states of cultural erosion and work routing (high and low). Each cell is annotated with the dominant impact to the team and the approximate time the progression takes. Each cell also contains the conversation sequence, with each conversation labeled by the week it occurs.

Figure 19: GYOR Speed vs. Cultural Erosion and Work Routing

When both cultural erosion and work routing are low, the ultimate danger is that you reinforce long-term mediocrity by moving slowly, but the immediate impact to the team is low. At the opposite end, when both cultural erosion and work routing are high, the team is experiencing pain, and you have to move much more quickly. You still have each type of conversation, but they are one of each at a week or less apart. Between these extremes are two situations that cause interpersonal stress or workload stress, but not both. They can be handled similarly to each other, with a bit more speed for interpersonal stress.

All these cases involve just a handful of conversations over a handful of weeks. You might talk with the person more often, but you have GYOR conversations on a cadence, and it is best to distinguish between casual check-ins and GYOR.

Figure 19 is just one way to engineer competent speed. What matters is that you have a rubric, work with intention, and use each experience to improve. Mastery brings speed.

Market Failures

The following lists the market failures referenced earlier in this chapter and in chapter 8, "Develop Mission Athletes." The first two scenarios can sometimes look like failures but are not.

[Not a Failure] They Are on Top of It; You're Just out of the Loop

You become concerned with someone's performance, but it turns out you're just ill-informed. There are many reasons for being out of the loop—managing a multitude of projects, not being in the trenches, just coming out of firefighting somewhere else. This is a reminder to always remain humble and inquisitive because if you're not, it's embarrassing for you but, worse, demoralizing for the other person. Beyond that, don't miss the opportunity to turn this into a clear win for the person—they are on top of it, and your concern was unnecessary. Celebrate that.

[Not a Failure] They Are Momentarily Blocked or Off Track

Coaching someone momentarily blocked or misaligned is the majority of coaching that entrepreneurial leaders do, and *how* you do that is a key driver of team culture. More than anything else, your actions here define whether you're a team that coaches toward mastery and aligned autonomy or one that demoralizes people for falling short. Culture is what you do, and you tend to do what you believe. So get your mindset on coaching and assume greatness until you learn otherwise.

The reasons for being momentarily blocked or misaligned span human performance. Here are just a few examples: having the wrong mental model, making tactical errors in execution or communication, lacking a skill, lacking experience, lacking confidence, being overwhelmed, getting too comfortable with their own level of performance, not being clear on team mission and priorities, or being distracted by something on the team or in their personal lives.

There is no one-size-fits-all solution, but there is a reliable approach—the medical two-step of diagnosis (defining the problem) and prognosis (defining the solution). Both problem and solution should be developed collaboratively, with you as coach. Expect these conversations to be relatively short, and don't worry too much about their frequency. It is the path forward that matters. And always remember to let the person drive the conversation to reinforce ownership.

They Have Reached a Plateau

In this scenario, a person cannot improve their performance beyond a plateau, despite coaching from you and effort from them. You generally land here after multiple coaching conversations bear no fruit. This is a market failure in personal growth that requires intervention of some kind.

If the person is not strong in other aspects of your success criteria, then the decision to exit is straightforward. Keeping someone on the team who fails to align with the basics and taps out on personal growth builds a low-performance culture.

If, however, the individual is strong in other success criteria, there are three possibilities.

- You have an organizational need for someone operating at this level.
- You identify another role potentially better suited, and experiment.
- You do not have either luxury, and you need improved performance in this role.

In the first case, you have essentially added a mid-organizational team member sooner than planned, and it is now time to find the next-level leader for that area. This is just a temporary fix, though, to buy time for the individual to break out of their plateau. Ultimately, everyone must be on paths to higher mastery to build a performance culture.

The second case is a common "dialing-in" practice where you help an individual identify a more aligned role as you get to know them (see "Dial in Success" in chapter 8, "Develop Mission Athletes"). I've repeatedly seen success here, but success means the person actually gets onto a mastery progression somewhere else. As I've said previously, to build a culture of mastery, you must dial in success, not mediocrity.

Finally, particularly when your team is small, you just might not have the luxury of finding another role or expanding the team, and this person has to exit. Again, if they are strong in other success criteria, you can take a bit longer to exit the person gracefully.

Inability to Meet Baseline Performance Standards

In this failure mode, the person fails to meet any success criteria for the role or team. This is the Type IV person described in "Success Criteria in Practice" in chapter 6, "Define Success." Most likely, this person is a mishire, but this situation also arises when an early team member becomes entrenched in the success criteria of yesteryear and fails to adapt to new criteria as the team matures. The 2x2 grid of effort and time (figure 19) offers a rubric for how to coach these individuals hopefully to a turnaround or, failing that, to exit.

Inability or Unwillingness to Live by Values

People in this group are missing one or more team values. If being unable to meet baseline performance standards points someone toward the exit, missing on values puts your foot on the accelerator. Remember, values are standards of behavior for the entire team that codify success strategies, and for them to have any weight, they must impact hiring, promotions, and exits.

Some value misses are easy to spot, such as a lack of transparency. Others, though, might take some time to play out, and might only come into full focus after a few coaching conversations and feedback from other team members. In the latter case, the team already knows what needs to be done and is waiting for you to do it. You should still walk through GYOR authentically for all the reasons previously discussed. If there are multiple value misses, though, you are likely already having Yellow conversations, so the remaining time and effort should be accelerated.

Anti-Alignment with Success Criteria

Being anti-aligned is very different from misaligned (previous scenario). Anti-alignment means the individual actively promotes the opposite of your team's success criteria, intentionally or otherwise, like resisting—beyond constructive feedback—vision, mission, values, and operating principles. These people are red alerts.

Anti-alignment can happen very quickly without an observable progression, like a behavioral trait that only comes out under stress or an operating belief that surprises the entire team. These people most likely put the team in the Pain quadrant of figure 19 and need to be exited quickly. It might seem total theater to do anything beyond a Red Talk and exit, and it absolutely would be if an issue breaks critical norms or laws. But if that's not the case, it's possible (though not probable) that the anti-alignment can be adjusted. In these cases, start with athletic coaching, but move quickly to Yellow and Orange due to the nature of anti-alignment.

Example: All-or-Nothing Engineering

I've worked with a number of senior engineers who all suffered from the same problem—an inability to iterate. It usually begins innocuously. Given a project, they come back after analysis and request the project scope be expanded to clean up a related part of the code. In itself, this is a normal request and is usually green-lit if the reasoning is sound. But these all-or-nothing engineers keep going, driving toward one of these two inevitable outcomes: never shipping anything or shipping a winner-takes-all, high-risk change that spans the code base.

At Roblox, some of these engineers suggested we rewrite the back end, rewrite the front end, or switch web stacks entirely—all in the name of adding a new feature. This behavior was quite literally an anti-pattern for Roblox, a culture steeped in iteration. Rapid iteration was a critical success strategy for early Roblox, as it is for other successful software teams. These engineers received clear feedback on our iterative approach as well as technical coaching on how to break up their project, but to no avail. I ultimately ushered all of them through GYOR to exit, and after a few of these hiring mistakes, we established the ability to iterate as a success criterion.

Unwillingness to Grow in Mastery or Autonomy

Mastery and autonomy (via ownership) are on my list of performance values described in chapter 2, "Live by Values." You'll also find them in the values of any high-performing entrepreneurial team you'll encounter, either explicitly so or implied through other terms. Unwillingness to grow in mastery and autonomy is covered, in part by the above two scenarios. Let's now consider additional details specific to these two values.

Unwillingness to grow in mastery or autonomy is very different from reaching a plateau, and it shifts the coaching decisively to out, not up. You can attempt to inspire mastery and autonomy through athletic coaching, but if a person is not interested in pursuing them, they are unlikely to contribute significantly to an entrepreneurial team. These individuals will undermine culture at its foundation. Don't expect anyone to tell you they are not interested in mastery or autonomy. Instead, you have to assess their unwillingness indirectly.

Here are some clues for mastery: They do not embrace feedback from anyone on the team and never use it to improve; they do not exhibit a passion for mastery in any area, even in personal projects; they always find ways to lower the bar and dial back objectives, and not for any stated performance or strategic reasons; and they consistently avoid what's hard rather than considering first what must be done.

And here are some clues for autonomy: They always have external reasons for performance misses and never take responsibility; they consistently assume the narrowest responsibility of a role and fail to act when the system fails outside their sphere; in the face of dynamically changing conditions, they blindly stick to the plan and then blame the plan for failure; they consistently fail to provide constructive feedback for improving the overall environment, focusing instead on problems; and they continue to seek approval at a fixed level of decision-making, rather than expanding their decision-making scope over time.

Coaching out conversations for these two values generally take a classic performance approach such as "This role requires X, and you are not meeting those requirements."

Example: I Know Enough

I was helping with an executive search a few years back, and as part of the process, we gathered together a sample of the reporting team to brainstorm on role requirements. During that conversation, we asked whether leadership mentoring was desired. I thought this was a slam dunk given that some of the leaders had rightfully complained that they did not have sufficient mentoring. One of these leaders, however, said no, this was not a requirement. When we asked why, he said that he had already learned a lot and did not need further coaching to do his job. Wow.

There were other issues at play that likely inspired this answer in part, but it was clear that he meant what he said. This person not only lacked a growth mindset but also any vision for his or the team's future. His response went a long way toward explaining why the person, while talented, wasn't really improving in his leadership skills. He had no desire to improve, having come to the belief that he had mastered his role.

Disrupting Macro or Micro Flow

Disrupting flow undermines mastery, whether it's the micro flow of an individual throughout the day or the macro flow of the team throughout a quarter (see "Mastery Through Flow" in chapter 3, "Institutionalize Mastery"). There are a number of reasons an individual disrupts micro flow, including boredom, an inability to focus, an insufficient workload, and prioritizing social interactions over mission impact. The reasons individuals disrupt macro flow include misalignment with plan, inability or unwillingness to use tools or follow team practices, inability to sustain focus, interpersonal conflicts, insufficient focus on mission, and a host of personal reasons.

All of these disruptions are destructive in nature—not disrupting plan because of lessons learned (as described in part I), but disrupting the productivity of a stable flow state. As with the previous scenarios, the response starts with athletic coaching (Green Talks) and follows the person where they lead, either to improved performance or to Yellow, Orange, and Red Talks.

Example: The Screaming Submit

One software engineer I worked with could not master our development tools, despite multiple rounds of coaching from multiple people, including peers. The tools were standard, and there was nothing unusual about them. The ongoing coaching he required was becoming a distraction for the team, but that was not the biggest issue. For reasons that still elude me, the engineer would often act rashly when using the tools, doing things that he seemed to know were incorrect. No one suspected malice.

One time, he dragged a bunch of existing code from one area of source control (a system for storing shared code) to another, breaking his build (code references to other code are often by file path). He then started yelling that he broke the build, to which others around him responded urgently that he should under no circumstances submit his changes. I remember his hand shaking over the mouse as I ran out my door to his desk. He screamed in panic and then checked it in, breaking everyone's build. He really was a nice guy, but he could not remain on the team after a few events like that.

The Spiraling Leader

There are times when a leader's performance starts spiraling downward, slow at first and then faster. It doesn't matter whether they are an executive or an individual contributor with broad responsibilities and influence. Their downward spiral has an increasing impact on the surrounding team and the overall mission. You still need to walk through the progression, from Green to Yellow to Orange then Red, and you can do it rapidly if warranted. But in addition, you also need to pull responsibility away after the first Yellow Talk or two. The amount pulled away and the rate at which you do it again follows the progression of the person.

There are a few reasons why I favor this approach. First, it legitimately gives the person more room for a turnaround because they have fewer responsibilities. Removing responsibility tests the possibility that they are overwhelmed. And because mastery is an uneven progression, not a continuous upward trend, they will have the opportunity to take on that broader responsibility again in their career, particularly if they recover. One step back might be just what they need to take two steps forward, and that would be my framing.

The other reason to take away responsibility is that it underscores the seriousness of the moment. Nothing says your job is on the line like actually losing part of it. If culture is what you do (it is), then backing up your last Yellow Talk before the Orange by removing responsibilities makes the situation unabashedly clear to all but the densest.

And finally, there is a third reason. It prepares the team for the person's potential departure, easing the overall transition and giving you subsequent space to fill the role properly.

Does It Get Easier?

There's a common question from those new to exiting a team member, particularly if that team member has an outsized role or influence. Does it get any easier? Yes, in two parts.

If you seek mastery in this area, you will move through the process more clearly and confidently over time. It will become easier to understand people, identify patterns of success and failure, and simultaneously embrace both obligation and decency—but only if you try. If you seek to get better at these, you will, and that does mean putting in the work early on. If instead you fail to embrace this part of the job, a part that has critical impact on the enduring performance of your team, then you will not get better, and everyone will experience not just short-term learning-curve pain but long-term institutionalized pain.

The emotional component should get easier too. If it doesn't, you are probably not framing the approach as I'm recommending. Every exit from a team means real impact to a real person. As a human, it is hard not to be affected by that, and you shouldn't want to close that off. But being too affected consistently might mean you are still holding on to the idea of indictment, not assessment, and definitely not narrow assessment. Remember, the ultimate decision in asking someone to leave is about *this* person on *this* team for *this* mission right *now*. Beyond that doesn't matter. And if you are transparent and constructive in your feedback, coaching out rather than firing, you have invested in that person's future. It does get easier if you seek mastery.

CHAPTER SUMMARY

It is critical for entrepreneurial teams to protect the productive from the disruptive. Otherwise, overall performance culture degrades, high-impact members leave, and the mission is at risk.

However, how you treat those who are struggling and how you exit those unable to course correct matter just as much as protecting the environment. That how is coaching out.

Coaching out is not a euphemism for firing someone but an approach that transitions organically from coaching growth to coaching a turnaround to asking an individual to leave.

Coaching out applies the same set of principles throughout someone's progression, regardless of trajectory. Those principles include honest feedback, human encouragement, objective assessment, and true opportunity for growth. They instill confidence throughout the team that everyone is treated fairly and has an authentic opportunity to respond.

To coach out effectively, leaders must understand these key building blocks:

- Disruptive people impact the team in the stress they directly cause and in the additional work people take on to protect the mission. People organically route around disruptors.

- You coach a continuum to higher performance or through turn-around or exit, following the individual where they lead and responding with appropriate feedback and actions.
- Performance assessments are just that—assessments. They are not indictments.
- It's not about being nice; it's about protecting the environment for the productive and then being decent to everyone who is unable or unwilling to contribute.
- You must require ownership in turnaround because mastery requires it.
- You operate exclusively against the probability of success, not the possibility of it.

These naturally lead to GYOR, a progression of talks from Green (athletic coaching) to Yellow (expressing concern), to Orange (stating that their place on the team is at risk), to Red (exiting).

Avoid common mistakes like having multiple Orange Talks. Guide effort and time by the severities of work routing and cultural erosion, and develop a market failure scenarios playbook.

CONCLUSION

This book is about the people and culture teams need for sustained innovation—a collective and enduring ability to disrupt the status quo through creativity, problem-solving, and impact.

I wrote this book for all those leaders who have earned their roles through subject matter expertise, a capacity for impact, and innate leadership skills, and who now face the challenge of building and growing innovative teams without any formal team-building training.

This book is for early leaders crossing the chasm from player/coach to team builder, much like products must cross the market chasm from early adopter to mainstream. And it's for seasoned leaders on the chasm's other side who question why their current strategies aren't working—why people are not aligned, not moving faster, and not innovating. And, finally, this book is for emerging leaders who want to embrace the road ahead with confidence and competence.

Entrepreneurial teamwork—collaborative disruptive creativity toward mission—is among the most impactful, rewarding, and fun things we can do together, but it is too often derailed by uninformed, misinformed, or just plain bad leadership.

I wrote this book to help leaders build engines of innovation in the behaviors they cultivate and the people they hire, develop, and retain—self-reinforcing systems that amplify and align creative effort to convert novel ideas into audience impact. And I wrote this book to address a number of common pitfalls leaders face when growing teams beyond a handful of people—diminished impact, lower productivity, culture dilution, disempowerment, focus loss, and hiring bursts followed by team-re-setting layoffs.

The central thesis of this book is that high-performance entrepreneur-ial culture can be summarized by a simple phrase—*the aligned autonomy of mission athletes.*

Autonomy is the organizing principal because only through autonomy can teams maximize the brainpower and horsepower applied to innovation and minimize the forces of soul-crushing bureaucracy. But while people need autonomy in order to unlock ownership and initiative, teams need *aligned autonomy* to effectively pursue mission. Entrepreneurial success is the result of the continuous and focused impact that builds audience pas-sion, not the inconsistent and diluted effort that builds forgettable utility.

Aligned autonomy is necessary for high-performing entrepreneurial teams, but it is not sufficient. Who you hire, promote, and retain is fun-damental to team culture and performance. My profile of the person most needed for these teams is the *mission athlete*—an individual committed to a shared mission who, like a sports athlete, seeks continuous improvement in personal and collective performance. The best athletes seek and apply feedback, measure themselves against benchmarks, embrace challenges, live by values, work by principles, and own their autonomy.

In addition to the overarching framing of aligned autonomy and mis-sion athletes, there are a few recurring themes in this book.

- Who you are matters—what you believe, who you work along-side, and what you bring to the mission and team every day.
- How you get stuff done matters just as much as getting stuff done, particularly over the long haul (lots of things work in the short term).
- High-performing entrepreneurial teams don't just innovate; they build engines of innovation in the behaviors they cultivate and in the people they hire, develop, and retain.

Given the breadth of the ideas explored in this book, I do want to be clear about the one thing as we close: The number one goal of an early-stage team is *survival.* For profit-seeking and service-seeking teams alike, survival means a sharp focus on product market fit, competent cash management, and a tight-knit, hard-charging team. That in turn means a commitment to three core values above all else: focus, urgency, and team health. Nothing in this book is contrary to this survival discipline, and that discipline is highlighted throughout, often through the lens of iteration. But there's also an important caveat.

Product market fit in my experience is seldom binary. You don't achieve it for your entire audience all at once. Rather, you find it for a cohort, and then you have to keep it, shape it, and expand it to other cohorts. Additionally, even with product market fit and the revenue or funding that might follow, growing an endeavor and disrupting a marketplace are harder than they seem, requiring a lot of horsepower and brainpower along the way. And for that journey, you need to build a team to create, innovate, and solve problems repeatedly and better over time—one that ultimately self-organizes and self-corrects around shared mission and strategy. That is the purpose of the innovation engine described in this book. Build it. Protect it.

Speed Is Culture

One of the most common topics in startups is speed—how to maintain it or how to increase it. Startups have a natural proclivity for speed. A small, tight-knit team of seasoned programmers, for example, working on a narrowly scoped project can typically move fast. But as this team expands, its pace typically slows due to increases in communications overhead and the greater need to socialize values and strategy. So how do you design for speed as you grow?

Tactically, there are a lot of things that can be done to drive speed, such as increasing the cadence of check-ins to set pace.[101] But strategically, speed is driven by the people and culture described in this book— the aligned autonomy of mission athletes. Speed is culture. Tactics can improve it, but culture creates and sustains it.

Speed is a summary of this entire book. Fast-moving teams fuel with purpose to inspire action intrinsically, and they institutionalize urgency as a core value. They unlock aligned autonomy to parallelize effort while maintaining focus. And they institutionalize mastery to reduce operating friction and improve effectiveness. Speedy teams also identify and attract those who are inclined to act with urgency. They then coach those so inclined to higher levels of mastery, promote those demonstrating competent speed, and exit those unwilling or unable to act with urgency.

One measure of speed is how fast a team can transform idea into impact, such as how fast it can respond to emergencies or how swiftly it can move day-to-day. Emergency response speed starts with the ability to rapidly detect and understand system deviations from norms. This in turn requires an understanding of the system, the ability to measure it, and the ability to distinguish signal from noise. The tools and expertise needed for this are only achieved through iteration toward higher levels of operational mastery, as well as commitments to urgency and impact.

Day-to-day speed is driven by a number of factors, including urgency, clarity of and focus on goals, low-friction tools and practices, time in flow state, and a degree of autonomy that reduces communication. As with the drivers of effective emergency response, these factors are all elements of the entrepreneurial culture discussed in this book.

The other critical form of speed needed on entrepreneurial teams is how fast the team can respond to changing conditions and deliver its first impact in a new direction. Like day-to-day operations, this kind of speed is driven by urgency, clarity, and focus. But it is also driven by the team's willingness to self-disrupt, the simplicity of its planning stack, the agility of its organizational structures, and a strategy of continuously scanning scenarios and options.

Speed is not doing something new every week or month without discipline. Enduring speed is measured by the impact of projects completed, not the hope of ones started. Speed is a consistent force applied in a direction long enough to have impact. But when self-disruption is needed, the ship needs to turn, and the lighter the ship, the faster the turn.

Design your system to institutionalize speed, not only in the team's people and values but also in the flexibility and agility of its planning stack to identify, understand, decide, socialize, and reorganize quickly. Speed is culture, so build one that creates and sustains it.

The Right Kind of Strength

Leading people is tremendously rewarding, but it also can be challenging. Exiting an individual or leading a team through significant change, for example, are among the hardest things I've done as a leader. And while knowing what to do might seem like the biggest hurdle, it's not. The real challenge is in resolving a tension between two constructive forces.

- The need to do what must be done with urgency
- The desire to be decent, which often takes some care

In my experience, the leaders who have failed to be decent have not generally discounted decency but simply lacked the tools and mindset. I for one did not always act with the decency I aspire to, but never once was that my intent. I was ill-equipped early on to resolve the tension above. I confused decency with being nice and was thus sometimes opaque and slow to act. I also didn't know how to be decent when I needed to move fast, or I didn't take the time to try.

But decency doesn't actually take much time. The decency that ultimately matters is respect—having the decency to be transparent and direct; explaining the *what* and the *why*; and recognizing that doing what seems right for the team is sometimes at odds with the individual.

When the task is easy, decency is easy. But when the task is hard, like asking someone to leave or terminating a project people love, it's far too easy to be accidentally callous. Here's my rubric for avoiding such accidents, and for resolving the tension between speed and decency.

- Drive decision-making and its urgency by obligations to mission and team.
- Be transparent to all and supportive to those negatively impacted by decisions.
- Then be willing to be thought wrong or disliked.

By transparency, I mean sharing your obligations, your rationale, your decision, and your ownership of that decision. By supportive, I do not mean keeping someone on the team who has little probability of future success; I mean hearing them and helping them transition. And with regard to the last bullet point, I am not comfortable with being disliked when I have missed something or failed someone in some way. I feel ownership for these outcomes. But when I've acted respectfully and met my obligations to mission and team, it's easier to live with the consequences.

There is one other issue with decency in our culture. It is sometimes considered soft. In the intertwined cultures of tech and the internet where people sometimes embrace being "alpha," decency often looks like being "beta."

Some of this critique is warranted, as when teams define decency as reducing all friction for employees and thus pull their punches. But as I've said elsewhere in this book, values like decency must be in service to mission, not replace it. Disruption and personal growth are not comfortable—they are challenging, sometimes demoralizing, and always require commitment. Attempts to remove all discomfort undermine mission and growth, which does feel "beta" to me.

But beyond this fair critique, it is also the case that some inexperienced leaders embrace callousness as a sign of strength—and it's not uncommon in seasoned leaders either. But the association of decency with "beta" by this group is a misconception of strength.

The strength needed to lead mission athletes is not fear-based power but an adherence to a code of conduct and a commitment to team and mission, often in the face of strong headwinds. It's doing the hard things that matter—an unwillingness to take the easy path when it's wrong, and a determination to make hard paths tractable with problem-solving. It is having the resolve to do what's needed and the commitment to putting in the work. It is the opposite of soft.

Culture is both the one you choose and the one you need for performance. Decency is indeed a culture many choose, but it is also key to leading teams that create, innovate, and solve problems. It is hard to do any of these in the face of people distractions, mistrust, and fear. If creation is the height of human achievement, then it's easy to imagine that we need to pair that with the height of human leadership—doing what matters with conviction and decency.

It's Doable

As I write this book, my daughter is in her final college year. And while she is well-adjusted and doing well, she often echoes what I hear about the challenges her generation faces—the stressors of COVID isolation, political polarization, institutional strain, internet-enhanced social pressure, environmental disasters, world disorder, social unrest, and a host of other crises and risks.

Regardless of who you think is to blame and what you think needs to be done, it seems that recent times have put stress on the optimism and health of young adults. This book is dedicated to my daughter's generation for a reason. It echoes what my mother told me in my youth—that there is nothing you can't do. And while I have interpreted this with more nuance as I've aged, the spirit in me remains.

I recently heard Jon Stewart expand on the phrase "the arc of the moral universe is long, but it bends toward justice"[102] by adding "but . . . you have to bend it."[103] To my daughter and her generation: go bend history. It's doable. You don't have to wait for permission, and you can't wait for others. Go change the world around you as you see fit.

You'll have to put in the work, be focused, and act with urgency. You'll also have to find *your* way—the path to impact that most speaks to your heart, your curiosity, and your talents. And for larger impact, you'll have to build teams to create, innovate, and solve problems. The teams may be formal or informal, hired or volunteer, private sector or public. But to change the world, people need to unite through shared belief, align on a path forward, and act.

The future is uncertain, but it has been for prior generations, and they have made progress. You can make your future as bright as you wish, and I hope this book helps even just a little.

ACKNOWLEDGMENTS

I am indebted to a number of people who helped me transform a collection of ideas into an actual book—something that flows, has a narrative, has examples, and addresses a specific audience. I am grateful to all of those who helped and encouraged me on this journey, and I am also incredibly humbled. I do not know what I've done along the way in my life to earn the support and encouragement I've received from friends and colleagues. All I can say is thank you.

Chief among this book's contributors is my wife, Lisa, who—as usual—was endlessly patient hearing me work through ideas on our morning dog walks. She asked great questions that forced simplicity and clarity in my thinking, and she helped me understand where my ideas had broader appeal. And without hesitation, she encouraged me to always keep moving forward.

I am also extremely indebted to Jared Shapiro and Chris Carvalho who waded through the embarrassingly raw first draft. I actually worked really hard on that draft for a year and would not ask a friend to read it until I thought it was at least decent. Looking back now from what is the fourth major revision, I see just how rough that draft was despite my efforts—so huge thanks. Chris's main feedback was about engagement—that the book was too often too academic, and he wanted many more stories and examples. The book is a much better read for this. Thank you, Chris. Jared's contribution will not surprise anyone who's worked with him: He read every page and was incredibly thorough. He had tons of questions and corrections, and he engaged with many of the ideas through additional comments. The depth and breadth of Jared's input took me a few months to incorporate, and the book benefited tremendously. I was always proud to work alongside Jared, and this was just another example of why I felt that way.

I am also grateful to readers of the third draft who helped bring the book into its sharpest focus yet, which allowed me to hone the narrative and jettison parts of the book that were no longer relevant. The result is much leaner and more accessible. In particular, thanks to Chris Fralic who asked me the same questions over and over again: Who is this book for? How does it help them? And then he'd add, "Go make the book about that." The answers to these questions not only made the book better, allowing me to reframe the introduction, but they also became the foundation of the book's pitch and marketing strategy. Thanks also to Jim Cloern, who read with an editor's eye and helped me see where—despite my efforts—the book was still too tech wonky. The book was much better after I worked through Jim's questions and suggestions. And thanks to Mark Coggins, Gabe Escobar, Simon Kozlov, Tim Loduha, Arseny Kapoulkine, and Tobias Harrison-Noonan. Your detailed and insightful feedback was incredibly helpful.

Special thanks to David Baszucki who generously wrote this book's foreword. Dave hired me right out of my doctorate, saying he needed my help to build the Mercedes-Benz of software engineering teams—he has always been a great recruiter, knowing how to inspire and excite. Dave ultimately hired me three more times, most recently at Roblox where we partnered together on building the product and the team. He's been both a mentor to me and a champion of my success, and he is responsible for introducing me to some of the most amazing teammates I've ever had—more than once. Thanks for everything Dave, including our friendship.

Thanks to all the other friends and colleagues along the way who gave me some great insights and always encouraged me to continue. Thank you to Anthony Lee, Jennifer Rosner, Bill Corwin, Judah Pollack, Christina Shedletsky, John Shedletsky, Anna Shedletsky, L. C. Crowley, Harold

Hughes, Karlene Cimprich, Alison Appling, Scott Rupp, Bryan Kramer, and Todd Sattersten.

And finally, thanks to my publishing team at Morgan James, including Krissy Nelson and Sofia Cresta. Thank you in particular to David Hancock, Morgan James' founder, who presented my first ever book offer and who has consistently been available to guide me through this process. Thank you, as well, to Becky Robinson, my launch partner at Weaving Influence, for being in my corner and bringing a wealth of resources to bear. And thanks to Aubrey Pastorek and Wendy Haan, my account managers at Weaving Influence. Thank you to Monét Rouse who helped with the book's diagrams and early cover ideas, and to Lawna Oldfield who created the final cover. Thanks to Julia Guagliardi, who built my website, helped with social, and conducted research. And thanks to Evan Blaser, my photographer. A final thanks to my editors, Sue VanderHook and Catherine Turner, who not only tuned up the writing but also gave me great suggestions on where it needed simplification and clarification.

ABOUT THE AUTHOR

Keith V. Lucas is a startup advisor specializing in product, growth, people, and culture. While Keith loves getting things done, his true passion is empowering people to get things done together—to focus on what matters, to create and innovate, and to have impact.

With almost three decades of entrepreneurial leadership experience, Keith has served as project lead, tech executive, and now advisor. At Roblox, a social platform for user-created games and virtual experiences, Keith led product and engineering, helping scale its infrastructure, product, team, and business. As COO of Instrumental, a company using AI to transform hardware manufacturing, Keith built out the company's financial modeling and helped advance its go-to-market strategy. Keith advises startups in AI, gaming, entertainment, social, and enterprise. He also advises nonprofits.

Keith holds a bachelor's in engineering from Columbia University, a PhD in aeronautics and astronautics from Stanford University, and a master's in public policy from UC Berkeley. Outside of work, he enjoys western horseback riding, fitness, travel, and learning new things.

NOTES

Introduction

1   Geoffrey A. Moore, *Crossing the Chasm: Marketing and Selling Disruptive Products to Mainstream Customers*, 3rd Ed. (HarperBusiness, 2014).

2   Steve Blank, *The Four Steps to the Epiphany: Successful Strategies for Products That Win*, 5th Ed. (Hoboken, NJ: Wiley, 2020).

3   Moore, *Crossing the Chasm*.

4   "History," Krispy Kreme, accessed January 14, 2025, https://krispykreme.ca/about-us/history/.

5   Daniel H. Pink, *Drive: The Surprising Truth About What Motivates Us* (Riverhead Books, 2009).

Chapter 1: Fuel by Purpose

6   Simon Sinek, "How Great Leaders Inspire Action," TEDx Puget Sound, September 2009, https://www.ted.com/talks/simon_sinek_how_great_leaders_inspire_action.

7   Jamie D. Aten, "The Impact of Human Purpose on Resiliency," *Psychology Today*, March 29, 2021, https://www.psychologytoday.com/us/blog/hope-resilience/202103/the-impact-human-purpose-resiliency.

8   Simon Sinek, *The Infinite Game* (Portfolio/Penguin, 2019).

9   Kent Beck et al., "Manifesto for Agile Software Development," *Agile Manifesto*, 2001, https://agilemanifesto.org/.

10 "Jobs at TED," TED, accessed June 13, 2024, https://www.ted.com/about/our-organization/jobs-at-ted.

11 "About," TED, accessed June 13, 2024, https://www.ted.com/about.

12   "About Us," Tesla, accessed June 13, 2024, https://www.tesla.com/about.

13   "Impact Report 2023," Tesla, accessed June 13, 2024, https://www.tesla.com/impact.

14   "Tesla Motors Reports First Quarter 2011 Results," Securities and Exchange Commission, May 4, 2011, https://www.sec.gov/Archives/edgar/data/1318605/000119312511126139/dex991.htm.

15   "History," Warby Parker, accessed June 13, 2024, https://www.warbyparker.com/history.

16   "History," Warby Parker.

17   Rajiv Bhatia and John Stauffer, "Reimagining How People Come Together through Communication, Connection, and Expression," *Roblox* (blog), October 19, 2023, https://blog.roblox.com/2023/10/reimagining-bringing-people-together-communication-connection-expression/.

18   "Corporate Overview," Roblox Investor Relations, accessed June 13 2024, https://ir.roblox.com/overview/default.aspx.

19   The demise of Kodak is an often-used example of missing a key inflection point because the team can't imagine losing the position of dominance it currently enjoys.

20   In a software company, product development is often shared across two macro teams—product and engineering. Product managers do market and audience research, define feature sets, work with designers, and then present requests to engineering. Engineering takes on the technical transformation of those requests into functioning software. On high-performing teams, the two groups have distinct responsibilities, but the ownership is shared. Every engineer should engage with the audience and use the product, and every product manager should think through work as an engineer and understand the technical trade-offs.

Chapter 2: Live by Values

21   "Building the Future Together," Roblox, accessed June 13, 2024, https://corp.roblox.com/leadership/.

22   Mug in my office.

23   "Our Core Values," Patagonia, accessed June 13, 2024, https://www.pata-

gonia.com/core-values/.

24 "Climate Justice Is Social Justice," Patagonia, accessed June 13, 2024, https://www.patagonia.com/actionworks/campaigns/climate-justice-is-so-cial-justice/. At least one form of justice Patagonia pursues is climate justice through its environmental value.

25 "Patagonia Founder Gives Away Company to Help Fight Climate Cri-sis," Reuters, September 14, 2022, https://www.reuters.com/business/retail-consumer/patagonia-founder-gives-away-company-help-fight-cli-mate-crisis-2022-09-14/.

26 Elizabeth Segren, "Patagonia Just Designed Its Warmest Coat Ever, and It's Made from Trash," *Fast Company*, October 24, 2023, https://www.fastcompany.com/90970505/patagonia-just-designed-its-warmest-coat-ev-er-and-its-made-from-trash.

27 Geoffrey A. Moore, *Crossing the Chasm: Marketing and Selling Disruptive Products to Mainstream Customers*, 3rd Ed, (HarperBusiness, 2014).

28 "Netflix Culture — Seeking Excellence," Netflix Jobs, accessed June 13, 2024, https://jobs.netflix.com/culture.

29 "Netflix Culture — Seeking Excellence," Netflix Jobs.

30 "Chaos Monkey," accessed June 13, 2024, https://netflix.github.io/chaos-monkey/.

31 "The Army Values," U.S. Army, accessed June 13, 2024, https://www.army.mil/values/.

32 General Stanley McChrystal, *Team of Teams: New Rules of Engagement for a Complex World*, with Tantum Collins, David Silverman, and Chris Fussell (Portfolio/Penguin, 2015).

33 Yuval Noah Harari, *Sapiens: A Brief History of Humankind* (Harper Peren-nial, 2015).

34 The "fun policy" also funded the courtship of one couple on the team until the policy shifted to "three or more." The policy shifted again when the couple added a "third wheel"—high marks for self-organization.

35 Simon Sinek, "How Great Leaders Inspire Action," TEDx Puget Sound, September 2009, https://www.ted.com/talks/simon_sinek_how_great_leaders_inspire_action.

Chapter 3: Institutionalize Mastery

36 Daniel H. Pink, *Drive: The Surprising Truth About What Motivates Us* (Riverhead Books, 2009).

37 Mihaly Csikszentmihalyi, "Flow, the Secret to Happiness," TED Talk, February 2004, https://www.ted.com/talks/mihaly_csikszentmihalyi_ flow_the_secret_to_happiness. In this TED Talk, Mihaly Csikszentmihalyi talks about this in the context of *flow*, a key ingredient for mastery; flow leverages skill so the doing of the work is a reward in and of itself.

38 Matt Smith, "What makes Olympic swimmers so fast compared to other swimmers?," Quora, https://qr.ae/psQDES. Matt Smith is a breaststroker and a D3 national champion, who swam in the 2009 World Championships.

39 M. G. Siegler, "'It Just Works,'" *TechCrunch*, June 8, 2011, https://techcrunch.com/2011/06/08/apple-icloud-google-cloud/.

40 Robert McKee, *Story: Style, Structure, Substance, and the Principles of Screenwriting* (ReganBooks, 1997).

41 "The sculpture is already complete within the marble block, before I start my work. It is already there; I just have to chisel away the superfluous material."—Michelangelo. https://www.goodreads.com/quotes/1191114-the-sculpture-is-already-complete-within-the-marble-block-before.

42 Momentum hiring is what happens when organizations hire simply from the weight of their size and structure—when each group develops an aggressive hiring plan based on its isolated mission and needs. A "butts-in-seats" strategy is the fulfillment of large hiring plans, however derived, in a short amount of time, decoupled from the capacity of the individuals recruited. And when people are hired without holding the line on mastery or because low-quality systems require people to scale nonmasterful work, overall team capacity suffers.

43 Pink, *Drive*, 117.

44 A distributed system of scalable back-end services and front-end applications that consisted of functionality that generally lived outside the game engine (e.g., social network and content management) and functionality that served the real-time, in-game experiences (e.g., content serving,

matchmaking, and data stores).

45 A collection of components (e.g., graphical rendering, physics, security, and networking) that operated together within an app (e.g., phone, laptop, console, game server) and communicated across apps in real time to deliver the Roblox multiplayer gaming experience and its creation tool, Roblox Studio.

46 "Extreme Programming: A Gentle Introduction," Extreme Programming, accessed June 14, 2024, http://www.extremeprogramming.org/.

47 In principle, mastery always matters, but in practice, it matters much more for things that relate to a team's differentiation and core intellectual property. That means holding the line on any audience impact that undermines core differentiation or advantage. Mastery is also in creative tension with speed and shouldn't always win.

48 Daniel J. Levitin, "Why It's So Hard to Pay Attention, Explained by Science," *Fast Company*, September 23, 2015, https://www.fastcompany.com/3051417/why-its-so-hard-to-pay-attention-explained-by-science. There is a hard ceiling of human processing capacity, and thus focus, of about 120 bits per second.

49 Julia Martins, "6 Tips to Harness the Power of Flow State at Work," Asana, January 14, 2024, https://asana.com/resources/flow-state-work.

50 Csikszentmihalyi, "Flow."

51 Pink, *Drive*, 115.

52 Alexandra Spiliakos, "Tragedy of the Commons: What It Is & 5 Examples," Harvard Business School Online, February 6, 2019, https://online.hbs.edu/blog/post/tragedy-of-the-commons-impact-on-sustainability-issues. A "situation in which individuals with access to a public resource—also called a common—act in their own interest and, in doing so, ultimately deplete the resource."

Chapter 4: Unlock Autonomy

53 Kristen D. Thompson, "How the Drone War in Ukraine Is Transforming Conflict," Council on Foreign Relations, January 16, 2024, https://www.cfr.org/article/how-drone-war-ukraine-transforming-conflict.

54   Zanny Minton Beddoes, host, *The Weekend Intelligence*, podcast, "Crunch Time for Ukraine: Is Ukraine Ready to Redefine What Victory Looks Like?," *The Economist*, September 28, 2024.

55   "How Drones Are Revolutionizing Search and Rescue," IEEE Public Safety Technology, accessed November 14, 2024, https://publicsafety.ieee.org/topics/how-drones-are-revolutionizing-search-and-rescue.

56   Thompson, "Drone War in Ukraine."

57   Minton Beddoes, "Crunch Time for Ukraine."

58   Thompson, "Drone War in Ukraine."

59   Minton Beddoes, "Crunch Time for Ukraine."

60   Thompson, "Drone War in Ukraine."

61   Daniel H. Pink, *Drive: The Surprising Truth About What Motivates Us* (Riverhead Books 2009). Also see the section "A Foundation of Intrinsic Motivation" in the introduction of this book.

62   Pink, *Drive*. Also see the section "A Foundation of Intrinsic Motivation" in the introduction of this book.

63   Pink, *Drive*.

64   "Extreme Programming: A Gentle Introduction," Extreme Programming, accessed June 13, 2024, http://www.extremeprogramming.org/.

65   Gary Keller and Jay Papasan, *The ONE Thing: The Surprisingly Simple Truth Behind Extraordinary Results* (Bard Press, 2013).

66   The immediate cause of the 1986 explosion of the space shuttle *Challenger* was a failed O-ring, but the root cause was ignoring eight years of warnings. The pressure to launch twenty-four flights per year by 1990 resulted in decision-makers down-ranking the O-ring risk, effectively casting the warnings as noise when they were collectively a critical signal. Boyce Rensberger and Kathy Sawyer, "Challenger Disaster Blamed on O-Rings, Pressure to Launch," *The Washington Post*, June 10, 1986.

67   Chris Sims and Hillary Louse Johnson, *Scrum: A Breathtakingly Brief and Agile Introduction* (Dymaxicon, 2012).

68   John Doerr, *Measure What Matters: How Google, Bono, and the Gates Foundation Rock the World with OKRs* (Portfolio/Penguin, 2018).

69   Eugene S. Bardach, *A Practical Guide for Policy Analysis: The Eightfold Path to More Effective Problem Solving*, 4th Ed. (Sage, 2012).

70 Mark Joyella, "Warner Bros. Discovery CEO David Zaslav on Killing CNN+: 'The Subscribers Weren't There,'" *Forbes*, May 18, 2022, https://www.forbes.com/sites/markjoyella/2022/05/18/warner-bros-discovery-ceo-david-zaslav-on-killing-cnn-the-subscribers-werent-there/?sh=5e8d8fca58e5.

71 Zack Sharf, "'Batgirl' Directors 'Saddened and Shocked' after Warner Bros. Killed the Film: 'We Still Can't Believe It,'" *Variety*, August 3, 2022, https://variety.com/2022/film/news/batgirl-filmmakers-shocked-warner-bros-killed-film-1235332526/.

72 Joe Flint, "David Zaslav Challenged the Streaming Industry's Orthodoxy. Now, Rivals Are Following His Lead," *The Wall Street Journal*, April 11, 2023, https://www.wsj.com/articles/david-zaslav-challenged-the-streaming-industrys-orthodoxy-now-rivals-are-following-his-lead-b38dfb1c.

73 Caeleigh MacNeil, "How the Sunk Cost Fallacy Influences Our Decisions," Asana, February 12, 2024, https://asana.com/resources/sunk-cost-fallacy.

74 Sims and Johnson, *Scrum*.

Chapter 5: The Cascade

75 General Stanley McChrystal, *Team of Teams: New Rules of Engagement for a Complex World* (Portfolio/Penguin, 2015).

76 Marc Andreessen, "Part 4: The Only Thing That Matters," *Pmarchive*, June 25, 2007, https://pmarchive.com/guide_to_startups_part4.html.

77 "Extreme Programming: A Gentle Introduction," Extreme Programming, accessed June 14, 2014, http://www.extremeprogramming.org/.

78 Henrik Kniberg, "Spotify Engineering Culture (Part 1)," *R&D Engineering* (blog), Spotify, March 27, 2014, https://engineering.atspotify.com/2014/03/spotify-engineering-culture-part-1/.

79 Interleaving is the process of taking distinct road maps (e.g., Project A, Project B, and Project C) and combining them into a mixed larger sort through project-based prioritization. This is also called a "stack rank" of the individual road maps. Interleaving works very well and is akin to the early-stage team's approach.

80   An example from Roblox: our "game engine" pod of pods with graphics, physics, and networking subpods. No subpod was autonomous, but the aggregate pod of pods generally was, barring web stack dependencies.

81   "All of Our Yammer Articles," *First Round Review*, accessed June 14, 2014, https://review.firstround.com/articles/yammer/.

Chapter 6: Define Success

82   Matt Dusek, repeatedly, from 2010 onward.

83   Private communication with James Cloern, Emeritus Research Scientist at the U.S. Geological Survey, Editor-in-Chief for *Limnology and Oceanography Letters*, Association for the Sciences of Limnology and Oceanography.

84   Lisa V. Lucas and Eric Deleersnijder, "Timescale Methods for Simplifying, Understanding and Modeling Biophysical and Water Quality Processes in Coastal Aquatic Ecosystems: A Review," *Water* 12, no. 10 (2020): 2717, https://doi.org/10.3390/w12102717.

85   Wayne Gretzky, quoting his father: "I skate to where the puck is going to be, not to where it has been."

86   Tina Seelig, *Insight Out: Get Ideas Out of Your Head and into the World* (HarperOne, 2015).

87   Korey Kasper, "Sports Training Principles," *Current Sports Medicine Reports* 18, no. 4 (2019): 95–96, https://doi.org/10.1249/JSR.0000000000000576.

88   Impact: competitive performance. Integrity: playing fairly, competing first and foremost with self. Ownership: owning their training, their results, and their improvement. Transparency: performance metrics and wins/losses are always public. Mastery: the daily improvement in skill through feedback. Urgency: prepping for a competition and competing (e.g., the last two minutes of the NBA Finals).

Chapter 7: Recruit Mission Athletes

89   Drafting is "riding in the slipstream of another rider ahead," saving about 30 percent energy. Angelina Palermo, "*Cycling Terminology*," USA Cycling, June 19, 2020, https://usacycling.org/article/cycling-terminology.

90   Examples: interactive brainstorming, road-mapping, or problem-solving session on real work facing the team right now. The experience should genuinely lead to useful contributions with collaborative engagement from current team members and the candidate. Software engineering teams often do this by inviting someone in for a day to fix a few bugs, typically some challenging ones that require an existing engineer experienced with the system. When I approach a new team to work with, I whiteboard directly with the people I will be working with most to gauge mutual alignment. To quote a good friend, I shouldn't be the one who cares the most.

Chapter 8: Develop Mission Athletes

91   Alexandra Spiliakos, "Tragedy of the Commons: What It Is & 5 Examples," Harvard Business School Online, February 6, 2019, https://online. hbs.edu/blog/post/tragedy-of-the-commons-impact-on-sustainability-issues. Shared goods fall into disrepair because their upkeep is greater than any individual's resources.

92   Costs are not borne by those producing an economic good, obfuscating the true costs of that good. Examples include factories polluting rivers downstream.

93   Carol Dweck, "What Having a 'Growth Mindset' Actually Means," *Harvard Business Review*, January 13, 2016, https://hbr.org/2016/01/what-having-a-growth-mindset-actually-means.

94   "Journey to Mastery," IDEO Design Thinking, accessed March 3, 2024, https://designthinking.ideo.com/journey-to-mastery.

95   IMVU is an avatar-based social network. My interest at the time was in its software engineering operations, which were pretty advanced. IMVU rolled out software to servers progressively, measured the performance across new and old code, and automatically rolled back code if performance dipped. This was a precursor to the continuous integration and deployment practices that have developed since then.

96   From an early reader: As an alternative to explicitly creating ad hoc challenges or quests, whether through a leveling matrix or not, "identify challenges in the [individual's] current work stream that align with skills

that an IC [individual contributor] has immediate opportunities to grow in and make sure that those challenges are given to that IC. There is no expectation that completing that challenge checks a box or makes them quantifiably more ready for some other title or responsibility, but just that by having that opportunity to work on something challenging for them, it increases their mastery incrementally and helps them grow in an open-ended way."

97   "Imposter Syndrome," *Psychology Today*, accessed June 10, 2024, https://www.psychologytoday.com/us/basics/imposter-syndrome.

Chapter 9: Coach Out

98   Martin Trinder and Mark Jabbal, "Development of a Smoke Visualisation System for Wind Tunnel Laboratory Experiments," *International Journal of Mechanical Engineering Education* 41, no. 1 (2013): 27-43, https://doi.org/10.7227/IJMEE.41.1.5, with permission.

99   Jeannie Kahwajy, CEO, Effective Interactions, https://www.linkedin.com/in/jeankahwajy/.

100   Ken Blanchard and Spencer Johnson, *The New One Minute Manager* (William Morrow, 2015).

Conclusion

101   Here's a longer list. Start with the end goal, and back-out the critical path; reduce project scope; change project requirements; cut deadlines in half, along with scope; increase the cadence of team check-ins; reduce larger team scope to add resources to a specific project; remove resources to reduce people complexity and accelerate collaboration; restate the problem to be easier to solve; rethink the solution to require less work; hack something now, coming back to it after audience traction validates investment.

102   Dr. Martin Luther King Jr., "Remaining Awake Through a Great Revolution" (final Sunday sermon at the Washington National Cathedral on March 31, 1968).

103   "Fareed Zakaria Global Public Square," *CNN*, accessed June 16, 2024, https://transcripts.cnn.com/show/fzgps/date/2023-03-26/segment/01.

A free ebook edition is available with the purchase of this book.

To claim your free ebook edition:
1. Visit MorganJamesBOGO.com
2. Sign your name CLEARLY in the space
3. Complete the form and submit a photo of the entire copyright page
4. You or your friend can download the ebook to your preferred device

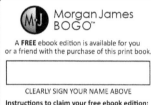

Morgan James
BOGO™

A **FREE** ebook edition is available for you or a friend with the purchase of this print book.

CLEARLY SIGN YOUR NAME ABOVE

Instructions to claim your free ebook edition:
1. Visit MorganJamesBOGO.com
2. Sign your name CLEARLY in the space above
3. Complete the form and submit a photo of this entire page
4. You or your friend can download the ebook to your preferred device

Print & Digital Together Forever.

Snap a photo   Free ebook   Read anywhere

www.ingramcontent.com/pod-product-compliance
Lightning Source LLC
Jackson TN
JSHW021918220725
88013JS00029B/99